Enforcing Exclusion

Law and Society Series

W. Wesley Pue, General Editor

The Law and Society Series explores law as a socially embedded phenomenon. It is premised on the understanding that the conventional division of law from society creates false dichotomies in thinking, scholarship, educational practice, and social life. Books in the series treat law and society as mutually constitutive and seek to bridge scholarship emerging from interdisciplinary engagement of law with disciplines such as politics, social theory, history, political economy, and gender studies.

Recent books in the series:

Jasminka Kalajdzic, *Class Actions in Canada: The Promise and Reality of Access to Justice* (2018)

David Moffette, *Governing Irregular Migration: Bordering Culture, Labour, and Security in Spain* (2018)

Constance Backhouse, *Claire L'Heureux-Dubé: A Life* (2017)

Christopher P. Manfredi and Antonia Maioni, *Health Care and the Charter: Legal Mobilization and Policy Change in Canada* (2017)

Julie Macfarlane, *The New Lawyer: How Clients Are Transforming the Practice of Law*, 2nd ed. (2017)

Annie Bunting and Joel Quirk, eds., *Contemporary Slavery: Popular Rhetoric and Political Practice* (2017)

Larry Savage and Charles W. Smith, *Unions in Court: Organized Labour and the Charter of Rights and Freedoms* (2017)

Allyson M. Lunny, *Debating Hate Crime: Language, Legislatures, and the Law in Canada* (2017)

George Pavlich and Matthew P. Unger, eds., *Accusation: Creating Criminals* (2016)

Michael Weinrath, *Behind the Walls: Inmates and Correctional Officers on the State of Canadian Prisons* (2016)

For a complete list of the titles in the series, see the UBC Press website, www.ubcpress.ca.

Enforcing Exclusion

Precarious Migrants and the Law in Canada

SARAH GRAYCE MARSDEN

UBCPress · Vancouver · Toronto

© UBC Press 2018

All rights reserved. No part of this publication may be reproduced, stored in a retrieval system, or transmitted, in any form or by any means, without prior written permission of the publisher, or, in Canada, in the case of photocopying or other reprographic copying, a licence from Access Copyright, www.accesscopyright.ca.

26 25 24 23 22 21 20 19 18   5 4 3 2 1

Printed in Canada on FSC-certified ancient-forest-free paper
(100% post-consumer recycled) that is processed chlorine- and acid-free.

Library and Archives Canada Cataloguing in Publication

Marsden, Sarah, author
Enforcing exclusion : precarious migrants and the law in Canada /
Sarah Grayce Marsden.
(Law and society series)

Includes bibliographical references and index.
Issued in print and electronic formats.
ISBN 978-0-7748-3773-6 (hardcover). – ISBN 978-0-7748-3774-3 (pbk). –
ISBN 978-0-7748-3775-0 (PDF). – ISBN 978-0-7748-3776-7 (EPUB). –
ISBN 978-0-7748-3777-4 (Kindle)

1. Aliens – Canada. 2. Refugees – Legal status, laws, etc. – Canada. I. Title.
II. Series: Law and society series (Vancouver, B.C.)

| KE4452.M37 2018 | 342.7108′2 | C2018-902066-0 |
| KF4454.I5M37 2018 | | C2018-902067-9 |

Canada

UBC Press gratefully acknowledges the financial support for our publishing program of the Government of Canada (through the Canada Book Fund), the Canada Council for the Arts, and the British Columbia Arts Council.

This book has been published with the help of a grant from the Canadian Federation for the Humanities and Social Sciences, through the Awards to Scholarly Publications Program, using funds provided by the Social Sciences and Humanities Research Council of Canada.

Printed and bound in Canada by Friesens
Set in Zurich, Univers, and Minion by Apex CoVantage, LLC
Copy editor: Barbara Tessman
Proofreader: Carmen Tiampo
Indexer: Judy Dunlop

UBC Press
The University of British Columbia
2029 West Mall
Vancouver, BC V6T 1Z2
www.ubcpress.ca

Contents

Acknowledgments / vii

Introduction / 3

1 The Creation and Growth of Precarious Migration in Canada: "Illegal" Migration and The Liberal State / 13

2 Status, Deportability, and Illegality in Daily Life / 37

3 Working Conditions and Barriers to Substantive Remedies / 63

4 Exclusion from the Social State: Health, Education, and Income Security / 100

5 Multi-Sited Enforcement: Maintaining Subordinate Membership / 135

6 Rights and Membership: Toward Inclusion? / 153

Postscript / 185

Appendix A: Migrant Participant Profiles / 187

Appendix B: Sample Interview Script / 189

Notes / 191

Index / 218

Acknowledgments

I would first like to thank the individuals who participated in interviews for this study. Their courage and generosity in sharing their perspectives and experiences gave life and meaning to this work. I am grateful for the trust, energy, and time they gave to this project. I hope that this work contributes in some way to the ongoing work of establishing inclusion for all precarious migrants.

The project owes much to the excellent research mentorship provided by Catherine Dauvergne, Geraldine Pratt, Emma Cunliffe, and Don Galloway. The painstaking work of obtaining government policy through Freedom of Information requests benefited from the research assistance of Rene-John Nicolas. I also had the privilege of working with two brilliant interpreters for this project: Liliana Castaneda Lopez and Jane Deasy lent this work not only their eloquence in word and thought, but also their flexibility, patience, and knowledge in reaching out within communities in Vancouver. The difficult and essential work of interview transcription was carried by Sandra Choromanski and Lauren Marsden. I also thank the anonymous reviewers at UBC Press for their comments on the manuscript, as well as Barbara Tessman for her careful copy-editing. My partner, Quentin MacMillan, supported this work with love, unwavering commitment, and even some formatting in early stages, and it would not have been possible without him.

I gratefully acknowledge the financial support of the Social Sciences and Humanities Research Council, which provided research funding as well as publication support through the Awards to Scholarly Publications Program, the Foundation for Legal Research, and the Liu Institute for Global Studies.

Enforcing Exclusion

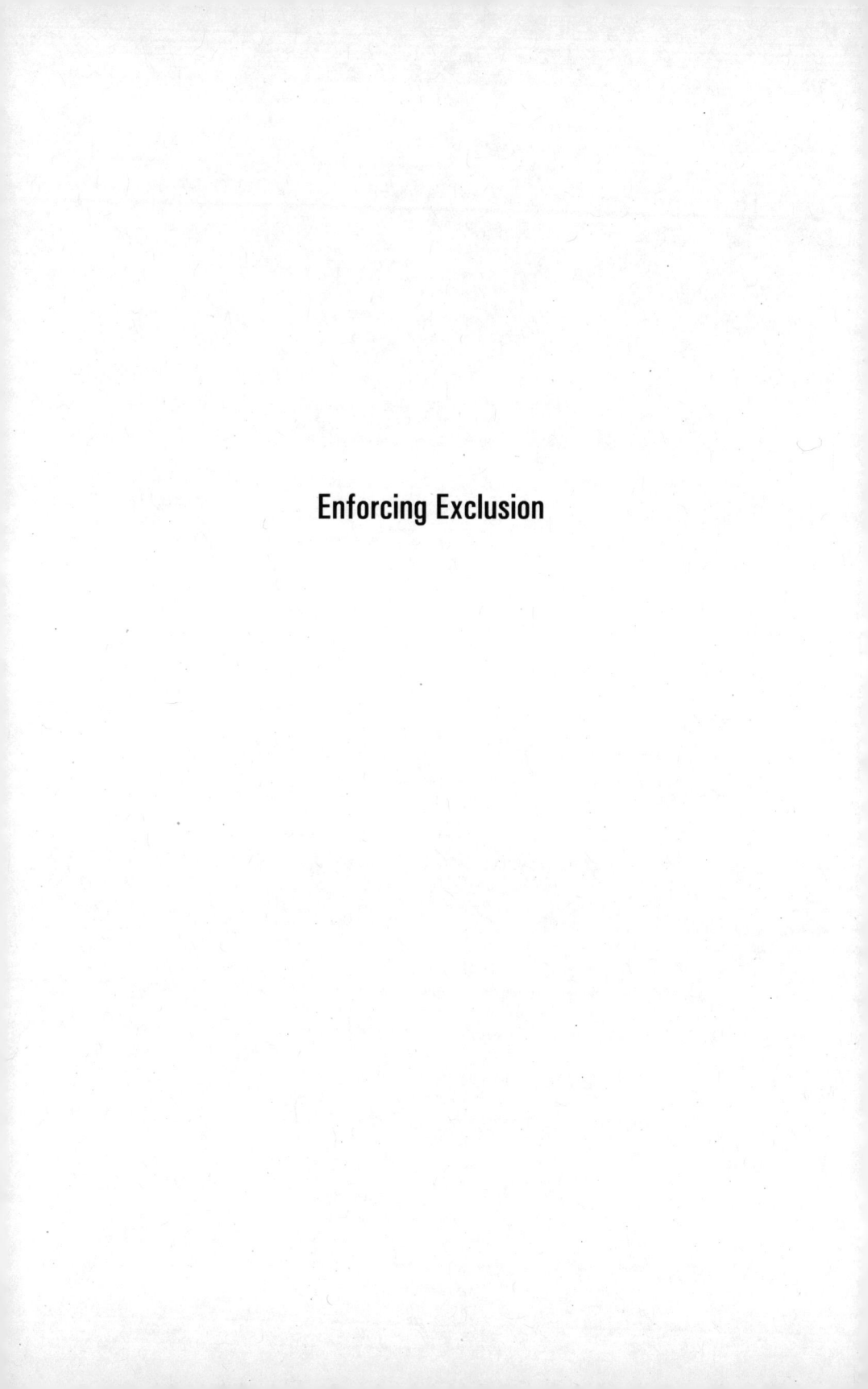

Introduction

Citizens and permanent residents in Canada do not have to worry about whether they are legally allowed to see a doctor or enrol their children in school. They may have difficulties securing enrolment in their school of choice, and the nearest hospital may have a long waiting list, but, once at the gate, permanent residents and citizens expect that, eventually, they will be allowed in. They may face unemployment, economic uncertainty, and discrimination, but they have no reason to question whether they have the right to go to work once they have found a job. And if they are laid off, they will be able to collect Employment Insurance if they've worked for the required length of time, and, if necessary, they can rely on social assistance to provide a basic level of income. Citizens and permanent residents who find that they have been paid less than minimum wage or who suffer a workplace injury can apply for compensation, and, while they may risk employer retaliation for taking such action, they do not risk removal from Canada or restrictions on their ability to work. The network of laws that upholds these entitlements for citizens and permanent residents is certainly imperfect. In the case of migrant workers, however, it takes on another role, functioning as a multi-sited force for social and economic exclusion, reinforcing the subordinate status of migrant workers, and foreclosing the possibility of full membership in Canadian society.

Permanent residents and citizens have the right to live and work in Canada and are entitled to health care, education, and income support when they need it. But a growing number of people living and working in Canada have less than full migration status – for the most part, they are in Canada with temporary status. Sometimes they lose their status or wait for months for their permits to be extended. Less frequently, people enter Canada with no status at all. Individuals sometimes become entitled to permanent status, but, due to processing delays, it takes years to obtain. Without either permanent or temporary status, people can be imprisoned or deported under Canadian immigration law. Indeed, the possibility of detention and/or deportation haunts non-permanent migrants even when they have status, because they know their status is fragile. It is also often contingent on an employer, a family member, or the discretion of a government decision-maker. Immigration law creates a hierarchy of status, but it does not do this work alone. Laws and policies governing social benefits also create distinctions between people with permanent status and people without it, usually with an exclusionary effect. Although laws protecting workers do not make the same distinctions, migration status profoundly influences workers' relationships with their employers. Unlike permanent residents and citizens, workers with less than full status risk losing their status if they report an employer's illegal activities or lose their job.

The lack of permanent immigration status not only limits the duration for which people may legally be present in Canada, but it also affects labour mobility, working conditions, and access to the health and social benefits that citizens and permanent residents take for granted. People with non-permanent status are categorically excluded from many benefits and protections in Canadian society. Based on information provided through interviews with migrants, as well as on analyses of laws, policies, and practices of multiple institutions, this book will explore how law and policy are implicated in this exclusion. I draw on the experiences of migrants without full status to understand the function of migration status in laws and policies that affect people's lives most deeply – in workplaces, employment standards, health law and hospital policy, school admission practices, and eligibility for income support. These areas have no formal connection to each other or to the laws and policies that govern immigration directly. Institutions like schools, hospitals, and workplaces cannot grant or withdraw migration status, but the way in which they administer services is directly affected by an individual's status. For migrants, a lack of permanent status is magnified through their interactions with such institutions, interactions that cannot be neatly separated from each other in the lived experience of migrants.

Merely having or lacking migration status becomes relevant to the lives of individuals through their interactions with such institutions, which often deny or reduce services on the basis of status. These practices lend power to status: for example, if a hospital did not require an individual to show his or her permit to prove status, the relevance of a work permit would be diminished. Given that migration status is a factor affecting access to multiple institutions that provide basic and necessary services, it shapes social and economic life on a large scale and contributes to the subordination of precarious migrants as a group. I was drawn to research on the exclusionary aspects of migration status through my involvement as a lawyer and advocate in the area of immigration and refugee law, and particularly through interactions with people whose status fell short of permanent residence. For the most part, the goals that clients articulated to me were about obtaining status, making their status more stable, or moving from temporary to permanent status. Several aspects of my professional experience compelled me to examine the area of status in greater depth. First, although migration status is intimately related to the operation of law, it is clear that people can have less than full migration status in a variety of ways that are not specifically articulated in statutes or policies. In addition, while laws list ways in which people can become entitled to status or maintain status, and policies often use specific types of status as a filter to determine treatment or entitlement, the ways migration status could shape and govern people's lives called for new research.

Second, it was clear that migration status was a major priority for the people I met, and for good reason – it was often entwined with people's ability to meet their most basic and urgent needs, including access to health care. One woman I met had entered Canada as a live-in caregiver from Mexico, overstayed her work permit, and become pregnant. Her employer was the father of the child, and he had not only withheld her pay but had also prevented her from leaving his home/her workplace at will. She was six months pregnant when we met, but because she no longer had migration status, she could not obtain regular prenatal medical care. She had managed to leave her employer's residence while he was away for the weekend, and she was obtaining free medical attention from a community doctor willing to see her off-hours. I gave her summary legal advice on her status situation. Her options to stay in Canada legally were few: without an employer's cooperation, the renewal of her work permit was impossible and the chance of eventual permanent residence was slim. In another instance of status compromising access to medical care, I spoke with a group of Latin American construction workers who had entered Canada without documentation. One of the workers had fallen and broken her arm but had not gone to the hospital because she was terrified that seeking medical assistance would bring her to the attention of the immigration authorities. For this worker, the status barrier existed even prior to contact with the hospital: if she had sought help, the hospital's answer to her would have been "no," or at least "not without paying," but her lack of status made her afraid even to ask the question.

Alongside health care, education is another area in which uncertain status can be a major barrier. I worked with a mother and daughter who were at risk of serious violence in Zimbabwe but had been deemed ineligible to make a refugee claim when they entered Canada. This family had made a further application for protection from inside Canada and they were hoping to have the merits of their case heard. In the meantime, the child's local school refused to enrol her unless she paid international student fees, which were far beyond the financial means of the family. The girl and her mother were not technically refugee claimants, but they could not be removed from Canada while their risk-based application was processed. Moreover, the federal government had suspended removals to Zimbabwe at the time, due to dangerous conditions in that country. Yet, although the mother was waiting to have her status determined by the government on the basis of risk, this circumstance fell short of what the school required to accept the child without fees. While the school was eventually persuaded to enrol the child without charging extra fees, its actual policy remained unchanged.

Finally, I was troubled by the contradiction of membership that arose repeatedly in people's experience: both the state and employers seemed to want migrants for their labour, but migrants had difficulty obtaining equal treatment both in workplaces and with regard to state-based entitlements. I thus wanted to examine the entire constellation of legal structures that would be likely to have an impact on the lives of non-permanent migrants in a systematic way, but I wanted to approach this examination primarily through the experience and aims of those governed by the law, rather than with respect to the law's prerogative in governing them. Both interview-based and traditional legal research methods were essential in this study, but I privileged interview responses, drawing on them to refine my focus on the laws, policies, and practices of institutions.

A growing body of research confirms the lack of access to social benefits by non-permanent migrants, and there is a wealth of documentation to show that people without permanent status suffer exploitation at work.[1] What compelled me to do further research in this area was the desire not only to add to this work but to focus specifically on how the idea of migration status itself operates in laws, policies, and practices. Put another way, I take the harmful repercussions of non-permanent migration status as a starting point, not a conclusion. Thus, rather than seeking only to confirm the detrimental effects of non-permanent status, I am interested in understanding how migration status affects social and economic standing, and what laws and legally governed institutions have to do with migration status. Take, for example, the refusal to enrol a child of parents without status in a publicly funded school. Starting from migrants' reports that schools require status documents to enrol their children, the following questions arise as to exactly how this plays out: Is migration status a specific requirement under the relevant provincial education legislation? If not, is this status requirement a product of written policy? Is it an informal institutional practice to require proof of migration status? Is migration status explicitly required, or is the status document ancillary to another requirement, such as proof that a family resides in the area served by the school? What is the role of the federal immigration regime, if any? This book asks and answers these questions in multiple areas that affect migrants' lives, including employment standards and workers' compensation, health care, education, and income support programs.

Both federal and provincial laws are relevant to understanding how migration status works in Canada. While federal laws determine who has status, provincial laws determine the allocation of social benefits and the enforcement of employment standards and human rights. The federal government uses the *Immigration and Refugee Protection Act* to determine who gets migration status as well as the conditions and time limits attached to this status. It is also within federal jurisdiction to enforce immigration laws through investigation, removal, and/or detention. Migration status originates in federal law, but it is relevant to a diverse array of laws, policies, and practices apart from the federal immigration regime. For example, laws governing workplace standards and safety are mostly provincial. While workplace laws do not explicitly require migration status to confer protection on workers, status becomes relevant to workers' access to these protections because it is entwined with the employment relationship: many migrants rely on the endorsement of their employers to maintain their status. Similarly, provincial laws determine health care coverage, eligibility for publicly funded education, and social assistance for low-income individuals, and each of these has its own manner of incorporating migration status as a requirement. A basic level of income is provided to qualified unemployed workers through Employment Insurance laws, which are not attached to federal immigration laws, but the absence of migration status can cause the disqualification of workers, as their work may be seen as "illegal."

In the abstract, it is possible to separate these various laws, and the institutions in which they are applied, but they are all bound together in migrants' lived experience. In order to consider the function of non-permanent migration status, I start from the perspectives of migrants themselves, moving from there to the content of laws, policies, and practices. In this book, I argue that migration status, as a legal construct, connects multiple legal and institutional sites, which operate together to exclude migrants from full status. I propose that this assemblage should be understood as a multi-sited enforcement regime in which the subordination of precarious migrants is created and maintained. The individuals I talked to in this study came from a range of migration status situations. They entered as temporary foreign workers, refugee claimants, or visitors, or without authorization. In many cases, their status changed during the time they were in Canada. Some worked or lived beyond the authorization given on their permits, some obtained permanent residence, and some were eventually deported. All of them, however, self-identified as having uncertain immigration status. While the federal immigration regime would label these individuals differently (for example, as "temporary foreign workers," "refugee claimants," or "visa overstays"), this book focuses on the common element of their lack of permanent status and on what they share with respect to access to rights and benefits. To do this, I use the term "precarious migration status" to describe the non-permanent status of these people. While precarious migration itself is not new in the Canadian context, the proportion of precarious migrants relative to permanent migrants has been greater in recent decades than at any time since immigration numbers have been recorded. Furthermore, shifting political tides have changed the social and economic reception of non-permanent migrants, making Canada's welcome ever more wary.

To situate the stories of the migrants I spoke with and the conclusions I draw, some background information is useful. In Chapter 1, I briefly discuss the historical and demographic context of precarious migrants in Canada and explain the idea of precarious status and why I am using it. I then describe the method I used to conduct the study. I introduce the primary themes of "work" and the "social state," as well as the questions and dilemmas that arise with regard to rights and membership for non-permanent migrants.

Migrant participants made it clear that migration status was a powerful feature of their lives, but the way they described it was not simply a repetition of the legislative taxonomy. Status is defined in the laws and regulations governing immigration and is applied through multiple other legal and institutional sites. Through the lived experience of participants, however, status emerges as something much more textured and dynamic than is obvious from the bare text of the law. In study interviews, status was prevalent as a framing construct of daily life and often served as a touchstone by which migrants assessed membership and belonging. In Chapter 2, after a brief overview of federal laws on status, I focus on the nature and effect of precarious migration status as elaborated by study participants, providing a rich definition of migration status that serves as the backdrop for subsequent chapters.

Working life is a central focus of this project. All of the participants were involved in the paid labour force in Canada, and many identified work as a primary site of their participation in and contribution to Canada. For precarious migrants, problems like wage disparity, poor working conditions, and inability to unionize are well documented.[2] In this book, I aim not only to provide further examples of the manner in which precarious migrants are subject to differential rights and entitlements, but also to implicate laws, policies, and institutional practices in the production of these conditions. In Chapter 3, I examine the role of migration status in the employment relationship, where precarious status functions to exaggerate power differentials, reduce labour mobility and bargaining power, and create barriers to enforcing workers' rights. Status becomes relevant in the sphere of work for precarious migrants in their relationships with employers, with the labour market generally, and with the legal institutions meant to protect basic standards in the workplace. I canvass job deskilling, labour mobility and stability, and working conditions, including pay, hours, health, and safety. Within these contexts, I consider the remedies offered through law and the effect of migration status, particularly with regard to provincial legislation designed to protect minimum working conditions and worker health and safety. While the text of the law does not discriminate among workers on the basis of migration status, the experience of workers nonetheless indicates that having precarious migration status in working life creates not only a risk of deleterious conditions but also barriers to legally available remedies.

The question of access to social state entitlements for temporary residents goes to the heart of what troubles the liberal state: if such people live and work alongside permanent residents, on what basis is it justifiable to exclude them from the benefits associated with membership in Canadian society? Entitlements to education, health care, and income security are often based on status, either directly or through policy and practice. Yet, even where migrants are legally entitled, they are reluctant to claim benefits because they fear it would have an impact on their status in some way. In Chapter 4, I examine the relationship between migration status and social entitlements, with a specific focus on health, education, and income security through Employment Insurance and social assistance programs. Laws and policies that govern the distribution of these entitlements often employ migration status as a filter through which benefits may be allocated or denied. Compared to workplace protections, social entitlements contain more explicit forms of exclusion and restriction, and also show deeper enmeshment with moral regulation and stereotyping of migrants.

Through laws, policies, and practices, migration status catalyzes state power. In both working life and in the social state, multiple sites function as locations of enforcement and discipline, which serve to exclude precarious migrants. Throughout these sites, the legal construct of migration status is often visible as a common factor. With respect to both working life and the social state, migration status is connected not only to issues of formal authorization, but also to migrants' ability to live and the conditions under which they do so. Migration status can have a profound effect on the way people earn their livelihoods as well as on their health, their material subsistence, and their inclusion in basic forms of belonging in Canada. The construct of migration status is generated in the legal texts of the federal immigration regime as an aspect of direct state control but is also picked up through other state structures, policies, and practices, many of which are present at a local level. Migrants are not only excluded directly through status requirements, but are also subject to disciplining effects through the implication that status could be removed at any time. The effect of migration status across multiple sites thus functions to create and maintain the economic and social exclusion of non-permanent migrants. In Chapter 5, I propose that this exclusion is best understood under the rubric of enforcement. Specifically, I argue that enforcement of membership boundaries is woven into institutions and relationships far beyond those of the federal state, within provincial laws and local policies and practices. In identifying the specific ways in which enforcement and discipline occur *beyond* the prerogative of the federal immigration authority, it is possible not only to document exclusion, but also to assess proposed rights-based strategies to increase inclusion.

In terms of rights, state institutions' membership determinations trump equality concerns for precarious migrants – in effect, because such migrants are defined as non-members, they are not considered to be rights bearing. In case law, the membership claims of precarious migrants can be denied on the basis of their contravention of immigration laws, and migrants' behaviour can be subject to moral scrutiny under the rubric of status. Membership is thus positioned as a necessary precursor to rights, and is precluded in reference to migrants' transgression of immigration laws, even when the benefit at issue is unrelated to migration. Informed by the rich literature on post-national membership and citizenship, I argue in Chapter 6 that, while contesting membership or "getting status" in a formal way is an essential component of addressing exclusion, this is not likely to be viable under current social and economic conditions. I conclude that, while it is worth working toward possibilities for greater inclusion of migrants at the local level, neither alternatives to national membership nor approaches focusing on human rights provide a pathway to complete inclusion.

1

The Creation and Growth of Precarious Migration in Canada

"ILLEGAL" MIGRATION AND THE LIBERAL STATE

Starting in the late 1960s, Canada's migration policy underwent a wholesale liberalization, characterized by the removal of explicitly racist laws, the introduction of procedural safeguards, and the acceptance of large numbers of refugees on humanitarian grounds, subsequent to the country's ratification in 1969 of the United Nations Refugee Convention. Economically based permanent migration came to the fore during this time as well. In 1967, the federal government established a "points system" by which applicants could demonstrate their potential for economic integration by reference to their formal education, language skills, and work experience.[1] For the first time, the primary focus of permanent migration was the economic potential of prospective individual immigrants, rather than their ethnic, national, or family affiliation. Shortly afterward, the federal government initiated a large-scale temporary labour migration program. Known then as the Non-Immigrant Employment Authorization Program, this was the first iteration of today's Temporary Foreign Worker Program. Beginning in 1973, this program allowed employers to hire foreign workers on the basis of labour market need, with the result that the number of temporary workers often rivalled or exceeded the number of economic-class permanent residents entering Canada.[2] Commentators have described the period from the early 1970s to the present as a time in which Canadian immigration policy moved generally from permanent to temporary migration, as well as from public to private interests (for example, basing admission on the needs of specific employers rather than the economy as a whole).[3]

In the early 1970s, the Canadian state also turned its attention to the issue of irregular migrants living in Canada, offering an estimate of an undocumented population of 200,000 in 1973, most of whom had originally entered Canada legally as visitors or workers.[4] The government provided a one-time regularization program for undocumented migrants in 1973. Although 50,000 people participated, this did not resolve the issue, and new program streams directed at refugees already in Canada further complicated the situation. In terms of public perception, the 1980s saw "an increasing public association [of] refugees, asylum seekers, and illegal immigration" as part of a pattern in which irregular migration became a "sometime social issue" in Canada.[5] Norm Buchignani described the division of precarious migrants into two classes in public consciousness: meritorious (though undocumented) industrious workers and deserving "compliant" refugees, on the one hand, and "bogus refugees" or "queue jumpers" on the other.[6] These themes persist in recent governmental discourse on the topic of refugees.[7] In public and policy discourse, migrants are often characterized using various "frames of deservingness" (with reference, for example, to vulnerability, demonstrated community contribution, law-abidingness, and/or economic performance) that may be internally incoherent (for example, a migrant without status to work cannot perform a job without also breaking the law and becoming "more illegal").[8] While these ideas of civic deservingness apply to citizens as well, they weigh more heavily on migrants, who, needing to prove themselves all the more, become the "guardians of good citizenship."[9]

In this analysis, notions of unfairness and illegality are deployed to condemn migrant groups that deviate morally or otherwise from the imagined deserving migrant. While there was considerable public support for amnesty for undocumented migrants in the 1970s, by the 1980s the increase in refugee claims was framed in public and media discourse as "threatening, inauthentic and large."[10] Such discourse contributed to a decline in public support for amnesty and an increase in controversy over backlog-clearance programs subsequent to the Supreme Court of Canada's landmark decision in *Singh v Minister of Employment and Immigration*.[11] According to commissioned reports on the issue of undocumented migration at that time, Canadians found irregular migrants socially problematic not for any measurable detrimental economic effect, but because their presence represented an offence to national integrity and sovereignty.[12] Policy and public rhetoric, both then and now, draw on the idea of the "bogus refugee" and other migrants taking advantage of Canada's social system to blame individual migrants and emphasize the "pull factors" that supposedly entice them to stay in Canada. These allegations do not point to any proof of a disproportionate burden on social systems by particular migrant groups, and there are no available data to support this conclusion. To the contrary, in this book I aim to show that migrants with less than full status face strong disincentives with respect to relying on social benefits at all, even those to which they are legally entitled.

The increasing presence of non-permanent migrants in Canada, an ostensibly liberal state, highlights liberalism's "basic dilemma" with regard to non-permanent migration: the contradiction of a liberal democracy maintaining a population with no political voice and with differential access to the social and economic benefits of membership.[13] Liberal values prescribe inclusion and non-discrimination, but the absolute right of the sovereign state to allocate permanent or temporary migration status means that some (permanent migrants) are more equal than others (non-permanent or precarious migrants). In Canada, law often justifies the exclusion of non-permanent migrants using the logic of border protection and restricting entry to keep people out or to determine who gets in. However, this logic is also applied to people who already live here, giving shape to the "illiberal tendencies" in Canada as an ostensibly liberal state.[14] Such tendencies are evident not only in the treatment of irregular or undocumented migrants, but also within the larger category of migrants with precarious status.

Beyond "Illegality": Defining "Precarious Migration Status"
Throughout this book, I use the idea of precarious migration status as a framing concept, drawing on the work of Luin Goldring and her colleagues. Migration status is precarious when it is marked by the absence of any of the following elements normally associated with permanent residence (and citizenship) in Canada: 1) work authorization, 2) the right to remain permanently in the country (residence permit), 3) independence from a third party for one's right to be in Canada (such as a sponsoring spouse or employer), and 4) social citizenship rights available to permanent residents (e.g., public education and public health coverage).[15]

This framework brings many legally distinct migrant situations together on a single spectrum – that is, on the basis of their less than permanent status and their resulting differential entitlement to benefits, rather than on the basis of the presence or absence of legal authorization in the federal immigration regime. The definition of precarity extends beyond those who are unauthorized or undocumented. For example, a sponsored spouse waiting for approval within Canada has precarious status while she is waiting to obtain permanent residency, as does an authorized temporary foreign worker with a closed work permit, because the permit may be revoked if he ceases to work for the single employer named on it. A refugee claimant in Canada waiting for determination of her claim has precarious status, and so does a migrant working beyond the terms of his permit or who entered without authorization.

The relevance of precarity as a unifying category becomes more visible by considering the array of situations in which status becomes pertinent for migrants. For example, when an authorized temporary worker is laid off after making a complaint about workplace safety, he is legally prohibited from working for another employer without that second employer's endorsement (a condition that would never be required for a worker with permanent residence or citizenship). Although he still has legal status in Canada, this worker may be vulnerable to exploitation through his limited labour mobility and reduced bargaining power. Because his permit is tied to a specific employer, he cannot circulate in the labour market; he has status, but his situation is highly precarious and contingent on an employer's whim. Similarly, a sponsored spouse in Canada who is awaiting an initial decision on a permanent residence application and who is faced with abuse from the sponsor may be forced to choose between remaining in the relationship with the hope of becoming a permanent resident and leaving the relationship with little chance of obtaining permanent residence through legal channels.[16] While both of these migrants would fall on the "legal" side of the legal/illegal migrant binary, their status relies on factors beyond their control and the real risk of deportation. Their situation is associated with the risk of economic and social marginalization in a way that is distinct from that of a person with confirmed permanent residence or citizenship.

As with other categorizations embedded in social and economic ordering, precarious migration status does not affect everyone equally;

rather, it interacts with factors such as race, gender, class, and nationality. Thus, while migration status should be understood as an aspect of social relations, it must also be understood in the context of the privilege and disadvantage that accrue by other means.[17] There are individuals with less than permanent status who enjoy labour mobility, wage parity, and full access to the social state, and there are those who are cushioned from the detrimental potential of their status by other aspects of their position. Precarious status will have a different impact on an English as a second language student from an upper-class Japanese family than on a construction worker from Guatemala. Empirical research establishes that precarity and vulnerability do affect those workers classified as "high skilled,"[18] but considerations other than class and skill level inevitably play a role in contributing to a migrant's vulnerability. In examining the way in which the use of migration status in multiple institutional sites contributes to inequality, my assumption is that, in a liberal state, the law should function to ensure that "all temporary migrants, not just the privileged, enjoy full social and civil rights."[19] Similarly, while this study demonstrates a clear line between those with permanent residence rights and those without, there is not an absolute dichotomy between citizens and non-citizens in Canada. Citizenship itself is not absolute in Canada: it may be subject to erosion and may reveal gradations that are "often connected with ethnoracial and ethnonational hierarchies."[20]

"Precarious migration status" is not a category within the law's own taxonomy of status. It serves well as a lens for analysis of the effects and functions of laws and policies because it does not rely on the definitions these laws and policies generate internally. Framing this analysis in a manner that is not limited to the binary of inclusion in or exclusion from legal status renders visible not only the effects of various degrees of legal status but also the function of the law in its categorization of migrants. Instead of accepting "legal" and "illegal" as the primary terms of reference and most relevant distinction between migrant groups, stepping away from these terms clarifies the effects that flow from the operation of legal distinctions themselves. Such an approach is also helpful in shifting the analytical focus from scrutiny of individual people as authors of their own status situation to the role and function of migration status in a larger sense, through laws, policies, and practices.

The concept of precarious migration status is also useful in providing a venue for exploring features such as labour vulnerability and lack of access to social services as characteristics that bind migrant groups. This disrupts the dichotomy of status/non-status and cuts across qualitative distinctions made between migrant groups in both policy and rhetoric. For example, the popular media may construct the "legitimate refugee" as a person fleeing persecution and violence and with no economic motivation to enter Canada, while framing the "economic migrant/bogus refugee" as entering Canada to improve his or her material conditions. (Ironically, in Canadian migration policy, the latter is seen as a highly desirable characteristic in permanent and temporary migrants who are *not* refugees.) In reality, these two apparently disparate situations may be entwined in complex ways. Many people entering Canada through the inland refugee process experience some combination of persecution and economic desperation: similarly, foreign workers may be motivated by risk-based factors not limited to the economy of the sending country. The concept of precarious status switches the focus from a preoccupation with a person's basis for entering Canada to an exploration of the effects of migration status itself.

The themes explored in this book are based on the lived experience of people who identified uncertain migration status as a factor affecting their working life or their ability to obtain basic entitlements such as health, education, and income security. All of the participants were living in the Greater Vancouver Area at the time of the study and had specific attachments to Canada through work, family, community, and social life. At the same time, they were excluded in varying degrees from health care, education, and income support, and were at particular risk of exploitation in employment situations.

At least 700,000 people in Canada have less than permanent status, and this number has increased over the past ten years. Federal government data indicate that, as of 1 December 2014, there were 353,448 authorized foreign workers present in Canada, up from 300,211 in 2012.[21] (These data do not include undocumented entries.) Recent legal and policy shifts form part of an ongoing pattern in which this number is likely to continue to increase, especially on the more vulnerable end of the spectrum.[22] Precarious migrants constitute a sizable and growing proportion of the population in Canada, and studies have shown that uncertain migration status may have detrimental socio-economic effects that persist even after regularization.[23] For these reasons, there is a pressing need to critically assess the role of migration status in the social exclusion of a growing number of people in Canada without permanent status.

Among this study's participants, the experience of various uncertain status situations had common features, and the importance of permanent residence was abundantly clear. Study responses suggest that the distinction between permanent residence and everything less than this makes a difference in the lives of migrants; those with temporary, but clearly "legal," status identified themselves as having uncertain status, alongside their counterparts without "legal" status. Across multiple status categories, migrants emphasized the importance of permanent residence rather than the distinction between undocumented and documented per se. Furthermore, possession of a valid status document did not necessarily legitimize all activities necessary to daily life. A majority of the participants possessed, or had possessed, some type of immigration status, but their interactions with the Canadian labour market were unauthorized, as they were beyond timelines or conditions specified on the permit. Even for those few who had never transgressed the formal limits of their legal authorization to be present or work in Canada, status uncertainty functioned as a limiting force within employment relations, state-based social protection, and day-to-day life.

Precarious Migrants in Canada: Foreign Workers, Refugees, and Undocumented Migrants

While migrant precarity exists in a wide variety of different status situations, there are three that deserve special attention. Temporary foreign workers, inland refugee claimants, and undocumented migrants not only constitute a large proportion of non-permanent migrants in Canada, but they also represent migrant groups entering or remaining in Canada for reasons of economic need and/or risk in their country of origin rather than for pleasure or tourism. All of the migrants I spoke with had belonged to at least one of these three groups during their time in Canada.

The number of people entering Canada with temporary work permits has been on the increase for more than a decade. In 2015, the federal government recorded 404,384 temporary work permit holders.[24] This group includes people participating in employer-driven work programs such as caregiver programs, the Seasonal Agricultural Worker Program, and working holiday programs, as well as people granted work permits for reasons of public policy or necessity. The top source nations for foreign workers at the time of the study were the Philippines, India, the United States, and Mexico. Significantly, the proportion of foreign workers classified as low skilled has been increasing for at least ten years. Low-skilled workers are particularly susceptible to exploitation and have fewer opportunities to become permanent residents of Canada.

Temporary foreign workers are precarious because they do not have the right to enter and reside in Canada on a permanent basis. Their status is contingent, given that it often relies on employers: about two-thirds of temporary foreign workers are permitted to work only for the employer specified on their work permit. This results in reduced labour mobility and bargaining power relative to citizen workers. In addition, work permits may be subject to restrictions, such as length of stay, occupation, and place of residence. People with "open" work permits, which do not restrict them to a single employer, are often spouses whose permits are contingent on their partner's status as a worker or student. With respect to residence, at the time of this study, live-in caregivers had to live with their employers in order to meet the requirements of their program and become eligible for permanent residence.[25] Temporary foreign workers are entitled by law to the same standards of hours, pay, working conditions, and compensation for workplace injuries as permanent workers, although, as will be detailed in the chapters that follow, they face barriers in accessing these protections. Foreign workers are legally entitled to participate in provincial health care and to register their children in publicly funded schools, but generally they do not have access to welfare. Although they pay into the federal Employment Insurance Program like all employees, they may be barred from its benefits because, as a result of their bonded work permits, they are not considered "available for work."[26] Finally, it is worth noting that temporary foreign workers classified as "high skilled" are much more likely to obtain permanent residence than those classified as "low skilled," regardless of other factors such as length of time in or connection to Canada.

Like temporary foreign workers, inland refugee claimants constitute a large proportion of precarious migrants in Canada. There is no formal cap on the number of inland refugee claims in Canada. While there is ongoing political and public interest in debating the genuineness of refugee claims and the legitimacy of claimants' presence in Canada, it is beyond the ambit of this book to take a position on the merit of claims or the procedure used to assess them. Rather, I consider the claimant population already in Canada as a subset of the precarious population on the basis of status contingency, physical residence in Canada, and participation in the labour market and Canadian social state. In the ten years preceding the study, the annual number of inland claims ranged from under 15,000 to almost 45,000. At the time of this study in December 2012, there were 89,385 unresolved refugee claims.[27]

Refugee claimants are entitled by law to obtain open work permits and basic services such as education and social assistance while they await claim determination. Prior to 2012, refugee claimants had access to health care benefits that were comparable to those of citizens and permanent residents. However, at the time of interviews with study participants, refugee claimants were eligible for emergency services only, and claimants from certain countries were ineligible even for those services.[28] This refusal of health services to certain categories of refugees was found to be unconstitutional by the Federal Court in 2014.[29] In 2016, after a change in government, the federal immigration authority restored health care coverage for all refugee claimants.[30]

There are no data on the labour market participation rate of refugee claimants, but it is safe to assume that, by necessity, most obtain work permits, and the data collected in this study indicate that they participate in work generally classified as "low skilled." Unlike temporary foreign workers, refugee claimants are eligible for welfare benefits in some situations. Compared to temporary foreign workers, they also have greater labour mobility, in the sense that their work permits are not bound to one employer. They fit within the category of "precarious migrants" because their status is contingent on the outcome of the refugee claim process, at which point they may become eligible for permanent residence or they may have their status terminated. Status precarity for refugee claimants is underscored by the fact that each person claiming refugee status in

Canada is issued a deportation order when a claim is made, which is removed only if a claim is successful.[31] While refugees engage in the labour market with relatively high levels of labour mobility and access to the social state relative to other groups, they still remain dependent upon status which is completely contingent on the outcome of the refugee claim process.

The final group included here is undocumented migrants. There are no precise data concerning the number of people in this country without status, but a 2009 federal report estimates the number of undocumented workers in Canada at 50,000–800,000. Although the report notes that undocumented migrants "are vulnerable to marginalization and mistreatment," it offers no analysis except the general recommendation to "stop the problem from getting any bigger."[32] While some individuals enter Canada without authorization, many others enter with temporary status as visitors, students, or workers, and then either are unable to renew their status or are without status for an interim period while waiting to restore or regularize their status. The structure of Canadian immigration law contributes to the population of unauthorized migrants in Canada, but enforcement of the law is relatively minimal, creating a situation in which undocumented workers are "unwelcome but tolerated."[33] There are no conclusive data on the specific ways in which this group participates in the labour market, but the lack of status or breach of permit conditions means they are unlikely to have labour mobility or bargaining power and will have little to no access to social benefits.

Data on temporary residents' engagement with the labour force is inadequate. One of the few overall sources is the Canada Revenue Agency's record of individual tax filers whose returns are based on a temporary social insurance number (SIN). These records show a considerable increase over the past decade in the number of tax filers with non-permanent status: in 2004, the number of tax filers who had been issued a temporary SIN was 193,250; by 2014, the number had increased to 463,720. These numbers represent a conservative estimate of the involvement of temporary residents in the workforce, as they capture only those jobs for which taxes are filed and paid and do not account for informal jobs, which are more likely a source of employment for precarious migrants.

Talking to Precarious Migrants

Migrant participants in this study came from various cultural, national, and class backgrounds. Participants self-reported with respect to uncertain migration status, concerns about the work, and access to health care, education, or income support. The group included twenty-eight migrants who identified their status as uncertain, as well as five participants from agencies that supported migrants. All agency participants were front-line workers at organizations that assisted migrants with uncertain migration status in their day-to-day work, whether as part of the organizations' formal mandate or otherwise. The migrant participants had a variety of current and past migration statuses, including lack of status, temporary foreign work permits (both open and closed), visitor visas, refugee claimants and post-determination claimants, and permanent residents who had past experiences of uncertain migration status. Migrant participants had been in Canada from several months to over a decade at the time of their interviews. Of the twenty-eight migrant participants, twenty-one were women and seven were men. In terms of nationality, eleven were from mainland China, nine were from Mexico, three were from the Philippines, two were from Colombia, one was from Bolivia, one was from Guatemala, and one was from Korea. (See Appendix A for basic profiles of the participants.)

A purposeful sampling strategy was used to assemble the participant group. Participants were enlisted through third-party recruitment and multilingual posters at migrant-serving agency sites and in high-traffic public areas. In addition, recruitment letters for both migrant and agency participants were produced in English and distributed by email to contacts among the legal community, paralegal advocates, and migrant-serving agencies. Posters and consent forms were produced in English, Tagalog, Spanish, Punjabi, and simplified Chinese. Interested participants were invited to contact the study by phone or email. I also relied on snowball sampling: study participants were offered copies of the recruitment letter and poster in the appropriate language and had the option of passing this information along to other potential participants.[34]

Because interviews were an essential source of data for this project, the research design demanded specific attention in this area. Rubin and Rubin provide a detailed overview of various approaches to qualitative interviewing based on the purpose of the research in question.[35] I wished to ensure the primacy of detailed experiential information as an entry point; I developed interviews loosely in the format of elaborated case studies, which sought to explore participants' recollection of events as factual occurrences and also to query their perceptions of the reasoning and motivation that underpinned their experiences. Of particular interest to me was the participants' perception of the factors underlying their experience and understanding of status and its relationship to employment situations and interactions with the social state. Closely related in the Rubins' taxonomy is ethnographic interpretation, which seeks to explore participants' perceptions of "key norms, rules, symbols, values, traditions and rituals"[36] that exist within groups in particular contexts. For my purposes, this ethnographic element added the dimension of exploring any specific "cultures" or organized responses to institutional governance, such as, for example, particular community perceptions of the impact of status on obtaining access to Employment Insurance benefits.

Applying an ethnographic approach provided access to information about unwritten policies and, in particular, cultures of policy implementation and understanding of specific texts that would not be evident from a reading of the text alone. This approach allowed me to focus on the real-life impact of front-line interpretation of legal texts and policies. Furthermore, the Rubins' model of "responsive interviewing" seems intuitive within the framework of institutional ethnography. They define it as follows:

> The term "responsive interviewing" is intended to communicate that qualitative interviewing is a dynamic and interactive process, not a set of tools to be applied mechanically. In this model, questioning styles reflect the personality of the researcher, adapt to the varying relationship between researcher and conversational partner, and change as the purpose of the interview evolves.[37]

In the context of this research, the use of responsive interviewing served both the methodological commitment to the concept of interactivity between text and interview, and the primacy of interview data and participant perspective. Although themes were established to a certain extent through recruitment and interview structuring, the majority of time spent in interviews was made up of more free-flowing conversation in which, although I was often asking the questions, I attempted to base them closely on the concerns and experiences articulated by participants. Because I approached this research as an outsider – and because a main target group of the research has been subject to oppressive and unequal relations on the basis of colonialist and imperialist legacies that persist in the organization of the Canadian state with regard to migrants – I assumed that efforts to "make room" in a general sense were unlikely to be sufficient to meet appropriate ethical standards or my own sense of responsibility. It was necessary to ensure that the format and content of the interviews was dynamic enough to allow participants' guidance and agency in terms of content and setting boundaries with regard to their own comfort level in responding. In addition, I made every effort to openly and appropriately recognize my individual stake and position with regard to the work within a complex set of colonial, racial, class, and gender-based relations. As such, I framed my own commitments in the interviews in terms of both transparency and solidarity, and actively pursued both during interviews. I worked to supplant the idea of the researcher as an objective, neutral observer with one in which I recognized my own place in the particular histories and relations that form the context of this work.

Specifically, in attempting to privilege the perspectives of participants as the basis for the analytical framing of this work, while remaining an outsider, I found it most appropriate to identify myself as an ally to the people and communities most affected by the legal and governance structures examined in this work. An ally position is not fixed. According to Vikki Reynolds, an ally position is, by definition, fluid and imperfect: one is always "becoming an ally."[38] In acknowledging the relative privileges I have and the consequences of my position within specific interactions in the research context and outside it, I actively maintained awareness of my own limitations alongside my willingness to act. Throughout recruitment, interviews, and writing, I remained cognizant of the risk of learning at the expense of study participants and took steps to reduce that risk, in terms of exercising discretion as to the extent and nature of questions and of giving priority to those issues that emerged as most important to the participants themselves. Reynolds ties this approach to respectful engagement, and specifically to obtaining what Paulo Friere calls an "authentic dialogue" in learning.[39]

Institutional Ethnography

This study draws on institutional ethnography, as described by Dorothy Smith, as a primary methodology. Institutional ethnography commits the researcher to start with the actualities of life for a person or group and move from there to consider how that experience is embedded in social relations and institutional functioning. For Smith, institutions serve as sites in which specific practices inform relations beyond the level of individual experience. After listening to study participants talk about the meaning of migration status, work, and access to legal protections, health care, education, and income support, I used the themes that arose during interviews to structure my next steps. Specifically, I used participant responses as signposts to guide me in conducting research on legal materials, including policy materials, legal texts, and case law. I traced back from participants' experiences to the statutes under which particular interactions were governed (for example, the *School Act* for interactions with schools and boards of education), as well as the court and tribunal decisions in which these statutes were interpreted and applied.

Smith describes institutional ethnography as "a method of inquiry into the social that proposes to enlarge the scope of what becomes visible from a specific site of interaction, mapping the relations that connect one local site to others."[40] By using local knowledge to understand translocal relations, it resists the objectification of people within sociological research and encourages inquiry that begins from inside their situations. Thus, while talking to people provides a venue for inquiry grounded within local experience, the objects of study are actually the specific institutions and structures themselves, rather than the people. In this way, institutional ethnography aims to "reorganize the social relations of knowledge of the social so that people can take that knowledge up as an extension of our ordinary knowledge of the local actualities of our lives."[41]

In order to commit to research that meaningfully included people and recognized my own position as an outsider/ally, I needed to ensure that participant data served to structure the direction and analysis in this study so that, in Smith's words, "[t]heir perspective and experience would organize the direction" of this research.[42] Smith's initial formulation of institutional ethnography was grounded in a feminist analysis that recognized the exclusion of women from the ruling apparatus and then expanded to provide a method of inquiry *for* people, rather than about them. The critical feminism inherent in this approach is appropriate for the present study, in part because the majority of study participants from both migrant and agency populations are women, a small sample of the larger-scale feminization of labour through migration. In addition to this direct connection to women's experience, however, is the idea that institutional ethnography as a feminist approach is appropriate for exploring not only women's experience but also the experience of all those who are categorically excluded from control of the ruling apparatus.

As Smith explains, institutional ethnography "may start by exploring the experience of those directly involved in the institutional setting, but they are not the objects of investigation. It is the aspects of the institutions relevant to the people's experience, not the people themselves, that constitute the object of inquiry."[43] Thus, the aims of the present research were not bound by specific hypotheses or causal relationships articulated at the outset; rather, they arose and developed through the process of exploration of people's experience within particular settings. The orientation and potential of institutional ethnography in terms of power relations are described by Campbell and Gregor as follows:

> Institutional ethnographers agree that the question of power is important to researchers, to those who are the subject of research, and to how research is used. We are particularly aware that the production of knowledge itself is integral to the relations of ruling and to the exercise of power in official, and perhaps even unofficial, ways. The radical potential of institutional ethnography is to rethink social settings taking existing power relations into account. Institutional ethnography is theorized and its research design developed in such a manner as to produce an analysis in the interest of those about whom knowledge is being constructed. It is that frame for the research that established the orientation of the analysis in the interest of those about whom knowledge is being constructed.[44]

An essential concept in Smith's institutional ethnography is the dynamic role of texts. Smith's application of the concept of the text is not limited to the written word, but spans various media and may include material transmitted through writing, speaking, or performing.[45] The key element of texts for Smith is their replicability. They may be reproduced and create interactions in multiple sites, with multiple actors, and can thus serve as a connecting and organizing force between disparate sites and individuals. Smith argues that, in contrast to direct, sense-based experience, texts perform a coordinating function as they play out within actions. Texts function to organize and connect people, meanings, and experiences in specific ways that depend on their context; texts thus function to render and organize the social.[46] Furthermore, Smith argues that institutional discourses function not only to prescribe particular actions, but also to produce patterns of "what participants can recognize as rational and objective" and "the terms under which what people do becomes institutionally accountable."[47] In this process, she says, texts subsume the particularities of lived experience by treating such actualities as instances of the categories already enumerated in the institutional text, displacing subjects except as institutional categories.

In practice, this methodology allowed me to trace the effects and relationships of specific texts and discourses through examples within lived experience and also to understand the function of texts in shaping migrants' experience. Thus, this methodology was an appropriate way to attempt to bridge the gap between findings that relate to the specific experiences of precarious migrants and the texts and institutions through which ruling relations are produced. Through this analysis, the data collected from specific people in specific sites were used to explore the way in which multiple institutional sites contribute to subordination.

Another fundamental concept in Smith's methodology is that of "institutions." There are many examples of institutional ethnography being used to study one particular site, exploring, for example, the management culture of one government department or corporate worksite. Yet, an institution is not limited to a single site, nor is it limited to government organizations. Rather, Smith defines institutions as "complexes embedded in the ruling relations that are organized around a distinctive function, such as education, health care, and so on [...] It is a specific capacity of institutions that they generalize and are generalized."[48] In addition, multiple institutions can be connected by a particular text. In this study, the construct of migration status functions as a text in this way: it plays a role in the federal taxonomy of citizens and non-citizens, in the determination of benefits and entitlements in provincial programs, and in individual work-sites. Importantly, it also serves to connect all of them in terms of migrants' lives and experience.

I posit that migration status functions as a text that is enacted in multiple sites through law, policy, and practice, forming a multi-sited regime in which subordinate socio-economic position is maintained. Migration status has a legal genesis, and is often applied on an individual basis, but, viewed using Smith's approach, its governing function through multiple coordinated sites becomes visible in ways that were not immediately evident from the standpoint of a more static approach to textual analysis. For example, it is the role of the federal government to determine and assign migration status and the consequences that flow from status distinctions, such as enforcement or removal. Through talking to migrants, however, it became clear that migration status was an extremely influential feature of their relationships with all levels of government and in their working and social life, in places and ways that are not overtly connected to the federal immigration authority. Flowing from this recognition, an exploration of regulations, policies, and practices revealed that the construct of migration status was a dynamic component of access and decision making for a wide scope of relationships, in addition to those related directly to the federal immigration powers. These various institutional sites can be understood by attending to "formal policies and regulations and the non-formal or substantive practices that together establish the terms that shape presence in legal status categories and access to their associated bundle of rights."[49] This book aims to give specific content to the types of conditions perpetuated by various institutional actors, but also to examine how they operate together in the lives of migrants.

Front-Line Discretion, Law, and the Administrative States
Belying its dull title, administrative law in Canada is a dynamic and compelling site in which the immediate impact of law on ordinary citizens can be studied. Many "life-altering" decisions[50] – including those related to

entitlements to necessary benefits such as income support, housing, and workers' compensation, as well as to fundamental rights such as basic employment standards and freedom from racial and gender discrimination – are not, for the most part, contested in the higher courts, but rather are made in the ostensibly mundane context of administrative bureaucracies. Law is, in part, a set of written statutes, determined by elected legislators through parliamentary debate; and these statutes are subject to interpretation and, in some cases, direct reshaping by higher courts, particularly in light of their compliance with the Constitution. However, the statute and its interpretation by higher courts do not provide a full account of the meaning and action of law in society.

Statutes may set out certain benefits and requirements in a broad sense, and these may be specified further in subordinate regulations that are enabled by the original statute. For example, the *Medicare Protection Act* provides that residents of British Columbia are entitled to medical care, but the subordinate regulation sets out a list of requirements for being considered a resident. Moreover, both a statute and its regulations, to have effect, must be applied, and they will be applied through specific agencies of the state. These agencies often comprise individual front-line decision makers, such as welfare or immigration officers. The work of these agents will make up a vast majority of the decisions under statutes, and, in carrying out their duties, they use further decision-making tools, such as written policies and the unwritten policies and institutional practices though which policy is also shaped.[51] Their decisions are generally subject to some level of internal review, as well as review by "arms' length" tribunals,[52] which can render tangible remedies – for example, if a benefit has been denied, a tribunal usually has the power to restore it. In some cases, there are only front-line decision makers (e.g., in the issuance of a work permit by federal immigration authorities) or only tribunals (as is the case with some provincial human rights regimes).

Front-line decision makers and tribunals are central to the law's power not only because they are responsible for a massive proportion of the decision making with respect to essential benefits, but also because their substantive exercise of discretion is by and large unassailable by courts. Judicial review of these types of decisions is available in most cases, but the remedies available are not substantive, and reviewing courts show significant deference to both front-line decision makers and tribunals. Decisions can be overturned if they do not give due regard to the evidence before them, or if the court determines the decision was made unfairly. Yet, even if this is the case, the court will not "re-weigh" the evidence or replace the decision with its own: the decision often goes back to the tribunal or office that made the original decision, for redetermination.[53]

Because front-line decision makers and tribunals are subject to very limited judicial oversight, the manner in which they apply laws is fundamental to the substantive rights affected by those laws. Discretion is exercised by individuals, but never in a vacuum. I do not subscribe to the traditionalist premise that "rules" (formal law) and "discretion" (decisions made beyond the pure dictates of the rules) are usefully separated. Instead, I proceed on the assumption that statutes, regulations, policy, and practice can be usefully assessed as a whole to understand what is produced in the application of law. I agree with Steve Wexler that "our unwillingness to face the reality of discretionary decision-making – our commitment to the myth of objectivity – prevents us from examining and redesigning our institutions to cope with either the present or the obvious future of the law."[54] In this book, I argue that the application of law across multiple sites creates an aggregate beyond individual discretion, reflecting and producing social relations through the use of the construct of migration status. I am not interested in implicating individual decision-makers with regard to the detrimental use of discretion. Discretion is embedded within an institutional framework in which the law is enacted in people's lives. Thus, I look at multiple institutional sites and draw on several sources of data, including migrants' responses as well as institutional policies and practices, to show that the entire aggregate functions to enforce subordination of migrants with less than permanent status.

Laws, Policies, and Institutions

To examine the basic legislative structures relevant to precarious migrants, I started by reviewing federal and provincial statutes and regulations in whose application migration status was likely to be relevant. Using the common experiences of non-permanent migrant clients as a starting point, I traced back from their experiences to the statutes under which they were governed. In terms of federal structures, I identified the

Immigration and Refugee Protection Act and the *Employment Insurance Act*. Among provincial statutes in British Columbia, I identified the *Medicare Protection Act*, the *Employment Standards Act*, the *Workers Compensation Act*, the *School Act*, the *Employment and Assistance Act*, and the *Employment and Assistance for Persons with Disabilities Act*. For these statutes and their associated regulations, I read through the text and selected those sections that were likely to be relevant to status, either directly or indirectly. In so doing, I kept in mind the language of migration status itself, as well as vocabulary in federal statutes and regulations associated with migration status (e.g., *work permit, temporary foreign worker, refugee*). I also selected sections that did not explicitly mention migration status but whose application would likely involve considerations of status (e.g., regulations about agricultural workers), as well as those that were of general application to all workers but were likely to present problems specifically for migrants (e.g., regulations governing hours of work and pay).

Having established a set of statutes and regulations and identified an initial subset of sections, I turned to their interpretation in case law through quasi-judicial tribunal and court decisions. The scope of jurisdiction for tribunals is limited to that which is given under the statute: they are limited to making certain kinds of decisions on the application of their home statute and empowered to provide only those remedies set out in that statute. I identified the tribunals in which migration status was likely to be considered in making decisions about workplace conditions or state entitlements – namely, the Board of Referees, the Pension Appeal Board, the British Columbia Employment Standards Tribunal, the British Columbia Employment and Assistance Appeal Tribunal, and the Workers' Compensation Board. Where a tribunal's decisions were available online, I used federal vocabulary associated with status (e.g., *work permit, temporary foreign worker, refugee*) as well as casual language associated with status (e.g., *illegal, without status, overstay*) to search for decisions in which status was mentioned. I also searched these decisions using the specific sections of the legislation I had previously identified and the language in them that I had identified as potentially relevant to status. Where tribunal decisions were not available online, I made formal Access to Information requests to each tribunal, requesting decisions in which migration status was a factor considered by the tribunal.[55] Where necessary, I followed up with tribunal staff to clarify my request and obtain copies of decisions.

In comparison to tribunals, courts are able to consider a much wider range of laws and remedies. While some courts are created by statute, and are thus limited with regard to the statutes within their jurisdiction, even those courts have a much broader role than any tribunal in terms of interpreting the law. Furthermore, courts are responsible for hearing judicial review applications of tribunal-level decisions; in this function, they may make findings that affect the manner in which tribunals render decisions, even if the court is in a different jurisdiction. In searching court-based jurisprudence, I used the same initial set of search terms that I employed for tribunal decision searches. My search included all courts in Canada, regardless of jurisdiction or geography. In addition, when I encountered language that was used by the court to make determinations relevant to migration status but that was not in the statute itself,[56] I added key terms to my search. Finally, I used CanLII's citation tools to see how key cases had been interpreted and applied in other case law, and whether they had been overturned.

With regard to the application of laws through the policies of first-level decision makers, I identified the government organizations responsible for the laws listed above, which included Service Canada, the British Columbia Employment Standards Branch, the British Columbia Workers' Compensation Board, the British Columbia Ministry of Social Development, the British Columbia Ministry of Health, Vancouver Coastal Health, Fraser Health, the British Columbia Ministry of Education, and all school boards in British Columbia. Some of these organizations publish policy manuals online, but I made formal Access to Information requests to all of them for statistics, policies, and materials concerning the application of migration status, which were tailored to the function of specific organizations.[57] I obtained initial policy data based on my existing knowledge of issues likely to arise for migrants; I then made amended requests to these institutions on the basis of information gathered through interviews, thus allowing the focus of the work to evolve with the input of study participants. As detailed in the chapters below, policy documents such as these figured critically in the provision or denial of benefits. It is worth noting that, although these policy documents were provided on request, only a fraction were readily available to the public other than by specific request (in contrast to statutes and regulations, which are always publicly available). Because these documents were so important in front-line decision making and in the application of the law, their absence from public fora could itself be seen as problematic in terms of transparency: without knowing what to ask for, it is difficult for people to make meaningful use of access to information laws to understand how laws will be applied to them. Even without such an intention, the result is invisibilization of information that is central to decisions affecting precarious migrants.[58]

Limitations

There are some important limitations in the sample used in this study. First, in designing this project, I recognized that there is a compelling need for reliable quantitative data concerning the numbers, locations, entry points, and social and material well-being of precarious migrants in Canada, particularly undocumented migrants. The fieldwork on which this book is based does not provide data that can be extrapolated to the larger population of precarious migrants with respect to these points. Similarly, the context in which my findings can be analyzed with regard to Canada's migration regime and other social and economic factors will be limited, as, at best, there exist only guesses about the exact numbers and locations of people currently without status and little or no data about those who have been without status in the past.

Second, the sample used in the present study is not random and thus may not be seen as "representative" in the traditional sense. Due to recruitment concerns described above, the study was not designed to obtain a representative sample. The data gathered may be limited in their application because they were obtained from applicants who were less at risk or more willing to participate for other reasons. My sampling process may well have missed migrants in the labour force whose experience might be different from those who were willing to participate. Another data limitation arose in tandem with ensuring ethical conduct. Making sure that source information was collected with due regard to the potential risk to the applicant meant a modest scope of questioning and the omission of interesting and important data, such as identification of employers and specific worksites or sites of social state interaction.

Who Belongs and Why?

The exclusion of non-permanent residents from social benefits is often justified on the basis of social closure or communitarian arguments – that a state has the right to determine its own members and to enforce its boundaries politically and territorially.[59] There is a distinction, however, between control of entry to a state and control of those already within it: this is the difference between "border control" and "migrant control." Linda Bosniak describes this distinction in terms of a citizenship model that is constructed as hard on the outside and soft on the inside. Those within the borders are treated equally as members, and those outside have no claims to such membership as long as they remain on the outside. However, she notes, this model is inaccurate insofar as it fails to capture the way in which "bounded citizenship often operates inside the community's territorial perimeters, especially by way of exclusionary laws on immigration and alienage."[60] Exclusion within Canada's territory is not limited to immigration laws, but includes multiple sites in the regulation of workplaces and the social state. A complex of laws, policies, and practices spanning various fields and jurisdictions is involved in the work of "structuring the vulnerability" of people who have migrated to Canada. This gives rise to the "paradox of democratic legitimacy," in which a closed polity necessarily excludes some of those who are subject to governance within it.[61]

As will be elaborated in the chapters below, exclusion of precarious migrants is not absolute, but can be understood instead as partial inclusion or, as Chauvin and Garcés-Mascareñas note, "subordinate inclusion," in which "illegality regulates mobility not through physical borders but through the creation of a hierarchy of rights."[62] An increase in the number of migrants in Canada with less than full status thus creates a "disjuncture between the reality of daily practice and legal status"[63] but also one between the fact of economic and social presence and the exclusion from the benefits of full membership in Canadian society.

Ethical arguments in favour of rights for temporary residents fall into two main camps, each of which understands the role of the sovereign state differently. On one side are arguments based on a universalist or cosmopolitan notion of rights, which include concepts such as global citizenship and international human rights, in which entitlements do not depend on association with a specific bounded community and state sovereignty is not the primary frame for membership.[64] On the other are those in which any rights are predicated on membership in a particular community and in which the sovereign state maintains a strong role.[65] This book falls squarely into the second camp – in Canada, domestic laws are of profound influence on the daily lives of migrants, and it is through interaction with the national state that membership is granted or restricted. The role of various state institutions needs to be addressed in order for rights and membership claims to become meaningful. In order to do this, it is not necessary or useful to frame the state as a singular entity, but rather as a constellation of texts, institutions, and practices united through the dispersion of particular functions, including the enforcement of status-based boundaries studied in this book.

2

Status, Deportability, and Illegality in Daily Life

Precarious migrants are preoccupied with their migration status. With status comes a sense of security; living without status generates uncertainty and fear. The state, too, is obsessed with migration status. In Canada, federal immigration law organizes people according to status, labels them accordingly, and authorizes their removal or punishment if they are out of place. At law, status does not exist as a simple binary but rather as a spectrum in which there are multiple statuses that fall short of permanent residency, with all subject to conditions, enforcement, and/or removal. Federal immigration law governs direct enforcement both at the border and inside Canada. For precarious migrants, however, migration status matters far beyond issues of entry, authorization, and deportation. This chapter starts with a brief overview of the structure in which migration status is formally determined through federal law, and then turns to a detailed account of the nature and effect of precarious migration status as defined by interview participants.

The manner in which individuals are legally authorized to be, to work, or to avail themselves of social protection in Canada can shape their lives in many fundamental ways, including in terms of physical and mental health, social life and community, wages and labour conditions, family relationships, and personal identity. In talking with migrants who identified themselves as having uncertain legal status, it was clear that the idea of status was a powerful and dynamic construct that affected their lives and relationships. Migration status is a state-determined assignment, which, far beyond merely labelling, functions to frame the terms on which people live, work, and belong. An isolated reading of laws and policies, however, gives only the most abstract sense of the meaning of status. An analysis limited to the federal classification of status would not only omit the significant role played by provincial legislation and its derivative policies and practices, but, more importantly, would fail to account for the manner in which status governs the lives of migrants. Because migration exists as a feature of multiple sites, the lives of migrants are not simply interrupted by occasional inconveniences due to lack of status – to the contrary, study interviews disclose a much more powerful and overarching role for status.

The power of status lies in the contingency it creates for migrants in the most primary aspects of their lives. Status affects not only the degree of entitlement to necessary services but also the very opportunity to make requests; unless or until individuals can demonstrate sufficient migration status, they are functionally non-persons from the perspective of state institutions responsible for the allocation of benefits. Migration status can be understood in its most basic sense as "standing." Differential and precarious status is established through territorial exclusion and through the creation of distinctions made within Canada's territory, by way of economic and social barriers that are conceived and maintained in a variety of relationships governed by law. Legal status thus conditions people's specific relationships to the Canadian state and affects the social and economic position of migrants.

In implicating multiple laws, policies, and institutions in which migration status tends to exclude precarious migrants, I first want to liberate the definition of migration status from the confines of federal immigration law. Migration is no doubt a creature of law in terms of its genesis and in the way it flows through multiple legal structures – it is, after all, the law and its application that form the focus of this book. But the assertion that status is a legal construct must be distinguished from the notion that the nature of migration status is best understood by reading statutes. To the contrary, the nature and effects of migration status give it potency only because they are lived out by people.

In talking to the migrants who participated in this study, all of whom identified as having uncertain migration status, it became clear that migration status was much more than a pre-emptive category or static label. Status influenced the ways in which participants identified themselves, organized their lives, and established a sense of belonging. Migrant participants spoke about status frequently, naming it as a causal factor in their negotiation of other aspects of life that we discussed in interviews, such as conditions of work and access to social protection. Status was of primary concern to migrants regardless of country of origin, actual migration status, job sector, family status, and gender.

I did not ask interview participants to define migration status, but many of the scripted questions I used (see Appendix B) referred to status – for example, questions about whether they had experienced times in which their status was uncertain and about the impact of uncertain status generally and with regard to particular matters, including conditions of work, enforcement encounters, and obtaining social entitlements. Furthermore, participants had been recruited on the basis of self-identification as having "uncertain migration status"; thus, the participant group consisted of people who had already determined that migration status was significant in their lives.

When I started reading the interview transcripts, it quickly became clear that participants revealed a diversity of experience that went beyond the scope of the specific questions. There were many responses that fell outside of direct information about enforcement, access to services, and conditions of work, but still described the way in which life was conditioned by migration status and how it was defined and understood. Participants depicted migration status from multiple angles: it could be a piece of paper, a precursor to geographic uncertainty, a social marker, or an omnipresent stressor. The manner in which migrants defined status was also of interest: it could be understood literally (e.g., in reference to legal standing), or through metaphor (e.g., through the idea of "not being here" or being "invisible"), in reference to self-identity and community, or relative to other migrants.

Migrants defined migration status in terms of its necessity as an identifier within legal, social, and economic structures, but also as a force enacted through multiple sites and through which they governed their own behaviour out of fear and uncertainty. Precarious migration status is a spectrum pervaded by uncertainty in which relatively more secure status is always desirable but may be contingent on unknown and known factors. In this spectrum, precarious migrants traverse both location and legality through their interactions with state and non-state actors. While migration status is unquestionably a legal concept, it gains potency through the lives of individual migrants; understanding the diverse ways in which the construct of migration status is received within governed communities is necessary to fully elucidating the function of migration status as a construct. By privileging the definition of migration status given by participants in interviews, I aim to enlarge the potential for critical assessment of the role of migration status in the application of laws, policies, and practices.

Migration Status in Federal Immigration Law

The power to make laws concerning immigration is an area of concurrent federal and provincial jurisdiction.[1] A province may pass laws pertaining to immigration into that province, and the federal government may pass laws concerning immigration into any or all of the provinces.[2] The federal power in this area takes primacy, however: any provincial laws in the area of immigration are constitutionally valid only insofar as they do not conflict with federal laws in this area. In effect, the power to define the basic legal categories and conditions of migration status rests with the federal government. Although provinces participate in the selection of both temporary and permanent migrants, they do not define, grant, or remove migration status. The focus here is therefore on the federal regime.

The federal *Immigration and Refugee Protection Act*[3] and associated *Regulations*[4] are central to the federal government's exercise of authority over migration status. It is through these laws that status is granted or removed and individuals deported or allowed to remain in Canada. At the most basic level, the *Act* divides people into three categories: Canadian citizens, permanent residents, and foreign nationals.[5] Canadian citizenship is available through three primary ways: automatically through birth on Canadian territory (*jus solis*); through Canadian parentage (*jus sanguinis*), with some limitations; and by naturalization for those who are already permanent residents, if they meet statutory requirements for citizenship.[6] Permanent residence in Canada is associated with many of the benefits of citizenship. Permanent residents are entitled by right to enter and remain in Canada and are able to freely participate in the Canadian labour market on par with citizens, with only a few exceptions (such as employment in the public service). They have access to education, health care, and social protections to the same extent as Canadian citizens, but they do not have voting rights. The status of permanent residents is less secure than that of Canadian citizens, as they are subject to minimum residency period requirements to maintain their permanent residence, and they may lose their status on the basis of serious criminality,[7] through misrepresentation,[8] or through failing to reside in Canada for the required period of time.[9] Furthermore, some categories of permanent residence are contingent on the fulfilment of certain conditions, historically in the case of migrant entrepreneurs,[10] but at the time of writing, also with regard to spousal sponsorships.[11] Permanent residents in Canada may face discrimination, deskilling, and barriers to social and economic integration but, given the rights and entitlements associated with their status, are not considered precarious migrants for the purposes of this study.[12]

In contrast to citizens and permanent residents, foreign nationals are defined by exclusion in the *Act*. Section 2(1) states: "'foreign national' means a person who is not a Canadian citizen or a permanent resident, and includes a stateless person."[13] Whereas both "citizen" and "permanent resident" can be said to denote a particular status, as each is determinative in terms of political, social, and economic membership, "foreign national" is a residual category, under which a wide variety of different status and entitlement situations are grouped. Foreign nationals include those authorized in be in Canada pursuant to the *Act* and *Regulations*, those without any legal authorization at all, and everyone else who is not a permanent resident, a citizen, or a "status Indian." There are three primary ways in which foreign nationals are authorized to come to Canada temporarily: as visitors, as students, and as workers.[14] All three categories are temporary by definition, but the law permits extension of status if the person can justify his or her stay.[15] People can also have what is colloquially known as "implied status" if they are able to make an extension request before their permit runs out. Visitors to Canada are authorized to enter and be present in Canada, but not to work or study. Visitors are excluded from both political membership and all social benefit entitlements. Students are generally authorized to study in a specific program (i.e., their permits are attached to a particular institution), are authorized to work in certain circumstances, and are eligible for participation in some social entitlements, such as state-funded health care.

Since the early 1970s, a complex federal regulatory structure has governed the admission of foreign workers. Admission has always been based on employers' labour needs.[16] Temporary worker programs in Canada attract much more political and academic interest than those governing either visitors or students. Because individuals are authorized to enter Canada specifically for the purpose of economic contribution, these programs engage questions of membership on a deeper level, as well as scrutiny of the conditions of work and level of social participation associated with being a temporary foreign worker. When their status is authorized, such workers are eligible for some aspects of social membership, such as Employment Insurance and state-funded health care, but they do not have the security of status that permanent residents enjoy and, as discussed in detail below, are often unable to realize the benefits to which they are entitled.

Frequently, temporary workers are admitted to Canada on the basis of a specific labour market need demonstrated by an employer. For the most part, preferential access to the Canadian labour market for Canadian citizens and permanent residents is built into the regulations: employers must obtain specific authorization to hire a foreign national by demonstrating that a suitable candidate is not available within the Canadian labour pool. Foreign workers may be admitted without this authorization pursuant to international agreements such as the North American Free Trade Agreement,[17] or on the basis of "Canadian interests," including significant benefit to Canadians and reciprocal working holiday agreements. With rare exception, in order to accept a job offer from an employer, a foreign employee is required to obtain a work permit. Such permits attach the worker to a specific employer. Workers with such permits cannot change jobs or employers without obtaining a new work permit, which relies on a new job offer and labour market justification based on employer demand.[18] For ease of reference, I will refer to work permits that bind a worker to a specific employer and occupation as "closed" work permits. "Open" work permits, in contrast, may be issued in the absence of a job offer or labour market need on the basis of public policy considerations. For example, the spouses of certain closed work permit holders and refugee claimants are eligible to obtain open permits as an incentive to the closed work permit holder (often a worker classified as "high skilled") to work in

Canada. While temporary, open work permits are not attached to a specific employer, and workers holding such permits are thus able to circulate in the labour market. A significant number of work permit holders, however, have closed permits and thus limited labour mobility relative to permanent residents and Canadian citizens.

Some temporary foreign workers can readily apply for permanent residence from within Canada after several years of work. For the most part, these workers are those whose work is classified as "high skilled" and who obtain admission pursuant to economic classes of permanent residence.[19] Workers whose labour is classified as "low skilled" are generally ineligible for these classes and thus much less likely to be eligible for permanent residence. There are large-scale federal programs for the temporary admission of foreign workers in certain categories of "low-skilled" work, notably in agriculture and domestic work. Unlike most workers classified as "low skilled," domestic workers are eligible to obtain permanent residence after two years of full-time caregiving work in Canada. The latter category forms the exception to the rule with regard to "low-skilled" workers and permanent residence under the auspices of the Live-in Caregiver Program.[20] At the time of the study, live-in domestic workers were eligible to apply for permanent residence after full-time live-in domestic service to an employer in Canada for two years within a four-year period.[21] Although this program offers eventual permanent residence to those who meet its requirements, there are many practical barriers, as discussed in detail in the following chapters.

Unauthorized migrants are not positively defined within the text of the *Immigration and Refugee Protection Act;* rather, they constitute a diverse residual category. Because the ways in which a person may have legal status in Canada are limited to citizenship, permanent residence, and permits for temporary visitors, students, and workers, those who do not fall within these categories are in Canada without authorization. In other words, the ways in which individuals may be legally authorized to be in Canada are few and limited, but the ways in which they can be unauthorized are many and varied. The federal legal structure describes the assignment of status in relatively clear terms: those who are authorized to be in Canada permanently or who temporarily have legal status. The ways in which a person may be without status are formed in the shadow of this authorization. A person whose presence in Canada is not authorized by law, whether through unauthorized entry or by overstaying their visa, is subject to offence and enforcement provisions. Enforcement and offence provisions also extend to people who have legal status but transgress the terms and conditions attached to their permit. Such transgression is often by way of unauthorized labour market engagement, such as working for employers for which a person does not have specific permission. An authorized visitor who works, an authorized worker who engages in work for an unauthorized employer or in an unauthorized job, and a student who works prior to obtaining permission to do so could all be subject to enforcement provisions, despite the fact that their presence itself is authorized. The legal structure holds many such opportunities for the creation and maintenance of precarious migration status, which come into sharper focus in the examination of the participants' interview responses below.

In addition to setting out a taxonomy of status in terms of authorization, federal immigration law contains enforcement provisions that govern the boundaries of status. It specifically prohibits people from remaining in Canada beyond the authorized period of time as well as studying and working without specific authorization.[22] It creates offences for those who contravene the *Act* or *Regulations* or who fail to comply with a condition – for example, contravening length of stay or the limitation of work authorization to one specified employer.[23] It is also an offence for an employer to employ a person who is not authorized to work; this imposes a positive obligation on employers to exercise due diligence to determine whether a person is authorized to work.[24] All of these offences are hybrid: the Crown has the discretion to treat them as either a summary offence or as an indictable offence. If they proceed by indictment, each attracts a fine of up to $50,000 and imprisonment of up to two years.[25] While enforcement and prosecution under these sections is relatively infrequent, as is discussed in Chapter 5, migrants' fear of state power and enforcement is often enough to make even the possibility of enforcement a major influence in their lives.

Identification and Belonging

Status, which is designated by the federal government, is often signified through a written permit. But when a permit runs out, the person does not disappear. In interviews for this study, both agency and migrant participants referred to status in terms of physical legal documentation, which was seen as conferring status and security. However, participants also described their relationship to the state beyond the conferral of formal status. Migrants often spoke of Canada as a unified whole, a place with which they had a relationship mediated through state institutions. Participants recounted their initial perceptions of Canada as a welcoming, diverse, and safe place. They expressed anger, frustration, and despair on encountering exclusion, and some attributed this exclusion to government action or inaction. For many, Canada had made promises through its migration programs that were not fulfilled, even when the migrants met the state's requirements. In an iteration of the liberal dilemma of presence without authorization, migrants' narratives disclosed a deep tension between the definition of identity through formal immigration status and their own sense of relationship with the Canadian state.

With respect to the use of federal documents as conferring status, an agency worker described status as being uncertain when a migrant did not have a permit physically in hand, regardless of whether she had legal status: "They experience uncertain status when [...] they are on implied status, waiting for a new work permit. Hopefully that work permit comes, but if it is refused, then they lack status." The document itself held power apart from the status it signified. Even when a person had legal status, that status was more difficult to prove without a document and was therefore less meaningful. Such a situation occurs, for example, when a person who has applied to renew status pursuant to the *Immigration and Refugee Protection Act* maintains the same status until a decision is made on his or her application for extension – something known informally as "implied status."[26] Without a document in hand, migrants in this situation experienced their own status as uncertain, despite the fact that their presence was clearly authorized. The certainty conferred by the physical document is also underscored by its practical relevance in terms of gaining access to social membership benefits. Migrants also reported being requested to provide proof of status by employers, schools, and landlords. As elaborated in Chapter 4, the gatekeepers of benefits require not only that a person have legal migration status to confer benefits but that they possess specific physical documents.

One migrant claimant elaborated on the identifying function of status documents: "The [work permit] helps you; it's a socio-political and legal way to know who you are. If you are a good person or you have committed a crime, the [work permit] is like a business card to society, and society is everyone." The paper permit carries meaning not only in terms of formal legal status, but also in terms of one's place in society more generally and the entitlement to hold such a place. In conveying legitimacy, it denotes membership beyond the basic permissions granted by law: it also renders the migrant visible to "society" or "everyone." However, this visibility is dynamic in the case of precarious migrants, because their status is, by definition, contingent. The possession of a status document can serve to protect a migrant or facilitate access to services. But it may also render the migrant more susceptible to enforcement, surveillance, or discrimination by identifying that person as a member of a "helot" group whose status is socio-economically subjugated relative to permanent residents and citizens.[27] While those without status, or without sufficient status, are visible in the sense of actual presence in working and social life, they need to maintain the "camouflage" of legal status.[28]

Migrant participants disclosed a variety of reasons for wishing to enter Canada. In so doing, they described their expectations and perceptions of Canada as well as their own place and potential within Canada. While a minority of migrant participants identified economic factors as a primary reason for entering Canada, most had other reasons. The live-in caregivers I interviewed, for example, did not cite economic reasons for coming to Canada. They were already well educated and multilingual and had sufficient opportunities to earn money in their countries of origin. As noted by one caregiver, "There were no economical reasons. To my knowledge, many of the live-in caregivers who come over from China don't have these economical problems." Migrant participants disclosed a broad range of reasons for coming to Canada, not limited to economics. These included political asylum; marital difficulties and a desire for distance; the belief that "Canada is a good country" in which to establish a new life; the need for a new direction; the belief that Canada is "a place of harmony and wealth and a friendly country"; and the idea that it would be beneficial to educate children here. Another reason was for personal development, as articulated by one migrant:

> I wanted more challenges in my life. If I didn't leave China, my life would remain a life that I don't admire. So to immigrate to Canada, it was as if

I opened a door to the world. Possibly by coming to Canada, I thought I could come here and somehow kind of ignite the innate abilities that I have and that are not yet discovered.

A Mexican participant employed as a construction worker articulated both personal and political reasons for wanting to migrate to Canada:

I decided to come to Canada 'cause I find this place with a wide world of opportunities. It's a better place to grow in your person and also your ideas and establish your future. Also, I find this place more comfortable 'cause of the diversity of culture and 'cause, I think, I guess, the people respect each other, 'cause they understand and they know the laws.

In both of these narratives, Canada is cast in positive terms – as an inclusive, diverse, welcoming place in which rights are respected and in which people would want to develop their lives. Specific economic and political factors did play a role, but these were usually embedded in more complex trajectories in which migrants' particular values were engaged; this provides a counterpoint to the stereotypical narrative of benefits-seeking migrants.

Study participants described frustration with Canada's failure to live up to its promises and their expectations with regard to status and inclusion. After observing extreme delays and failure to permanently regularize caregivers, one caregiver who had studied law before coming to Canada questioned whether Canada's immigration law was "really not a law." Migrants' perceptions of Canada's immigration programs were often initially formed before coming to Canada:

When I was in China before I came to Canada, I was told that if I was continuously employed for two years after arriving in Canada, within eight months I would receive a maple card [permanent resident card]. This policy is always changing, and there was an open period of one year and a half, and it may take even longer to eventually become a citizen. It's uncertain.

An agency participant implicated Canadian government–based pre-departure programs in making promises with regard to permanent status and family reunification:

> Interviewee: The thing is, when they leave the Philippines, they really believe that they can stay here. And that's what many of them are saying that in the pre-departure seminar that they have in the Philippines, they are really convinced that Canada is the best country where you can work, because of the possibility of becoming an immigrant. They never talk about that this is only for two years or four years and then you'll have to come back again. They never talk about that.
> Interviewer: Are those CIC [Citizenship and Immigration Canada] pre-departure or are they from the recruiters?
> Interviewee: No, that's from the government.

This respondent also identified the contribution of foreign workers in expressing her frustration at the inequality she observed in clients' experiences: "If there are workers, if they are contributing to the development of Canada, if they are making Canada rich, why can they not be considered as workers and given the rights of other workers?"

A caregiver analogized her relationship to the Canadian state to a contract:

> At the time when we signed this contract, this means three years, right? It's in there. It's a part of it. It's like as if you sign a contract and once somebody goes into that agreement, there should be an obligation for the government and their part with everything that was initially said, being fulfilled. And after that, a year ago, you must know that they are trying to change the policy in favour of nannies. And then we all expect that would be shorter the time but [...] they're way more longer than that.

Another caregiver saw the Live-in Caregiver Program as part of Canada's strategy to attract migrant investors, with associated obligations to those brought in as caregivers. However, she felt that despite her status as a "foreigner," it was still reasonable to expect to be treated fairly by the government: "I feel that the government needs caregivers to provide for the investors that the government so desperately wants. I can understand the concern of the government. We are foreigners here in this country. We still have hope that the government could possibly treat us with dignity and humanity."

An agency participant described the bitterness and disappointment of migrants upon encountering exclusion in Canada. The respondent cited the case of a migrant who spent eight years trying to regularize his status and obtain health care before he passed away of HIV-related complications: "There are a lot of people who, through this process, come to this place and come to hate Canada [...] His frustration, he was an educated man, and I don't think this is what he expected his life to become."

While migrant participants recognized federally issued documents as one way in which status was symbolically conveyed as an identifying feature, they also described a relationship with the Canadian state based on values and expectations and the particulars of Canadian migration programs. Apart from the issue of formal status, precarious migrants viewed Canada as accountable for maintaining their rights and the obligations it had accrued through its relationship with them, and they recognized when these obligations were often not fulfilled. While migrants certainly were aware of the need to appear "deserving," as discussed in detail in Chapter 5, these responses demonstrate their agency beyond the construct of deservingness. Canada not only identifies itself in terms of liberal egalitarianism but is identified as such by these precarious migrants. While study participants did not refer to human rights protections specifically, this expectation of equal treatment invites a human rights response on the basis of equal treatment and dignity of the individual; and, in Chapter 6, I return to the issue of human rights to assess strategies through international, national, and subnational human rights regimes.

Contingency and Uncertainty

Migrants spoke frequently of fear and stress when talking about status; this was true for those who had legal status as well as those who did not. Some migrant participants attributed this stress to processing delays while waiting for documents or status changes. This issue was most evident in talking with participants in the Live-in Caregiver Program. The majority of interview participants working in this field first came to Canada under the impression that they would be able to obtain permanent residence after two years of full-time work in Canada and that, at that time, they would be able to reunite with their family members, whom they could not bring with them when they initially came to Canada. Their interpretation is consistent with federal immigration law: live-in caregivers are eligible to apply for permanent residence after working full time for two years within a four-year period. However, there is a long administrative delay between the time when workers complete the two-year work requirement and the government provides an "open" work permit under which a worker is free to work in any job and for any employer (a permit given in anticipation of permanent residence). Even in the most straightforward situation, when live-in caregivers complete two continuous years of employment with their first employer, they are limited to working for that employer for the time it takes for their open work permit to be processed unless they find another employer willing to obtain a Labour Market Opinion and work permit for them.

Participants had often experienced years of delay on the way to securing permanent residence. In addition to lengthy waits for the initial open work permit, they faced subsequent delays between the issuance of the open work permit and the permanent resident visa. During this time, although workers do have improved labour mobility, owing to the open permit, they do not have permanent status and are unable to reunite with their families. Many of the participants in this study were separated from their children for from four to six years. Furthermore, if a worker had to change employers for any reason during the initial two-year work period, the total processing time would be increased by the length of time it would take to process a new work permit, often five or six months. During those months, workers are still subject to the restrictions of the first work permit and cannot work legally except for the first employer. Even if caregivers had left their employers because of abuse or had been laid off, they were not legally able to work anywhere else until they obtained a new work permit, and obtaining a new work permit required not only finding work but relying on a new employer to support the process of obtaining a new permit. One migrant participant gave an example of a delay that was representative of migrant responses:

> I feel like the Canadian government, their policies towards us live-in caregivers, the time in which we can immigrate, the time frame is too

long because we have to stay with one employer for two years. If I have to change employers in the middle of this time frame, there would be a waiting period of five to six months. So the time line goes on again. And after that period ends, we have to wait an additional sixteen to seventeen months but in actual fact, the combined amount of time is five years. We have to wait for an open permit for eighteen months. And we need to stay with the same employer for two years and then we apply for the open permit. So that's a total of three and a half years. And once the open permit comes down, we have to wait an additional twenty months. So from start to finish, it's about a five-year period.

In this period of waiting, participants reported feeling uncertain, even when their temporary status was legally secure, and even when they had already obtained an open work permit. A caregiver who had obtained an open work permit, but had not yet obtained permanent residency, explained: "It's been over a year since I made that application for permanent residency, but I feel like my only choice is to wait, to wait for this liberty, to wait for this freedom." Many participants described the anxiety of waiting, including expressing the fear that they would never be able to receive "a solid status" and the inability to "expect or predict the result of getting status." In addition to lack of labour mobility, they also experienced uncertainty with regard to other specific material aspects of social life, such as the lack of opportunity to learn English and delayed reunification with their families.

Many participants related that they were afraid to assert their rights, owing to the fear that they associated with having uncertain status. One (non-caregiver) migrant who was waiting for her refugee hearing noted that, as long as her status was uncertain, she was afraid to ask her employer to improve poor working conditions. In her words: "I was afraid for my status.[29] I don't get a fair trial [...] I was afraid I didn't have the same rights or something." The use of the term "trial" with reference to obtaining immigration status illustrates not only workers' apprehension concerning state power but also their perception of a connection between the employment relationship and the eventual outcome of a legally unrelated immigration proceeding.

Other work permit holders echoed this sentiment: "If you have a temporary status, you are always in fear, like, I might not be able to complain about my rights. There is always that fear." Migrants were also afraid of damaging their potential to become permanent residents, of losing their livelihood, and of not being able to return to Canada. In the latter case, one migrant noted that a work permit was not enough to allay the fear: "It has to be a permanent status. If you have a work permit, you can be denied." For migrant participants, this uncertainty was connected to both the actual and potential operation of law; illegality and deportability are thus emphasized in legal institutional contexts beyond the federal authority over immigration. Even when migrants held formal legal status, and even when they possessed status documents, their lives in Canada were conditioned by uncertainty flowing from bureaucratic delay and the protraction of bonded work-permit situations. This uncertainty was closely associated with a sense of fear and lack of control. The impact of this uncertainty with regard to specific rights and entitlements will be discussed in more detail with regard to work (Chapter 3) and access to social entitlements (Chapter 4).

Migration Status as a Spectrum

In contrast to the fixity and objectivity implied by the legislation governing status, interview participants saw status as relative and dynamic. Participants often framed their own status in terms of other kinds of status – whether "better" or "worse" – or the potential loss or gain of status. When this topic arose in interviews, I asked participants to speak about the difference between various status situations, including no permit, a closed work permit, an open work permit, and permanent residence. Many participants aspired to permanent residence, and this was a primary motivating factor in their decision to come to Canada. The perceived potential to gain or lose status was particularly influential on working life and employment relations. Although permanent residence or citizenship served as a general yardstick of "certain" status, participants identified their own positions comparatively.

When considering the difference between a closed work permit, attached to one employer and one job, and an open work permit, participants often highlighted the lack of labour mobility: "With an open work permit, I could look for other forms of employment. Now that I'm tied down to one employer, it's difficult because I would have to work even if I don't want to. I would [have to] just have patience and hold in those emotions." A participant in the Live-in Caregiver Program noted the impact of this lack of mobility on her conditions of employment and on the power or "personal jurisdiction" of the employer in her life:

Interviewer: From your perspective, do you think your situation would be different if you were a permanent resident? What would be different for you if you were a permanent resident or had an open work permit?
Interviewee: The differences would be huge. I would never do a job like this if I was in that situation.
Interviewer: Tell me more about what the difference would be.
Interviewee: I could do any job I desire. As a live-in caregiver under someone else's roof, there is a phrase, "you have to look at the eyes and the colour of one's face," which means that you'd be at their beck and call and under their personal jurisdiction.

Participants also noted the impact of differential migration status in terms of family reunification, socio-economic status, and autonomy. One migrant participant who had already obtained an open work permit compared her situation to permanent residence and its associated benefits: "If I eventually receive a maple card, I will be able to reunite with my son, my family. The economical stress and burden would be greatly lessened." Another migrant noted the difference between any kind of work permit, open or closed, and permanent residence in terms of socio-economic potential: "If I were to get my maple card, it would be completely different because I would be able to further integrate into society. I would be able to learn. I would be able to work in my areas of interest. I'd be able to become more acquainted with the law of Canada." A third participant attributed the termination of her employment to her status as a closed work permit holder, in which her employer had to meet specific requirements, as compared to a citizen: "My employer said that if he hired a Canadian, there would be no issues with the application, so my employer's letting me go."

The potential to lose the ability to apply for permanent residence overshadowed participants' negotiation of employment relationships. Many workers said they tolerated substandard or abusive working conditions because they thought that reporting them could have a detrimental impact on their permanent residence application. This fear is relevant to live-in caregivers but also to other workers hoping to obtain an employer's endorsement for a provincial nomination program, in which a worker can gain access to permanent residence based on provincial needs, or to qualify for other economic categories of permanent residence. One live-in caregiver summarized the situation as follows: "Even though we work under some kind of situation [in which] we're not happy, we have to do it because we want the time [to put toward permanent residence]." Employers held power inasmuch as their reference or confirmation was needed to prove employment for permanent residence: "If you want to find a new employer, you can't offend your former employer in any way [...] You can't make them feel like you're going to leave them or ditch them." Another caregiver put it plainly: "If I had permanent residency, there would be no way I would do a job like this. This job is torturing."

Migrant participants spoke directly about the impact of status differentials in their relationship with the law, particularly with regard to rights. One participant described the difference her status made to the potential of the law to protect her through the enforcement of her contract. While working for a new employer without authorization, she said, "I felt like I was protecting myself and the contract did not protect me." After receiving a work permit for a new employer, she said, "I feel like the contract is protecting me." A worker in the restaurant industry who was originally from Mexico echoed this sentiment: "You need to be careful what you are doing, and that's the big difference. I know that I have rights because I become a resident. Before, you only struggle with one employer." An administrative manager originally from the Philippines also described the difference between temporary and permanent status in terms of the fear of exercising rights:

Interviewer: What is the difference between being here as a foreign worker or being here as a permanent resident?
Interviewee: Mostly it's the security – that you are part of the Canadian residents and entitled to the same rights and benefits.
Interviewer: What are the major differences in rights and benefits?
Interviewee: You can actually complain – sometimes, if you have a temporary status, you are always in fear, like I might not be able to complain about my rights. There is always that fear.

This extract highlights the distinction between awareness of legal rights and the ability to pursue rights claims. Migrants with precarious status knew that they had rights, but they also assumed that they could not exercise these rights without permanent status. Read in isolation, this could be construed as simply a misunderstanding on the part of the migrant; however, as described in detail in Chapter 6, the perception that rights are predicated on membership is borne out on a large scale in Canadian law. Thus, this type of response should be read as an internalization of the state's exclusionary practices at the level of membership.

Neither Here Nor There

Another common thread through the narratives of migrant participants was the association of uncertain status with tension about location, often expressed in terms of a pressure or contrast between disparate locations. This discordance was expressed directly in terms of space and nationality, but also by the use of metaphor to evoke a sense of stress flowing from multiple, incompatible trajectories. The articulation of this sense of "being neither here nor there" as part of the experience of status uncertainty was striking in its similarity across a diversity of national backgrounds and status situations.

One caregiver from China expressed this tension as an aspect of her employment relationship and the necessity of keeping a new employer happy in order not to endanger status: "If I have a new employer, who somehow decides halfway through this application process not to work with me, what do I do? I'll be left with two sides empty with two feet in two little boats. I should decide some place to stand. I want to continue living." In reflecting on life as a refugee claimant whose status was yet to be determined, one participant explained that permanent residence "would be more stable and you wouldn't have this doubt, this dilemma of staying or having to go back to Mexico." A student from Korea described the need to maintain multiple options while she waited for authorization to work: "Here I had to wait, not knowing my status in the future. I always think about two options, two plans – what if I go back to Korea." A Colombian migrant who had experienced a delay of years in obtaining his permanent residence subsequent to a positive refugee determination echoed this description and tied it in to a sense of belonging in neither of two places:

> Because we don't know what is going to happen [...] I have my license, I have a work permit, I have my social [insurance number], but then it's like feeling that I don't belong here but I don't belong there. We can't think in the future because we don't know what's going to happen. It's been two and a half years in the same situation and nothing happened.

A participant from Mexico who had successfully obtained refugee status also explained that this feeling had an enduring effect on her sense of belonging, even after her refugee case was positively decided and permanent status granted: "I already had it [the ability to obtain permanent residence] but, like I'm saying, I feel all the time that I am one foot here, one foot outside; I don't feel security at all." This is consistent with Landolt and Goldring's research showing that the detrimental effects of precarious migration status are "sticky": even after they obtain permanent status, many migrants who had experienced precarious status continue to experience its negative socio-economic effects on a long-term basis.[30]

In struggling to regularize their status in Canada, many of the migrant participants spoke of the possibility of returning or being returned to their countries of origin in terms of not being able to go back because of political or economic risk or of having "nothing to go back to." Some expressed that they could go back if options were exhausted in Canada. Many mentioned that they wished to be able to go back temporarily to see family but had difficulty in doing so because of legal restrictions on re-entry, lack of time off, or fear of losing status in Canada.

Multiple participants closely associated uncertain status with the sense of not being able to move either forward or backward. A business owner from China, one of the few participants in the study whose work would be categorized as "high skilled," described a feeling of being unable to return to China after years of temporary status in Canada with no permanent residence options on the horizon: "I decided not to practise law there anymore because I wasn't willing to engage in corruption and bribery, so I went into business. So after all these years, it would be very difficult for me to go back to that environment, so I don't dare to think of the road ahead of me." A live-in caregiver expressed the same dilemma in terms of risk, cost, and the resulting sense of powerlessness and stress:

> Even we can't move forward or move backward. Move forward is not [within] our control. We want to move forward and think, no, forget about that, Canada, I want to go back to China. I don't want to give up the four years of trying so hard, but, I mean, I can go back to China and to live there, but I couldn't. This status, when you ask them, they say you are not supposed to go back, "we will not guarantee you can come back [to Canada]." We didn't dare to do that, to take that risk. In this situation, it's really nothing. I feel like I have no hope right now.

Lack of information and uncertainty about options also increased the feeling of tension, as described by another caregiver from China: "My work permit expires on this coming nineteenth of December and I'm not sure what to do. I'm personally in conflict. I would really like to study but I'm not sure if I can extend my work permit or if I can get some kind of study permit. I'm not sure of my options."

A non-profit worker commented on a similar duality at play with regard to the law's failure to facilitate regularization. She spoke about people who had entered with work permits and were unable to obtain legal status to remain in Canada, despite their ongoing social and economic roles in Canada. Many workers instead went "underground." She described it as follows: "In Tagalog we say, 'you are holding onto a two-edged sword.' Because there is nothing else for you. You know that the law is not going to help you." Another participant expressed the contradiction in the role of law and the resulting paralysis in similar terms: "Now I need to make a claim for EI [Employment Insurance] before I get a record of employment, and I am working illegally now. I'm stuck. I can't go ahead and I can't go backward."

In the theoretical world of immigration legislation, location is contingent on status authorization, and presence or work in Canada can be initiated or curtailed on the basis of permits and at the whim of employers. The situations described by migrants reflect a more complex reality, evoking the tensions of connection to Canada without permanent status. In consideration of the various risks, relationships, and trajectories articulated by participants, location emerges as something in which status is a complicating factor, rather than a determinative one.

Illegality and Illegalization

In recruitment posters and letters, as well as in the interviews themselves, I specifically avoided using the language of illegality. However, migrant participants regularly referred to illegality as a way of describing their actions and conditions. Migrants reported an acute awareness of the potential of being "illegal" or doing "illegal things" in relation to state power when their status was uncertain:

Interviewer: Was your status uncertain at any time since you came to Canada?
Interviewee: I feel like it's time waiting where I follow the policy and I don't do illegal things and I wait. I don't feel like I'm secure.

For this participant, the fear of being seen as illegal was strong enough that she became reluctant to speak about it during our interview, regardless of the confidentiality of her answer:

Interviewee: I needed money so I began to work while I was waiting for my permit.
Interviewer: You only worked at that second job for two months, right?
Interviewee: I don't think this is a good question. According to the government's legislation, this is most probably illegal so I feel kind of nervous.

Migrant participants used the language of illegality to describe various situations that are quite distinct in the legal structure that governs status. They used such language to describe entering Canada without authorization, residing in Canada or the United States without authorization, and staying after the expiry of a permit. Participants also used the term "illegal" when referring to situations in which people had migration status but were – or thought they were – in breach of the conditions attached to their permits. Migrants used "illegality" to describe their very presence in Canada and applied the term to both unauthorized workers and their labour.

The potential for being seen as "illegal" or being asked "if you are illegal" also functioned proscriptively in the lives of precarious migrants – for example, as a disincentive from seeking police assistance. In social life, migrants indicated that they had actively tried to make sure no one became aware that they, or their friends, were "illegal." One migrant described the need to "avoid [having] the evidence that I was working illegally." Being "illegal" was also something that prevented migrants from asking for better work conditions and/or higher pay from their employers. Illegality was described as something to be feared and avoided, and migrant participants made it clear that when they were "illegal," it was due to circumstances they could not control, often resulting from the termination of employment and always related to the need to support themselves financially: "I'm in a situation where I'm not willing to do anything illegal, but at the same time, I don't have any choices." The concept of illegality, like status contingency, also seemed to function to isolate the worker from state protection, particularly in employment relationships: "I know that working unauthorized is illegal but during that time I was only depending on my employer." Such sensitivity to questions of legality contrasts with stereotypes of the non-law-abiding migrant.

The concept of illegality within the lives and experiences of migrants provides insight into the ways in which the law is activated through experience. Migrants used the term both descriptively (in terms of actions, work, or themselves) and proscriptively (to denote things that they should avoid doing or being). In both senses, the concept appeared to function to condition migrants' agency through the avoidance of actions that would create, increase, or draw attention to what they perceived as illegal. Many of the conditions they described as "illegal" do have corresponding offence provisions in the *Immigration and Refugee Protection Act*, although, as described below, actual direct enforcement is relatively infrequent. But nowhere in the legislative texts are persons themselves described as "illegal." Rather, the fact that status distinctions and enforcement are enshrined in law gives rise to the discourse of "illegality." Migrants described "illegality" not only as the opposite of "having legal status" but as something more pervasive that could attach to actions or persons regardless of status. Furthermore, migrants described an acute awareness of the potential to attract punishment through illegality, even when such illegality was a necessary consequence of actions taken to ensure survival.

The documentation of migrants' experiences of illegality does not carry the implication that the migrants themselves are the source of illegality; on the contrary, these experiences provide a view on the operation of particular forms of governance that enlist illegality and deportability. As noted by Nicholas De Genova, "[t]here is nothing matter of fact about the 'illegality' of undocumented migrants." Rather, he argues, illegality is produced by immigration laws and is "lived through a palpable sense of deportability."[31] As was the case when De Genova was writing in 2002, some irregular migrants are deported, but many others stay, and the symbolic power of deportability is profoundly influential in the lives of those who remain. While the construct of migration status does arise in the context of immigration law, it is also reproduced in multiple institutional sites, all of which carry by association the power of deportability and illegalization.

Conclusion

Federal laws draw lines around those with status, creating a large residual category of those without. In the text of the federal statute, this approach determines the potential for enforcement on the basis of unauthorized presence or activities. According to this legal schema, so long as individuals comply with the conditions of entry and of ongoing presence, work, or study in Canada, there should be no negative effect attached to their temporary status. Furthermore, in provincial legal regimes, various entitlements, notably those pertaining to access to education, health care, and basic minimum income, require a basic level of migration status, and such benefits are presumed to be available or unavailable on the basis of a person's status as determined by the federal structure.

My interviews with migrants illustrate that the nature of status is much less dichotomous: a majority of the people involved in this study had some kind of legal migration status that was certain according to the text of the law. Nonetheless, these individuals described their status primarily in terms of contingency and uncertainty. This was an unexpected result of recruitment: I assumed in the initial design of the study that those who considered their status "uncertain" would be those who would be considered completely "out of status" or "undocumented" at law. In the end, migrants who had never had status were not well represented in the study, likely as a consequence of the perception of risk in disclosing their status in any forum. Yet, a majority of participants at some point had been either out of status or otherwise acting beyond their authorization in Canada. The idea of "uncertain" status as identified by study participants represented a variety of status situations, and they were all precarious. The ways in which migration status can be authorized through the state are discrete, limited, and well defined in the statute, but the ways in which a person can lack status are varied, and their effects are rendered much more visible through migrant narratives than they are in the statute.

Alongside situations in which they lacked status or had somehow breached conditions, migrants identified as "uncertain" various authorized legal migration situations, including open work permits, closed work permits, and refugee claims both pre- and post-hearing. None of these situations would fit into the statutory understanding of "non-status" or "undocumented," yet, in the experience of migrants, they shared common fundamental traits in terms of the manner in which status was experienced and understood. These traits associated with status uncertainty demonstrate an order and shape beyond that visible in a static analysis of the legal text per se. That migration status was ever-contingent, relative rather than fixed, and fraught with tension over location for those whose status fell short of permanent residency, regardless of whether they had migration status at law, underscores the utility of precarious migration as an organizing concept.

Although the nature of status from the perspectives of governed migrants is expansive and divergent relative to the status/non-status dichotomy in law, it is by no means less "legal." Indeed, the power ascribed to legal authority is perhaps even more evident in this perspective than in the text alone. Although I did not introduce the language of "legal/illegal," either in recruitment or in the process of interviewing, it emerged as a major concern for migrants, even beyond the "specter of deportation."[32] (Il)legality arose as a circumscription of behaviour, as a precursor to enforcement, and as affecting behaviour in relationships with employers and the social state and within social and family life more generally. Thus, participants understood migration status not only descriptively, but also, and essentially, proscriptively, because they understood it to be inextricably legal. The concept of illegality, which was pervasive in the interviews as a governing factor in the lives of migrants, arises not so much from the specific content of status laws as from the very existence of laws in which status may be determined and enforced. In this way, law is not only lived but also lives through the experiences of the governed. By considering the particular nature and content of the legal construct of status as informed by the perspective of those who are governed by it, the relationship between this construct and social relations can be more closely followed. In the following chapters, the identification of a category of migrants whose status is precarious, and the understanding of status as a dynamic governing force, will inform a closer examination of the subordination evident in the context of employment and interactions with the social state.

The experience of uncertain migration status, evident from the themes and patterns in migrant and agency interviews, provides an expanded definition of the nature, content, and effect of migration status. The idea of status is based in legal structures and applied through regulation and policy, both formal and informal. Attending to the information gathered from a group of migrants identifying their own migration status as uncertain makes visible particular features of status that would remain undetected in a reading of the legal texts alone. Migration status does not cease to be a legal construct in its application or lived effect: in contrast, migration status gains potency as law through the diverse situations in which its effects are lived out. The definitions of the nature and function of migration status arising from the foregoing discussion will thus provide a frame through which to examine the social relations evident in employment relationships and encounters with the social state.

From migrants' understanding of status, there also arise specific understandings of the role and nature of the state. Although participants described encounters with various state institutions that are legally and jurisdictionally separate,[33] they tended to see the state as a unified whole, which they identified as Canada. Furthermore, to this unified entity they often ascribed a specific role in their lives and a set of obligations associated with their relationship with Canada. This perception, while not accurate in terms of law and jurisdiction, provides insight into the function of migration status: when migration status becomes relevant in multiple sites, the state can appear as a unified but unpredictable whole, which lends power to the enforcement of status distinctions and the exclusion they entail, as well as to the creation of subordinate membership within the state.

3
Working Conditions and Barriers to Substantive Remedies

Without exception, the migrants I spoke with had spent time working in Canada. Like all workers, they worked to provide material support for themselves and their families, and many carried the additional burden of repaying debts they had incurred in coming to Canada. Across different cultural and national backgrounds and types of status, all migrant participants were engaged in Canada's labour market, often in areas of high labour demand and low pay, such as domestic, construction, and service work. Migrants shared stories of their own labour trajectories in coming to Canada, often to lower-skilled work for which they were overqualified. They described working extremely long hours, being underpaid, and experiencing problems with health and safety at work, all of which was compounded by a lack of job security and mobility. Participants were acutely aware of the power their employers had over them, which they often associated with working conditions ranging from inadequate to abusive. For all workers, there is a power imbalance inherent in the employment relationship. But for workers with precarious migration status, this imbalance is amplified at a structural level: as a function of their less-than-permanent status, workers often rely on specific employers for their status and have limited labour mobility.

Many of the participants' workplace problems should be, in theory, addressed through the enforcement of minimum standards through the employment standards system and the workers' compensation system, both of which are governed under provincial law. In British Columbia, these laws include all workers regardless of migration status. According to the text of the law, all workers' rights are to be protected, and injuries should be reported and redressed universally. I asked the provincial Employment Standards Branch and the Workers' Compensation Board about claims by precarious migrant workers, and the information provided by these institutions show that some such workers do assert their rights through these systems. It is impossible to know quantitatively the extent to which workers hesitate or fail to report illegal working conditions, but, during interviews, migrant participants explained the reasons for which they were reluctant to make rights claims with regard to employment. All of the migrants I interviewed reported incidents or conditions that breached employment standards or workers' compensation laws, but few had asserted their rights through these legal mechanisms. Of those who did, the dynamic of the employment relationship often impaired or delayed the workers' pursuit of remedies.

Before entering into an analysis of the study data, there are a few background considerations relevant to the way "work" in conceptualized in this study. First, I rely on feminist critiques of the definition of work. While work as remunerative labour figures prominently in both the narratives of participants and the definitions given by legal texts, I do not intend the use of the term "work" to refer exclusively to paid labour or to omit non-remunerated forms of work. I consider the remunerative work situations described here as part of a range of work, which includes not only unpaid physical labour but also the work associated with maintaining family relationships, cultural bridging, and navigating institutional structures.

Second, I contest the idea that migrants' remunerative capacity should be the main reason they are entitled to membership. The economic advantages of migrant labour to both state and employer are well established, and the financial contribution of migrants supports arguments in favour of their rights and entitlements.[1] While it is important to take account of this economic contribution, it is also important to resist the neoliberal idea that people's labour alone is the primary basis for recognition of their belonging. Participants revealed a sense of belonging and entitlement beyond their function as workers, and identified multiple non-economic factors motivating their own migration, spanning the social, familial, and political. "Work" in this chapter thus refers to just one example of the multiple ways in which precarious migrants are present as participants in Canadian society.

Finally, while the focus of this chapter is the working life of precarious migrants, precarity in the labour market is a reality for a growing number of workers under conditions of globalization. Worldwide, both resident and migrant workers face increasing casualization, contract work, and temporization of labour.[2] Increasing precarity of labour affects both citizen and non-citizen workers, but precarious migrants are likely to bear the brunt of this trend.[3] The workplace problems I discuss here are linked with precarious migration status. But rather than framing this as an exceptional phenomenon, it should be understood as one particular manifestation of labour precarity on a greater scale.

Migrant workers' access to legal protection in the area of work is shaped by migration status in several ways. First, although it is not explicitly mentioned, the construct of migration status is implicit in laws and regulations because they are premised on the unspoken assumption that all workers have permanent status. While employment laws do not exclude migrant workers, they are blind to the particular labour situation of non-permanent migrants. By failing to account for classes of workers whose labour mobility and security are, by definition, limited, such laws have a differential effect on precarious migrants. Second, federal laws concerning migration status interact directly with the employment relationship to create a power disparity between worker and employer that is categorically greater for non-permanent migrants than for other workers. This increases the likelihood of detrimental working conditions and decreases the likelihood of worker reporting or redress. Migrant workers rely on employers to endorse them through confirmation of employment or Labour Market Opinions that justify the place of the migrant worker in the Canadian economy. Without this endorsement, workers' status is at risk. Lacking permanent status, such workers are more likely to experience job insecurity and, by definition, are limited in their labour mobility. Third, even where employers have less direct power over the worker's status, the construct of impermanent status itself imparts a fear of reprisal and loss of status to workers. As confirmed by migrants' experience, this fear discourages workers from reporting or seeking redress for illegally low pay, long hours, sexual and other abuse, and often extreme deskilling, and confirms the characterization of the labour of precarious migrants as what Fudge and MacPhail call "an extreme form of flexible labour."[4]

Labour Trajectories and Deskilling

During interviews, I asked migrant workers about the type of work they were doing in Canada, as well as their work and educational experiences before coming to Canada. Although the vast majority of participants were doing low-skilled work in Canada, many disclosed postsecondary education of some kind, whether in trades, college, or university.

Study participants had worked in the following fields while in Canada: domestic work and childcare, including both live-in and live-out domestic work; construction, painting, and site labour; food service and kitchen work; administrative assistance; and agriculture. Domestic and childcare workers were, without exception, women. Workers in the area of construction-related fields and agriculture were almost all men (one was a woman). Only two migrant participants identified themselves as working in high-skilled fields: one woman who had student status and was working as a researcher, and a man who had entered Canada on a high-skilled work permit in order to work for a business of which he was part owner.

A majority of the migrants who worked in the domestic field came to Canada under the Live-in Caregiver Program, and most had high-skilled work and post-secondary education. Before coming to Canada they worked as nurses, teachers, doctors, and businesspeople. They had university degrees in business administration, business English, nursing, education, and medicine.[5] The deskilling of caregivers in this study was consistent with previous research documenting the prevalence of university credentials among live-in caregivers.[6] Although some told me that they would never choose to do domestic work if they had legal status that allowed them to do otherwise, one caregiver drew a direct connection between her role as a medical doctor in the Philippines and her work taking care of children in Canada. This worker described a psychologically abusive work environment in which she was "emotionally injured", yet she maintained an ethic of care toward the family she worked for:

Interviewer: You were trained as a physician. I'm interested to know how you feel about doing this kind of work.

Interviewee: Realistically speaking, I feel that back home I was taking care of sick people. Now I am taking care of this family, and they are quite similar.
Interviewer: Do you feel like you have a chance to use your skills?
Interviewee: I often recommend certain lifestyle recommendations and choices to this family [...]
Interviewer: Is there anything else you want to share about your experiences that we haven't talked about already?
Interviewee: I feel like coming here to work, you need a certain sense of endurance. Even at the beginning, if it's extremely difficult, I feel that one can conquer these difficult situations. I'm still full of hope, even for these people I'm taking care of, even if they treat me badly. There is no way I could willingly hurt them or harm them. So I still believe that the future is quite bright.

Deskilling was not limited to caregivers. Participants who worked in construction, painting, warehouse labour, and similar positions also had university-level training, skilled trades certificates, and management experience. Workers without authorization worked in informal labour markets where having documents mattered less, notably in construction and related work. Workers ascribed the shift to lower-skilled work to their limited ability to speak English and the lack of opportunity to convert their certification and education to a format that would be recognized in the Canadian labour market.

Deskilling trajectories are not unique to precarious migrant workers. For new permanent residents in Canada, there is also evidence of significant labour deskilling on arrival, including barriers to labour market advancement related to language, certification requirements, and racial/cultural bias.[7] Because of the particular disentitlements and limitations associated with less-than-permanent status, however, precarious migrant workers experience these barriers in a categorically distinct way. Unlike many of the workers' concerns discussed in this chapter, deskilling is not subject to any specific rights or protections at law. Yet, because precarious migrant workers are overrepresented in lower-skilled, lower-paid, or otherwise undesirable work, as well as within the informal economy, the deskilling of labour is an integral part of the context in which migration status and the law operate in the lives of these workers.

Non-permanent migrants require a permit in order to work legally; in this way, immigration law directly limits workers' mobility. Workers' labour paths can be determined by the type of permit they have. For example, both the Live-in Caregiver Program and the Seasonal Agricultural Worker Program recruit foreign workers into particular labour segments, and these workers are limited to working with named employers. Workers outside these programs who hold closed work permits are also limited to a particular employer. Even though they are not specifically restricted to a labour segment, the requirements to change a work permit are onerous and rely heavily on employers. Even for open work permit holders, who have a relatively greater degree of labour mobility, types of work may be limited by the fact that employers can readily identify them as temporary work permit holders on the basis of the "9" designation on their social insurance number. Regardless of status, all non-permanent migrants are susceptible to a lack of labour mobility, and specific permit requirements give shape to this limitation.

Foreign worker programs in Canada and elsewhere are often associated with work that is dangerous, dirty, or difficult (sometimes referred to as "3d" labour),[8] work that cannot be done offshore and is not paid well enough to recruit permanent resident and citizen workers.[9] In the Canadian situation, although both "high-skilled" and "low-skilled" temporary workers are recruited through authorized foreign worker programs, "low-skilled" workers constitute a growing proportion of total foreign workers admitted to Canada.[10]

In British Columbia, at the time of this study, the largest labour segments for which employers hired foreign workers were harvesting labourers, domestic workers, and cooks and other restaurant service and kitchen workers.[11] All of these occupations were represented in the interview groups. Construction workers are not identified in government data as a major labour segment for hiring foreign workers, but they did respond to the call-out for this study. Construction workers could be underrepresented in government data due to the prevalence of informal labour within the construction industry; because it is easier to work without authorization in this field, there would be fewer authorized foreign workers to record. Of study participants who identified having been completely without status at some point, many had worked in this occupational group. Without official data on occupations for unauthorized workers and workers with open permits such as refugee claimants, it is difficult to determine with any precision the industries in which workers without industry-specific permits are working. Several study participants also referred to workplaces in which authorized and non-authorized workers worked side by side. Government data do not paint a complete picture of the jobs that are filled by foreign workers in Canada but, even using limited government data, it is clear that foreign workers are doing necessary labour, often in low-paid, "low-skilled" work.

Both the deskilling of individual workers and the increasing concentration of precarious migrant workers in lower-skilled occupations[12] are part of how migration status shapes people's working lives. When they come to Canada, workers without permanent status face the likelihood of working in jobs at a much lower skill level than that for which they are trained, and often in conditions that permanent residents would not accept. Because their labour is categorized at law as being lower skilled, their ability to obtain permanent residence is also impaired.[13] This deskilling thus bears directly on migrant workers' socio-economic position, from which they encounter problems with labour mobility, security, and working conditions.

Job Security and Mobility

Precarious migrants rely heavily on employers' discretion in order to obtain work permits. Federal legislation casts the individual employer as the arbiter of labour market need. In order for them to obtain permission to hire a foreign worker, the federal government requires employers to provide evidence of a need to fill a specific job vacancy that other workers (i.e., Canadians or permanent residents) will not fill at the wage offered by the employer (although wage rates must meet specific minimums, according to the federal labour market taxonomy). Because foreign worker regulation is premised on the concept of the free market, and is designed to meet the labour needs of employers, there is little consequence to an employer who refuses to supply the required documentation for a work permit. The consequences for the worker, on the other hand, can be paralyzing, and may include loss of status or, at best, a waiting period of several months while another employer makes an application for a new authorization for the worker, during which time that individual cannot work legally.

The people I interviewed raised job security and mobility as pressing concerns, which they often associated with their lack of permanent status. Participants identified job insecurity and problems with pay as issues for those outside the formal labour market. In one example, a painter had been told by his employer that he was a "contractor," despite strong evidence that he met the legal definition of "employee." Consequently, his employment proceeded as a series of short projects. This worker linked both sporadic pay and lack of a formalized work arrangement with job insecurity: "There is insecurity in terms of getting paid and there's no stability because it's not something formal."

Workers across multiple labour segments highlighted lack of continuity and sporadic work as a feature of status uncertainty. One agency worker reported that, within the Seasonal Agricultural Worker Program, workers who were sick or had a medical condition were reported to the recruiting program and were more likely to be refused work permits in the following year. This pattern was confirmed by a migrant worker enrolled in the program. The same logic applied to women agricultural workers who had reported sexual abuse or harassment on the job. Thus, the potential for discontinuity of work arising from the refusal of a work permit functioned as a disincentive to report illness, injury, or abuse on the job.

For live-in caregivers, job security is tied directly to the potential to obtain permanent residence, which requires two years of full-time work within a four-year period. Immigration law requires employers' endorsement in order for workers to obtain a new work permit, and only authorized work counts toward permanent residence. As such, threats to job security are amplified by the risk of loss of existing status, as well as the risk to future permanent residence. Migrant participants noted that disruptions to job continuity were beyond their control; they were often the result of the changing needs of their employers, including the start of full-time school for young children, or alternative care arrangements for older adults, rendering the caregiver unnecessary. One caregiver felt that longer-term status would improve her job security, stating that a four-year work permit would "protect [her] work, without unemployment."

Workers reported that employers threatened termination in order to ensure compliance with substandard conditions of work. Even where employers did not make this threat, workers were reluctant to complain or request changes to working conditions because they feared job termination and the resulting loss of legal status. In one case, the employer used the worker's status directly in their threat to terminate, by stating that they would communicate with immigration authorities: "The first time I was doing something wrong and I assumed I made a mistake. I arrived late at work, and that was my mistake, and for that I was fired. The thing I really don't like is that they gave me a letter and in the letter, they [told me] that they were going to inform immigration about it."

Job security and mobility are related: where job security is not possible in one job, the ability to move easily to different jobs can provide an alternative safety net. Yet labour mobility for precarious migrants can be particularly elusive. Migrant participants emphasized the difficulties they had in being able to leave a job or find a new job. Closed work permits are issued based on the needs of employers, must be initiated by employers, and bind the worker to one employer. As one worker noted, "The thing about the work permits, right, it's really tricky, people have to get one employer that named on the work permit." Another elaborated:

> In my case, I always got the temporary work permit, and they were restricted. I was only allowed to work for that employer. That makes a big difference. If they treat you well or not, they know that you are all the time willing to do whatever they want and this is a big problem. I left the place and there is one girl still working there, and I know that they don't treat her very well because they know that she will do whatever they want because they are the boss. If not, all the time there will be the pressure in the background, "We can fire you. We can fire you. And we did it once so we can do it twice."

Once they obtain an open work permit, workers are able to circulate in the labour market without being bonded to a specific employer. Despite this, some workers found that discrimination in hiring on the basis of temporary status was also a barrier to labour mobility. A construction worker encountered bias in hiring once employers found out that he had a "9" on his work permit:

Interviewee: Because when you have the 913 social security number is what they tell you, they say on the paper that you can find a job in whatever. But, bottom-line, this is not true because you are not applying for certain job and, especially with government job, they no accept you. They reject you because you have social security in 9.

Interviewer: Tell me more about that. Did you get rejected or did you get discriminated against because of your 9?

Interviewee: Yeah, because of 9.

Interviewer: So tell me more about that.

Interviewee: Because you know when you apply, I was unemployment for so long, I was on welfare, because when you apply for certain jobs, for example security guard, they not accept you. I went and took the course and everything, but when they see you have the number 9, I have my BST 1 and my BST 2,[14] because they sent me to jobways,[15] to help me find me a job, but the problem was not to find a job. The problem was the social security with a 9.

Interviewer: Did they tell you?

Interviewee: Yes, because when they see 9, they not give a job at the time.

Interviewer: How many times do you think that happened?

Interviewee: So many.

A live-in caregiver also reported that her employer was unwilling to sign the paperwork to obtain a work permit for her because her social insurance number started with a "9." Every foreign worker allowed to remain in Canada has a social insurance number with a "9," and it seems illogical for an employer to reject such a worker when the employer's explicit aim is to hire a foreign worker. At least one larger study in Canada has confirmed that having a "9" designation on the social insurance card restricts job searches and contributes to irregularization, strengthening the connection between precarious status and precarious work.[16]

The power differential between workers and employers was amplified for the migrant workers I spoke to, through labour mobility barriers associated with deskilling, but also through the employers' power in individual employment relationships. Migrants identified mobility barriers not only in terms of lateral movement between employers in the same field, but also with regard to movement between labour segments, and in particular the movement from low-skilled work to work closer to that for which they had originally trained:

> Once I have an open work permit, I'm not obligated to continue with the same employer. I can make use of my qualities and my skills. I can go to Kindergarten to teach piano, singing, dancing. I am very willing to serve on behalf of the children of Canada. In China, I was considered to be an outstanding teacher. I could teach them Chinese language. I was very good. I was of high standards. I have this intention to serve.

As described above, on arrival in Canada, foreign workers are streamed into jobs less skilled than those they are trained for, and the closed work permit system functions to preclude labour mobility once workers are here. This compounds deskilling, as it limits the chances of finding and being available for higher-skilled jobs. Migrant workers feared what would happen if they attempted to leave their jobs, as in this case:

> Interviewer: You mentioned that you could only obey. Can you tell me a little bit more about that? Why was that?
> Interviewee: I was working for them and I was living in their house, so I had to follow by their rules.
> Interviewer: What would happen if you didn't?
> Interviewee: I was afraid of causing trouble because we had a pre-existing contract and also, I know it's difficult to change employers and it's not easy to have a consistent employee-employer relationship.

The migrants I spoke with also described employers' refusal to supply references and recommendation letters as a threat to workers; this, too, has an impact on labour mobility by making it harder for migrants to secure another position.

Employers' power is underscored by the ever-present risk of losing authorization. Two caregivers described how the potential to lose one's job with a particular employer further cemented this risk. As one observed,

> Under the Live-in Caregiver Program, you are not allowed to work with anybody else unless with the one who is on the contract. That is the hardest part, and, like in my situation where I am not being released by my employer, I was not able to look for another job. It's just like taking the risk of working unauthorized.

The other noted, "I'm completely without a will. I don't dare to resist because my contract states that I have to stay with the same employer for two years. So I have to listen to them. I have to obey. If I don't listen, there are huge implications in changing employer."

Canada has no statutory protection for job security and mobility. A minority of workers in Canada may enjoy such protection as a result of membership in a collective bargaining unit, but none of the workers who spoke with me belonged to a union. While provincial employment standards legislation does provide a "floor" of basic entitlements for workers, labour mobility and job security are not among them. Federal Employment Insurance, which is discussed in the next chapter, aims to provide a certain level of remediation for unemployed workers, but there is no legislated right to stable, suitable work and free circulation in the labour market per se, for any worker. Given the pivotal role of the employer in determining the immigration status of non-permanent workers, however, the effect of reduced job mobility is of a different nature than that faced by workers who are permanent residents or citizens. These aspects of labour market involvement are conditioned in specific ways by migration status, and they form an integral part of the context in which precarious migrants are engaged in the labour force.

Job security is also shaped by precarious migration status, in terms of reasons for unemployment as well as the ability to regain employment. Although unemployment can be detrimental for any worker, it takes a particular form for workers lacking stable migration status. In such cases, the employer's ability to unilaterally terminate the employment relationship or dictate conditions is greatly enhanced due to the particular vulnerability of workers in this situation. For temporary foreign workers with closed work permits, employer power is also categorically greater, as the process of obtaining and maintaining a work permit relies on the employer's whim and participation.

The precarious migrant's relationship with the state changes the stakes of both employment and unemployment. For example, workers without status or with a closed work permit may be compelled by poverty to accept unauthorized work even while they are aware of the potential consequences, particularly as they are likely to be ineligible for social assistance. Because precarious migrants experience particular barriers to participation in state-based social protection, they are more likely to be in a position of poverty and less likely to have access to financial alternatives to unauthorized work. Both the impetus to work without authorization and the stakes associated with undertaking such work are formed in the shadow of precarious status. Precarious migration status also changes the stakes: where a citizen worker risks material privation in exercising their labour mobility, a precarious migrant risks deportation, criminal sanctions, and loss or preclusion of their ability to reside legally in Canada simply by seeking and accepting work.

Hours of Work and Wages

Because it is harder for them to circulate in the labour market, workers with temporary or precarious migration are particularly susceptible to low wages and long hours. Although minimum wage, maximum hours, overtime, and breaks are all prescribed by law, the migrants I spoke with described regular violations of these standards as well as a climate of impunity, often because workers were afraid to report their employers.

In British Columbia, the *Employment Standards Act* governs employment standards, and it applies to workers without reference to immigration status.[17] It covers minimum wages, hours of work, leave, notice of and basis for termination, advertising of work, and recruitment practices; in addition, it provides a framework for complaints, enforcement, and appeals of employment standards decisions. The *Act* requires meal breaks after five hours of work, eight hours free between shifts, and thirty-two consecutive hours free from work each week.[18] It also requires the payment of a minimum wage,[19] which in early 2017 was $10.85 per hour.[20] During the time period covered by the study, the statutory minimum hourly wage ranged from $8.00 to $9.50 per hour. Despite piecework provisions of the *Regulations*,[21] which exempt farm workers from the minimum hourly wages under the *Act*, foreign workers under the Seasonal Agricultural Worker Program must also be paid on an hourly basis that is consistent with the statutory hourly wage.[22]

Under the *Act*, employers must pay overtime after an employee has worked more than eight hours a day or more than forty hours a week, at 1.5 to two times the regular rate of pay.[23] The *Act* also limits total working hours, stating: "an employer must not require or directly or indirectly allow an employee to work excessive hours or hours detrimental to the employee's health or safety."[24] The *Act* includes protections specific to domestic workers, including live-in caregivers. Employers must provide "domestics" with a written contract indicating hours of work, duties, wages, and room and board. The same section explicitly includes the requirement for the employers of domestics to pay for overtime hours beyond the regular hours of work stipulated in the contract.[25] The *Act* also states that employers must pay all employees at least semi-monthly.[26]

Workers reported unpaid overtime in multiple labour segments, but some of the most extreme examples came from the Live-in Caregiver Program. One agency worker described a particular caregiver as "practically enslaved" by her employer, working six days a week from six a.m. to at least nine p.m., plus working an extra job on Saturday as a cleaner. Based on those hours, this worker was working at least ninety-eight hours a week, assuming an eight-hour day for her part-time job. This was not an unusual number of working hours for a worker in the Live-in Caregiver Program, as the following exchange confirms.

Interviewer: Can you talk a little about the difficult conditions with your employer?

Interviewee: The biggest issue I have currently is that the employers very rarely respect the eight-hour work limit. You usually have to work over eight hours.

Interviewer: Can you give me some examples of that?

Interviewee: The first employer had two children and I had to wake up and start working at seven in the morning. I would work all day with one hour of break in between.

Interviewer: When did you your work day end?

Interviewee: In theory, it should be that I should stop working at seven in the evening. Because sometimes the employer, the parents of the children, would be busy with different events and activities such as school activities, PTA meetings, or, if the husband came to Canada at that time, the wife would have to go socialize with the husband, and sometimes I would finish work at eight and the latest was eleven thirty.

Interviewer: Did you ever talk to your employer about that?

Interviewee: I'd be afraid to voice those concerns. Once I expressed any dissatisfaction with the work conditions, the employer would be unhappy.

Another caregiver described very similar conditions:

> I had to work seven thirty a.m. until nine thirty, fourteen hours in total. My friends who also apply for this program and work for the Live-in Caregiver Program, they all seem to work a lot of overtime hours like myself. When I came to Canada, I was completely alone, I didn't know anybody here, so when my employer demanded to me work whatever hours, I complied.

Live-in caregivers were not paid hourly but instead were paid a fixed amount per month, calculated on the basis of the theoretical forty-hour workweek at minimum wage. This means that the actual hourly rate at which they were remunerated was much lower than the statutory minimum wage, often $6 per hour or less. One caregiver explains:

Interviewer: Were you doing the jobs that were described in your contract?
Interviewee: Yes. It was the job description that was stated in the contract. However, the house was large, and I was doing everything, and I was working non-stop.
Interviewer: Were you paid by the hour or were you paid a certain amount each month?
Interviewee: Each month.
Interviewer: How much were they paying you?
Interviewee: The total sum was about $1,400. In the contract it stated that room and board would be deducted and after room, board, and tax, I was left with about $900, and that was going at eight hours per day, forty hours per week.

In another case, the employer had overtly factored in about 6 hours per day of unpaid overtime on a written work schedule:

Interviewer: Do you find that the pay and the hours are more or less than what they're supposed to be with your employer?
Interviewee: Lots of overtime.
Interviewer: How many hours a day do you have to work?
Interviewee: At least ten hours. I forgot to bring a document over today. I'm not sure if it's important or not, but my employer prepared a document that

stated a daily schedule of what I should be doing from seven a.m. to nine thirty p.m.

Interviewer: How many hours are you getting paid for?

Interviewee: Eight hours.

Migrant workers noted that overtime work per se was not an issue; rather, the problem was the terms under which overtime work occurred. Many migrant participants would likely have accepted overtime work if it had been voluntary and paid at an overtime rate – or at all. Migrants across several labour segments felt they could not decline unpaid overtime, or unpaid regular time, because their status was associated so closely with their relationships to employers.

Several caregivers also reported that when they needed to find a new employer, which was often due to either a layoff or poor working conditions, prospective employers would demand a "trial period" during which the worker would be forced to work without authorization, and sometimes without pay, while the employer decided whether to help renew the worker's permit. Until 1995, live-in caregivers were specifically excluded from the minimum wage provisions of the *Employment Standards Act*. While the inclusion of caregivers in the statutory minimum wage requirements is undoubtedly a step toward equality, subsequent research found that many employers disregarded the law in this respect,[27] a pattern still clearly evident today.

Wage problems were not limited to caregivers: a worker in the restaurant industry reported that she was making more money per hour as a babysitter than she was at her regular restaurant job. Another restaurant industry worker without authorization described working shifts without any meal or rest breaks, and also being required to do extra work and a variety of tasks beyond her job description (e.g., cashier and kitchen work) without receiving any extra pay. She was paid a total of $200 for two months of work.

Participants reported unpaid overtime in construction work. One worker, who was a naturalized Canadian citizen at the time of her interview, described an employer's preference for lower-paid unauthorized workers and "immigrants" as follows:

Interviewee: Yeah, they pay the minimum [...] they pay $10 to me, but the rest of the peoples, the illegals people they pay the minimum $9, when they work most time they augment to $9. My husband, for example, get paid for $9 and they make people to work for many, many hours [...] Because they need more people and there was no more people available to work night and days, so I saw many people from Mexico, they didn't sleep during the week. And I couldn't understood how they do that, because I was working for eight hours, maximum ten hours, and I was exhausted, yeah. So at the beginning, I was surprised why they do that, why they cannot sleep. I arrive to work, and they say, "oh, I didn't go to sleep yesterday" [...] I was start feeling, like, weak, because I was able to work only eight hours with my break [...] At the end they fired me because I was weak; they say this company is to make money [...]

Interviewer: What do you think is the real reason they fired you?

Interviewee: Because they knew I was Canadian.

Interviewer: And what does that mean to them?

Interviewee: That means Canadian, we know our rights, and I know this pay is too low; the Canadian people know much information about dangerous materials and they have information safety and they have information about human rights. They have information about salary too.

This worker's husband was in Canada without authorization at the time, and she reported that he was working nineteen hours daily.

Another construction industry worker commented on the impact of status differences on both wages and tasks at his workplace:

They pay less [to workers without status] ... and I know people who work and they don't get paid ... because they are always afraid that the police are going to be stop them and to be caught, and it's hard to live like this. For me, it's stressful to live with constant fear. I lived six years in the US illegal, and it's difficult [...]

Let's say there is this roofing company and there are ten people working on a house. There are light, heavy, things that are more difficult, and people who have papers get more than $15 per hour, the rest is less. So the heavy work always goes to the person who is getting less, and the other people who are getting more are just outside with a little flag, or a sign, or doing something really easy or small. But who has to put themselves with shelves or any other material is the people who work for $15, which is me.

Even where the wage was above the statutory minimum, the lack of sufficient or regular working hours was also a problem for workers, particularly where employers would attempt to limit the working hours, in spite of a full-time contract, in order to reduce the cost of the worker. One migrant participant who worked as a painter had been paid from $12 to $14 an hour, which he said would be sufficient to support his family of four if he were to be given regular hours – that is, of about fifty hours per week. His hours were sporadic and fell short of regular full-time work, so he was not able to earn enough to meet the family's needs. As with other conditions of employment, negotiating for more work hours would be more difficult for a worker with precarious migration status.

Migrant participants in the study who performed both authorized and unauthorized work stressed the inadequacy of their income to meet the basic costs of living, and they also related this to their migration status. The wife of a migrant worker described the impact on his earning capacity of his not having status:

> Because it was a short time, the period he was working for, and he couldn't work a lot of hours. So before I came here, he had to pay for his rent, his pass, his transportation; he had to send money to us for our kids' school and food for us. It wasn't enough he was making in comparison to the expenses.

One caregiver reported that she was being financially supported in part by a friend in order to make ends meet. She noted the discrepancy between her wages and expenses: "Since you know how much wages is for nanny, and [I am] paying taxes, I am paying for my MSP [medical services plan], life insurance, and everything, it's not enough."

Workers from various communities and in various job types told me that it was a struggle to cover basic necessities of life, and that payment from employers was uncertain. Two migrants said that income was sufficient for the basics, but barely: one respondent indicated that even welfare plus a job was "enough to live on," but not declaring income to welfare authorities is an offence, which makes this strategy risky. Another migrant participant who had a student permit and was working in various authorized and unauthorized situations in low-wage jobs said that she was receiving "barely enough." In contrast to other responses, one caregiver indicated that she had saved enough money to support herself during a time when she was without work.

For those who were underemployed or unemployed, the impact of low income on food security also arose in interviews. In one refugee claimant family, one of the parents explained: "It's hard for the couple because I didn't eat so my wife and my kids could eat, or both. We took not so much food because the kids had to eat." An agency participant described an interaction with one of her clients:

> They live on a very, very limited budget. I had a client today, for example, who does not have a job yet. She doesn't have her work permit yet, and it's been so long since her application has been at CIC Vancouver. So, she doesn't have any money. So I saw her for about an hour and a half, helping her to prepare for her work permit interview, and I said, "I've got another appointment. Can you wait for another hour and I'll see you again after that?" She said, "Yes. But the problem is, I'm really hungry." And she was obviously ashamed of telling me that.

A further factor bearing on the wages on migrant workers is recruitment debt. Several workers, most notably women caregivers from China and the Philippines, went into debt by using a recruitment agency or "middleman" to come to Canada. Workers from China reported paying recruitment fees ranging from $10,000 to $25,000. Charging such fees is not legal in Canada, but the recruitment fees are paid overseas. For many, the debt was incurred before they left for Canada, and they planned to pay it off from their working income once here. This not only imposes an immediate burden on already low wages, but it is a debt that migrants associate specifically with the potential to obtain status in Canada. Recruiters represent themselves as providing people with the chance to work in Canada, and migrants who have used recruiters often see them as a non-negotiable aspect of getting a work permit. Recruiters are also often the first source of information for potential migrants – this is how some migrants find out about working in Canada. Once they arrive in Canada, some migrants are saddled with debts that would challenge even those in less uncertain circumstances. None of the workers I spoke with had refused to repay the debt. Although repayment could not be enforced by the recruiters in Canada, presumably it could be enforced formally or otherwise against family members in the country of origin.

While inadequate pay, work beyond the job description, and illegally long hours are not unique to precarious migrants, the way in which these realities are experienced is shaped by migration status. Unlike permanent residents and citizens, precarious migrants are subject to circumscription of their ability to legally reside and work in Canada, which bears directly on their experience of the employment relationship. The power differential in the employer-employee relationship is exaggerated when a worker has fewer options in the labour market, when there is a recruitment debt in the home country, or when the worker depends on the employer's authorization to maintain legal status in Canada. Thus, while employment standards legislation does not formally exclude precarious migrants, it fails to account for the role of migration status in the employment relationship.

While employment standards law does not prevent employers from changing job descriptions or duties, workers generally expect to perform the role for which they are hired, pursuant to a written or verbal contract. Live-in caregivers are subject to standard employment terms in a written agreement which specify their role, but interview participants reported that they were required to work beyond the job description for which they had been hired. For example, live-in caregivers are hired to care for children, the elderly, or disabled people, and, on paper, their jobs are limited to a related set of tasks. However, caregivers regularly reported doing extra work in housecleaning, cooking, and shopping, as well as cleaning and maintenance outside the home. One caregiver reported that her job was terminated when she refused to do the extra work associated with cleaning an eight-bedroom house for the family by whom she was employed, and another stated that she was terminated for taking on a second job in her off-hours. For these workers, working in a role other than that for which they were hired could constitute a breach of their work permit conditions; what for other workers would be a stress or inconvenience thus rises to the level of risk for precarious migrants.

Safety and Health at Work

During interviews, study participants emphasized difficulties with health and safety at work. As with employment standards, migration status was relevant to both the conditions of work and workers' capacity to seek redress.

The *Workers Compensation Act* governs workplace safety in British Columbia. This law defines workers broadly and includes work contracts that are express, implied, written, or oral.[28] As with employment standards, there is no requirement that workers have a specific immigration status; indeed, the Workers' Compensation Board has gone a step further, confirming that its policy is that "a worker is a worker," regardless of immigration status. The Board has also posted a presentation specifically with regard to "newcomer" workers, which actively states that foreign workers, both documented and undocumented, are covered by workers' compensation in British Columbia.[29] The same presentation discusses work vulnerability for such workers and strategies to increase access to the workers' compensation system, notably by way of services in languages other than English.

In the British Columbia workers' compensation system, workers are entitled to compensation, including benefits for lost wages and for health care and rehabilitation, when an injury arises "out of and in the course of employment."[30] In a recent addition to the *Act*, mental disorders arising from work-related stressors, including bullying and harassment, are now specifically covered as part of workers' compensation where they are confirmed by a psychiatric diagnosis.[31]

The *Workers Compensation Act* also mandates reporting of injuries by both workers and employers within a specific format and timeline. Workers are obligated to report injuries to employers as soon as possible,[32] and employers must supply the means for workers to file a report. Employers are required to make a report in a specified format to Workers' Compensation of every injury claimed by a worker and must do so within three days of the injury. Failure to do so is an offence pursuant to the *Act*.[33] The associated *Occupational Health and Safety Regulation* requires employers to maintain a safe workplace.[34] It provides physical safety standards and also specifically mentions violence and threats as creating potentially dangerous working conditions.[35]

Most of the injuries and conditions reported by migrant workers in this study would be covered by workers' compensation – if their injuries were reported. In interviews, participants spoke of workplace injuries resulting in both chronic and acute health problems. In terms of physical health problems arising in the course of employment, migrant participants reported skin problems, joint mobility problems, arthritis, compound limb fracture, fever, chills, headache, and stress and anxiety resulting in physical symptoms. One worker attributed illness to living without heat in accommodation provided by an employer, and another said that she thought insufficient food provided by an employer in a live-in situation caused her to become sick.

While workplace stress affects many workers in Canada, the stress arising from the impact of uncertain migration status on the employment relationship is specific to precarious migrants:

Interviewer: What was the impact on you of having that uncertain status or the difference for you between having the status you have over having permanent residence or an open work permit?
Interviewee: There's a huge difference. There's a huge psychological and mental stress. People in my situation, it really is a stress because the way the employer treats us, it's so different from a regular person.

The impact of stress on worker dignity also came up frequently in interviews. Some sources of stress were linked directly to insecure migration status, such as delays in obtaining documents, reliance on the employer for immigration support, and interactions with immigration authorities. Other sources were less acute, but were nonetheless associated with status, such as being unable to plan for the future, separation from family members, and pressure to enter into relationships for migration purposes. Migrants also reported stress based on material conditions of work, including low pay, sexual harassment, sexual assault, and humiliation by employers.

Live-in caregivers, in particular, chronicled humiliating and degrading treatment by their employers. Employers scrutinized and monitored domestic work to an extreme degree, blamed workers for various broken items and household problems, some unrelated to caregivers' work, prohibited workers from leaving the house, monitored and placed restrictions on food consumption, and refused to allow workers to have private phone conversations with their family. In talking about humiliation in the domestic employment relationship, one worker described being forced to go through the garbage when her employer was trying to enforce rules about food consumption and conservation:

> Basically, they don't respect your character, your individual person. When I cook for the children, the remaining food that the children do not consume, I have to eat that food. If I don't eat that food, my employer will be unhappy. There was one day I cooked a thick soup made with eggs for the children. The child coughed some kind of residue on the egg, and I didn't eat that piece. I threw it away. When my employer saw these, she asked me, "Where's the remaining part of that soup?" I said, "I threw it away." My employer said, "Who told you to throw it away? Do you know how expensive eggs are?" I said, "I've thrown it away this time; I won't do it the next time." My employer proceeded to say I'm wasting this food. I said, "Okay, I'll give it back to you. I'll buy an egg and reimburse you."
>
> On that same day, there were seven cherries remaining from the previous day. Of those cherries, three of them had gone bad. There were four good ones and three bad ones, and I ate the four good ones [...] My employer saw the three remaining cherries on the table and proceeded to ask me, "Where are the three cherries?" And I said, "Three of the cherries had gone bad so I threw them away. The four remaining, I ate them." [...] My employer didn't believe me that I threw away the bad cherries. I said, "I truly did dispose them in the garbage." My employer then proceeded to say, "Go find the cherries." I found the cherries in the garbage and I took them to my employer. I was basically rummaging in the garbage and finding these three missing cherries that my employer wanted to see.
>
> My employer then proceeded to say, "These are edible; they are completely acceptable." And I had nothing to say. I had no words to reply to this. And I said, "For you to do this to me, I feel I have lost face. I feel like I've been humiliated and I have lost a sense of dignity."

Another caregiver talked about the diminishment of dignity in her employment dynamic:

> I feel that, at the beginning, I was in a state of feudalism where I was a slave. I had no dignity whatsoever. To now, where I feel like I have a dignified life because I put some financial matters and distractions aside. This isn't even the point, but the point is that I can get through this period of time strongly, to change this dynamic.

Both migrant and agency participants reported employer abuse at worksites. Women workers reported sexual abuse and/or harassment across several labour segments, including the restaurant industry, agricultural work, and domestic work. One participant talked about a restaurant worksite where part-time women workers were exchanging sex with employers in order to obtain the extra hours to make a full-time wage. This participant cited the fear of being reported and the potential for the employer to refuse to renew the work permit as reasons why a worker might not report sexual abuse at the workplace. Another migrant worker in the restaurant industry attributed her employers' abuse to their need for profit: "People who have money are making money abusing workers."

Many migrant workers described being regularly monitored and criticized by their employers. This was prevalent particularly in the case of live-in caregivers, who were subject to close scrutiny by their employers. Workers' failure to perform specific demands to the standards articulated by the employer resulted in discipline, even when the work was outside the workers' job description. For example:

Interviewer: Are the jobs you're doing the same jobs listed in the contract or are you doing other things that are not agreed in the contract?
Interviewee: My contract stated that I have to take care of children and to attend to simple domestic tasks. Now I am a cleaner and they live in a big house. I do everything except tending to the rat holes in the house and cleaning the roof. Everything else, I do it. We have a large gate outside the house, and they asked me to scrub the fencing, and if there's certain areas I can't get, I have to use a toothbrush to clean the small areas. I have to do that work in the rain while holding an umbrella.

Live-in caregivers also reported that their employers would blame them for items that were broken in the household and demand reimbursement. For example, one employer deducted $250 from a caregiver's paycheque, claiming that she had used the wrong finger to press a button on the stove, causing it to break.

One worker thought the employer's unreasonable demands were attributable to her status vulnerability:

Interviewee: My employer wishes me to work to a level of 100 percent satisfaction.
Interviewer: Do you feel like even if you were perfect, you could meet her standards?
Interviewee: It would be impossible for anyone to meet her standards. These episodes would be closely related with her moods. If her mood was somehow bad or negative, she would find an outlet.
Interviewer: Why do you think your employer thinks it's okay to talk to you that way?
Interviewee: Because, first of all she's paying me and she knows that I need to work two years before I can begin my immigration.

One caregiver, a woman who had worked as a doctor in her country of origin, adopted a unique strategy to deal with an abusive employer: she refused to accept pay, in order to give the employer the message that she was not working only for pay and that she could not be paid to tolerate abuse:

Interviewee: She would constantly say, "I'm paying you to work." And I wanted to let her know that I wasn't working for the money. What I wanted to do was to help the family within my abilities.
Interviewer: When you had that discussion, did it change the dynamic?
Interviewee: I think that after that conversation, it's slightly amusing, after that it seemed like on the exterior there were not many changes but I noticed that she now thinks and now that I'm not a person who holds onto the money issue and I'm not connected to money that closely.
Interviewer: So did that change the dynamic between you and your employer? Did that give you something?

Interviewee: I felt that she'd still be angry or criticize me but I felt like I had a little bit of collateral to reply in certain instances.

Caregivers regularly reported that employers attempted to control basic aspects of physical life, such as access to food, their private space, sleeping hours, and their ability to enter and leave the workplace. Even though caregivers often cooked for the entire family, which was beyond the scope of their contract, some reported being prohibited from sharing freshly prepared food or subject to other food restriction. In one case, where the worker had digestive problems that she attributed to lack of fresh fruit and vegetables in her diet, she explained that she felt compelled to comply with the employer's demands:

Interviewer: You are talking about your employer prohibiting you to eat fresh fruits and vegetables. How did they express that to you? How did they enforce that?
Interviewee: It was just face to face. She said, "You can only eat stuff in this area." Just like that.
Interviewer: How did you feel about that?
Interviewee: I could only obey and say okay.

Live-in caregivers also reported employers' control over their access to community services such as English lessons.

When the nature of the work gave rise to acute injuries, some participants related that employers failed to take steps to protect them, or created barriers to health care. An agency representative gave one example:

Let me explain one case, the case of a migrant worker with an ear infection. He asked the manager, because that's usually the normal procedure, for them to ask the manager for permission to go to a walk-in clinic. The manager ignored him. Three days he asked him, "Could you please take me to see a doctor, I need to see a doctor." Ignored again. A week later, he started bleeding, then the manager brings him to a physician that has some kind of affiliation with the farm owner. And all these things cause lots of problems because what happens is these physicians that are somehow affiliated with the farm owners will not do a proper assessment, will not fill out all the forms, neither, for example, if the migrant worker needs to rest for a couple days, for a week. Of course, they are not going to do that because they work with the farm owners.

Such responses echo the results of empirical work documenting the negative psychosocial effects of precarious status on individuals and families, particularly with regard to mental health,[36] as well as the identification of migration status as a social determinant of health.[37]

Like employment standards, workers' compensation laws do not exclude workers on the basis of migration status. But precarious migration status both increases the risk of health and safety problems at the workplace and decreases the capacity of workers to obtain support in dealing with them through the legal remedies that are available.

Remedies

In British Columbia, aspects of working life are protected by employment standards and workers' compensation laws. Some migrants do assert their rights to such protections, but the potential to activate these rights is clearly affected by migration status. In this section, I briefly describe the remedies available through both systems, review the available data relating to precarious migrants' use of these systems, and explore the ways in which migration status shapes the law's protections in the field of work.[38]

Employment Standards

The British Columbia *Employment Standards Act* empowers the Employment Standards Branch to assess fines, file orders in court, seize property, and otherwise enforce its decisions.[39] The *Act* established the Employment Standards Tribunal, to which parties can appeal if they do not agree with the decision of the Branch.[40] Pursuant to the *Act*, any employee, former employee, or other person may make a complaint about a contravention of the *Act*. In order to obtain a remedy at the Branch, workers must provide their complaint through a "self-help" process, and the Branch forwards complaints to the employer for response. These requirements are waived where there are language difficulties or where the employee is a farm worker or domestic worker.[41] The process of registering complaints directly with the Branch should make the system more accessible to precarious migrant workers, as it would allow them to file a complaint without having to engage their employer directly in a dispute. On request of the worker, there is also the option to make a confidential complaint, in which the worker's identity is not disclosed to the employer.[42]

The Employment Standards Branch keeps track of complaints made by "foreign workers," which includes both those with temporary work permits and those without. In the first three years after it started tracking this information in January 2008, the Board heard between fifty-six and ninety-eight complaints per year from this group of workers and has made determinations of contraventions of various sections of the *Employment Standards Act* by employers, including the following:

Section 8 – making false representations with regard to the availability of work, type of work, wages, or conditions of employment
Section 10 – charging money to employee for hiring or job placement
Section 12 – operating as an employment agency without a licence
Section 16 – failure to pay minimum wage
Section 17 – failure to pay wages within the prescribed
Section 18 – failure to pay wages on termination
Section 21 – unauthorized deductions from wages
Section 27 – failure to provide written wage statements
Section 28 – failure to produce payroll records
Section 40 – failure to pay overtime wages
Sections 45 and 46 – failure to pay statutory holiday pay
Section 58 – failure to pay vacation pay
time
Section 63 – failure to pay compensation for length of service
Section 83 – mistreatment of employees because of a complaint or investigation by the Branch[43]

Records show that many of the complaints that foreign workers made were abandoned, withdrawn, or settled voluntarily. Of those for which a formal determination was issued against the employer, the Board, in addition to ordering compensation for the worker, issued penalties against employers ranging from $500 to $2,500 per complaint.[44]

Individual decisions of the Employment Standards Branch are not publicly available, but the Employment Standards Tribunal, which handles appeals, does publish its decisions. While the Branch likely deals with matters concerning precarious migrant workers, Tribunal decisions involving people with precarious migration status are rare; they occur primarily in reference to the Tribunal's interpretation of the Labour Market Opinion (LMO),[45] which, for many workers, is a necessary prerequisite to obtaining a work permit.

In one 2009 decision, the Tribunal considered an argument from an employer that he should not be required to pay the wage rate he had promised in the LMO.[46] The employer argued that the Tribunal did not have jurisdiction to enforce the terms set out in the LMO. The Tribunal found that the wage rate in the LMO was relevant evidence of the agreement between the parties and could be considered by the Tribunal, and found in favour of the worker. This finding has been confirmed in more recent cases in which the Tribunal has upheld the use of the LMO as a strong indicator of the wage rate that the employee should be paid.[47] In another 2009 case, the Tribunal did not rely on the LMO rate specifically, but it did uphold the standard form contract used for low-skilled and live-in caregiver workers that was attached to the LMO.[48] In so doing, it ordered workers to make payments to their employers for room and board as indicated under the terms of the contract.[49]

Although workers are afraid that "illegal" work precludes them from being able to use employment standards to recover wages, at least one Tribunal decision shows the opposite. In considering an application made by multiple agricultural workers from Mexico, the Tribunal heard an argument from the employer that it should not have to pay wages to the workers for the time they were asked to do non-agricultural work. The employer argued that this was outside their authorization as seasonal workers and contrary to the Seasonal Agricultural Worker Program through which they obtained work permits. The Tribunal dismissed this argument as "absurd," holding that the workers' compliance with the federal migration program was irrelevant to its determination on wages, and that because what they were doing was clearly "work," their wages should be paid.[50] This irrelevance of worker migration status is double-edged: while in the latter case, it increased the workers' entitlement to wages, it can also result in the absence of a remedy. For example, the Tribunal has found that it had "no jurisdiction to award damages based on mistreatment of a foreign national working under visa" unless the worker fit within existing statutory standards.[51]

Clearly, the employment standards system in British Columbia is not hostile to migrant workers; their inclusion is consistent with work in other jurisdictions demonstrating that formal labour rights are commonly extended to migrants, including undocumented migrants.[52] The employment standards system may uphold their contracts and may find that lack of status or authorization does not impede the enforcement of their rights. This is encouraging, but, given the barriers faced by workers without full status, it is not enough. This formally equal treatment of workers fails to account for the categorical vulnerabilities of precarious migrant workers, which render them both more likely to experience breaches of their rights and less likely to enforce them. Indeed, my findings add to the existing research documenting the need for a "complaint-based system which specifically addresses the particular vulnerabilities of migrant workers."[53]

Workers' Compensation
In the area of worker health and safety, the Workers' Compensation Board is empowered to make awards to workers, and also to make orders with regard to the safety of workplaces and employers' dealings with workers, including the unusual remedy of ordering employers to re-hire workers in certain circumstances.[54] In response to a Freedom of Information request, the Workers' Compensation Board disclosed records of worker claims for temporary and undocumented workers. Data were available for the number of claims, the gender and age of the worker, and occupation type, dating back to the 1960s. Although the specific outcomes were not available in this information release, it was clear that applications for benefits were processed regularly for temporary and undocumented workers. Over the years just prior to the study, claim numbers ranged from several hundred to over a thousand per year in both 2009 and 2010, across a wide variety of industries.[55]

Workers who disagree with the initial assessment of their claim can use an internal review mechanism, after which they can appeal the decision to the Workers' Compensation Appeal Tribunal (WCAT). This

Tribunal has considered several cases in which the migration status of the worker may have affected the decision. In one case involving a temporary migrant worker on a construction site, the worker argued that a language barrier and lack of information about how to report injuries prevented him from reporting an injury that he subsequently claimed; the Tribunal did not accept the argument in the specific facts of that case.[56] In another case, the Tribunal considered the situation of a temporary foreign worker originally hired as a truck driver. The worker did not meet certain licensing requirements, and the employer did not allow him to work as a truck driver as originally agreed. The worker ended up living at the employer's house and doing various household tasks without pay, which he understood as being in exchange for room and board. The worker was injured while painting the employer's house. The Tribunal found that the injury in this case did arise "in the course of employment,"[57] even though he was working outside the terms of his permit and his work would have constituted an offence under the *Immigration and Refugee Protection Act*.

On the surface, workers' rights laws seem to benefit precarious migrants, who are at law equal in entitlement to protection and compensation without regard to status. Both employment standards and workers' compensation systems are clearly cognizant of the presence of precarious migrant workers in British Columbia and have not excluded them from protection on a categorical basis. From talking to migrants, however, it is clear that considerations related to status form a barrier to such protections for precarious migrant workers, regardless of whether or not they have status. For workers without status, this lack and the consequent fear of deportation amplify the inequality of the power dynamic with their employers. For temporary workers with status, the threat of losing status serves the same function. Even where employers did not threaten status directly, actual or potential lack of status contributed to workers' reluctance to speak up about workplace concerns. For workers with temporary status, even when they were totally compliant with immigration requirements, the fear of losing status governed the employment dynamic. As one study participant expressed, "Without this status, without the status we need, we can be easily abused or mistreated. Because there is no extension of justice into this realm of our lives, she [the employer] could very well say that white is black and black is white."

Some migrant workers view passivity, including the avoidance of asserting one's rights through health and safety or employment standards processes, as an unavoidable aspect of their working lives while they have temporary status. As one caregiver noted, "This passivity, specifically speaking, means we have to be obedient toward our employers. Secondly, we have to listen to the government and what they say about our lives and our situations; we have to abide by their regulations in order to wait out this period. That's it." This view was echoed by a third worker, who saw consent to poor working conditions in Canada as being implied by workers' silence: "If you are silent, silence means yes here in Canada."

I spoke with a caregiver who said her employer made oblique threats, and the worker interpreted them as being specific to her status:

Interviewee: My employer would say to me, "You know, if you don't work up to my standards, I have more severe ways to treat you."
Interviewer: What do they mean when they make these threats?
Interviewee: My employer knows that I am completely reliant and dependent on them for reference letters and my immigration application. They know you have no friends here, no people to help you.

Pursuant to the *Employment Standards Act,* employers can terminate workers unilaterally, but, if they do so without just cause, they are required to provide compensation for length of service, in order to allow the worker time to obtain a new position.[58] For citizen and permanent resident workers, this provision may suffice, but the benefit of this provision for workers with precarious migration status is less clear. With a closed work permit, such workers will not be able to obtain legal authorization to work for a new employer unless they can find one willing to offer them a job and obtain a Labour Market Opinion, which takes months. Thus, although status is not directly specified as a requirement to benefit from protection from arbitrary termination, such protection is ineffectual for those without permanent migration status.

In interviews, participants talked about the protections available through the *Employment Standards Act*. Agency workers were aware of these protections and saw them as a viable means of securing rights – one pointed out that the Employment Standards Branch will continue with workers' complaints after deportation. But agency representatives also confirmed that the fear of deportation or losing status could stop workers from making complaints: "One of our legal advocates focuses on employment standards complaints. And she helps a lot of caregivers with that. Clients will do it, though not all of them. There are a lot of them that are reluctant to do it because they are afraid it will affect their immigration status."

Of migrant participants who commented on the Employment Standards Branch process, one stated that, when she arrived in Canada, she and other workers knew "nothing about laws." Another migrant participant thought that working "illegally" might prevent her from making use of this option:

Interviewer: Did you ever think of doing anything legal to try and get money from that employer friend who didn't pay you or compensation from your first employer?
Interviewee: I would like to do something to recover money from my friend, if I could say "friend." But I don't know what I could do because I was working illegally right.

One worker saw her assertion of rights as a determinative factor in her termination:

Actually it happened for the first family [...] because I talked to them when I know more about Canada and the laws and talked to them after three or four months, and then I just said, "It's in the contract that I should work eight hours and how much I should be paid." And then they agreed, and I think that's why they let me go at the end of the year, because they were not expecting that to happen.

With respect to workers' compensation, one worker I spoke with reported receiving compensation with no problems. However, the threat of immigration enforcement was a barrier for others: "Compensations, they don't qualify because the owner is not reporting them and they are scared to be deported if they are in an accident. Some accidents, they prefer to deal by their own, seeing a doctor who doesn't require any documents, just a payment." A woman who had worked in the construction industry while unauthorized saw her involvement with the informal economy as a bar to workers' compensation processes:

Interviewee: I said unfortunately I cannot do anything about my ...
Interpreter: Accident.
Interviewee: Accident before because the condition to work was cash, yeah, and if I work cash, I cannot go to the authorities to ask for protection once I had my accident.
Interviewer: Why not?
Interviewee: Because I work cash.
Interviewer: And you were worried about something happening?
Interviewee: Yeah, because I work cash, so that's why I couldn't go to the authorities.

An agricultural worker working with a work permit described direct interference by the employer in the workers' compensation process:

Interviewer: Did you ever have any issues with your employer or with your workplace?
Interviewee: Yes. So this is my second year working with him. Three weeks [previously], when we started to work, I felt unwell. I had some problems, some health problems. And on June twenty-ninth, I asked him to see a doctor.
Interviewer: What happened?
Interviewee: I mentioned to my boss that I wanted to see a doctor, and he had a friend who was a chiropractor. But there was no result for me. So I talked to WCB and that bothered my boss. He wanted to fire me, and his father didn't let me take the cab to go to therapy, and then I was reported to abandon my job and that was sent to Colima to the Consulate of Mexico. And I have no support by any agency. I don't know what to do. My boss gave his version, and it's his word versus my word.
Interviewer: What kind of injury did you have?
Interviewee: The injury was muscle inflammation from the neck to the lower back because of the weight of the liquid [carried on the worker's back as part of his duties] [...]
Interviewer: Do you remember what your boss said to you?

Interviewee: That he was going to take me to his friend. And there was not going to be any problem with the pay and that I should go to work. So I have witnessed that he put some pressure on me to make a three-day work on one day.

Interviewer: So this was at the same time you were injured?

Interviewee: Yes.

Interviewer: Was it possible for you to work at that time or was there too much pain?

Interviewee: I was taking pills and I didn't feel the pain. But the pills got to a point where the pills didn't work anymore, and I couldn't stand it. And that's when I reported to WCB.

Interviewer: So how long was the time from when you got injured to when you reported to WCB?

Interviewee: After three weeks of work, on June twenty-ninth, I told my boss [...]

Interviewer: Did the boss declare that you abandoned your job?

Interviewee: My boss [...] he said I abandoned my job.

In this example, the employer directly delayed a worker's claim for compensation and report of an injury, which is contrary to law. According to the worker, the employer had followed through on a threat to report to the embassy that this worker had "abandoned" his job. Such a report can have serious consequences for a migrant worker because the renewal of his or her status and livelihood through the Seasonal Agricultural Work Program depends on the employer's selection of the worker for the next harvest season. The worker in the preceding interview had legal status in Canada and was covered by workers' compensation. However, because his status was tied closely to the employer's power to report him as having abandoned his job, his migration status effectively mediated his access to workers' compensation, rendering the stakes of reporting much higher than they would be for a worker with permanent status. The risks to workers in situations such as this are multifaceted: an injury may worsen if a worker is forced to continue working, a worker may receive less compensation if an injury curtails his or her ability to work, and an unsafe worksite may cause risk to other workers if unreported. This dynamic is not unique to the agricultural workers' program: it is a risk in any situation in which a worker relies on an employer for status continuity, including all those involving closed work permits. Employers are obligated by law to report injuries, but when the injured worker is a precarious migrant, the employer can refuse to report injuries, with little fear of reprisal.

Conclusion

Paid work is a primary axis of life for precarious migrants who live in Canada. It is one venue through which they become socially and economically connected to the country and in which they spend much of their time and effort. For the migrants in this study, working life was marked by deskilling and by limitations in both job security and mobility. All of these conditions are connected to their status and shape the context of employment relationships. Federal immigration law empowers employers by making migration status contingent on their endorsement. The workers I spoke with disclosed breaches of employment standards and health and safety concerns, but few had used the legal protections available to them, and most were afraid to do so because they did not have permanent status. Although neither employment standards nor workers' compensation schemes exclude workers on the basis of status, these regimes also do not adequately account for the fear and power imbalances that can arise from precarious migration status. Differential access to protection against exploitative and unsafe working conditions thus functions to create and maintain a class of workers whose labour is welcome and necessary but who work without equal benefit of protective laws and who are deprived thereof on the basis of a specific shared trait – namely, precarious migration status. The data provided by participants in this chapter show that inclusive legal structures exist alongside the reality of differential treatment. Through the mediating effect of migration status, inequality becomes structurally entrenched, regardless of the liberal gestures of the law in the field of work.

Precarious migration status is produced and reproduced in the federal immigration system,[59] where it often functions to exclude migrants from secure or permanent status. But migration status also operates in the sphere of work, affecting relationships with employers and access to workers' rights processes that are beyond the ambit of federal immigration law. Alongside immigration law and enforcement, working life is a further site in which migration status tends to result in exclusion, another place in which legal migration status matters, often to the detriment of migrants. The potency of migration status in the workplace is cemented by constructions of deportability and illegality in which employers are prime agents. The workplace is thus a central site in which "deportability is produced as a value in itself in the informal economy, resulting in lower salaries, poor working conditions, and general uncertainty. In that sense, deportability is an institutionalized concept that verges on being commoditized; its meanings and values are evident to employers, landlords, middlemen, and irregular migrants." In the workplace, migrants live with the manifestations of deportability in the shape of "lower wages, longer hours, poor working conditions, and above all the risk of dismissal."[60] Furthermore, employers' withholding of endorsement for work permits necessary to maintain legal status functions as a specific manifestation of deportability.[61]

Work is not the only axis of membership and belonging, however, nor is it the only place where status matters. The next chapter will explore access to the social state, following precarious migrants' interaction with social entitlements commonly associated with membership in the Canadian state, such as health, education, and income security.

4

Exclusion from the Social State

HEALTH, EDUCATION, AND INCOME SECURITY

Work is not the only area in which migration status functions to the detriment of precarious migrants. I spoke to migrant participants at length about the other ways in which status mattered to them, and, specifically, about their experiences related to health care, public education, and income security. It is difficult to imagine a life in Canada in which a person would not make use of publicly funded social benefits at some point. For citizens and permanent residents, the experiences of obtaining a health card, enrolling children in school, or applying for income support on termination of employment are bureaucratic but routine. Precarious migrants can be excluded entirely from these basic services, and even when they are included, their access to the services is fraught with fear and complication.

Although other marginalized groups also face barriers to accessing social and health benefits,[1] for citizens and permanent residents, entitlement to these benefits is associated with membership as a matter of right. This entitlement is not extended to non-permanent residents, who encounter formal or informal institutional barriers to the social state specifically as a result of their migration status. Although the federal immigration regime is largely silent on the issue of benefit entitlement, governments and the media use such migrants' potential access to social state entitlements to justify exclusion or restriction of status, drawing on the perennial stereotype of the lazy migrant or bogus refugee greedily draining Canada's bountiful social system. This chapter focuses on the law in four cornerstones of the social state – namely, publicly funded health care, education, Employment Insurance, and income assistance (welfare), looking specifically at how these laws play out in the lives of migrants with precarious status.

Health Care
Canadian law and culture entrench public health care as a highly valued aspect of permanent membership in Canadian society. Canadians view universal health care as a major contributor to Canada's image as a humane and equitable society, particularly in comparison to the United States.[2] These qualities are repeated in the text of the *Canada Health Act*, which governs the transfer of federal funding to provincial health care plans.[3] At the same time, some politicians and media outlets tout the exclusion of those identified as non-members from publicly funded health care as a moral victory against those who purportedly seek to take advantage of Canada's generosity.[4] For many precarious migrants, the need for health care is shaped by the particular conditions of work they encounter, which may include a heightened risk of injury or illness in the course of employment or employer-based barriers to health care, including those explained in Chapter 3.

The primary requirement for health care in British Columbia is residency, not migration status. But hospitals and health agencies incorporate a further requirement of definite immigration status as a necessary component of residency. For those migrants subject to federal health coverage through the Interim Federal Health Program (primarily refugee claimants), access to coverage at the time of the study was explicitly tied to status. Study participants experienced barriers at points of service, including medical offices and hospitals, and in trying to obtain proof of status from immigration authorities for health care purposes.

Legislation
In its preamble, the *Canada Health Act* refers to "access to quality health care without financial or other barriers" and establishes basic requirements for provinces to establish non-profit, publicly funded health care with accessible care for "insured persons." The *Act* does not refer to immigration status in its definition of "insured persons"; rather, the category is delineated by residence. It encompasses all residents of a province, other than those still serving a waiting period to become residents, and those covered by

specific federal plans.[5] The definition of "resident," however, does involve immigration status, if indirectly. The Act defines a "resident" as a person who is "lawfully entitled to be or to remain in Canada," who resides in the province in question, and who is not "a tourist, a transient or a visitor to the province."[6]

The provinces are responsible for health care for most of their residents, with the exception of refugee claimants, for whom the federal government is responsible for funding health care. At the time of writing, federal health care for refugee claimants was administered under the Interim Federal Health Program (IFHP). Difficulties may arise between federal and provincial authorities when it is not clear which is responsible for the health care of an individual, or where policies are inconsistently applied. Furthermore, IFHP documents have a specific expiry date and must be renewed prior to that date in order for people to have continuous coverage. For migrants covered by this policy, the provision of health care is tied directly to their ability to obtain an IFHP document, which is separate from their immigration documents. Participants reported that the federal government's delay in providing a renewed IFHP document was a complete barrier to health care – without it, they could not obtain treatment from doctors or hospitals. This exclusion occurred both upon expiration of their immigration documents and during the delay in waiting to obtain the IFHP document, even where immigration status was continuous.

Health care falls under the authority of the provinces pursuant to Canada's constitution.[7] In British Columbia it is governed by the *Medicare Protection Act*[8] and associated *Regulations*.[9] The *Act* itself does not make specific reference to temporary migrants, but entitlement to the Medical Services Plan (MSP) in the province is determined on the basis of residency. This *Act* defines a "resident" as a permanent resident or citizen who "makes his or her home in British Columbia" and is present in British Columbia for a minimum of six months out of each year.[10] The *Regulations* also create a secondary category of "deemed residents," which includes study or work permit holders who have had legal status for a minimum of six months, some temporary resident permit-holders, and spouses and children of residents where an application for permanent residence has been made or sponsorship has been confirmed.[11] Medical insurance coverage for temporary residents is limited to the dates specified on their temporary permits.

At first glance, authorized temporary status seems to be coextensive with medical coverage, at least for workers and the others mentioned in the *Medicare Protection Act* and the *Medical and Health Care Services Regulation*. But there are situations in which even those with temporary status are unable to obtain care. For example, people waiting for their renewed work permits after the expiry of previous permits have implied status under the *Immigration and Refugee Protection Act*, as detailed in Chapter 2, cannot obtain provincial health care coverage. Yet migrants in this situation are not "out of status": they are waiting for an updated work or study permit as *confirmation* of the status they already have. People with implied status may be unable to extend their provincial health care coverage while they wait for their status document to arrive. In interviews, two participants commented on the challenges of this situation:

> So it is a big problem when clients don't have status, because MSP won't extend their coverage. We had one case where it was critical that the caregiver have access to health care coverage because he had chronic renal failure and he had to be hospitalized, and, because he didn't have coverage, he ended up with a medical bill of $50,000.

> I needed to retake a pap smear because I took one before and it was irregular, so they ask me to take one after six months. So that was something that was kind of important, and I need to do it soon. But my care card was expired, and when I called them, they told me to just keep waiting. But nothing ever arrived, so I had to go to the free clinic because, as a foreigner, I find medical service really expensive here.

Lack of access to care can have serious, even fatal, consequences. One agency worker described a young HIV-positive man dying without health care after his study permit expired:

> There was a meeting of a bunch of different service agencies about a year ago for a young man who was in a situation where he was unable, he maybe wasn't connected to community services, his education visa had ended, and then he was in need of health care, and somehow fell through the cracks and died. I don't even know if he was thirty at the time.

The interaction between federal and provincial health care systems also created barriers to care for people with temporary status:

> The people who don't have access to IFH[P] are in this nebulous time period of maybe trying to get work permits, and TRPs [temporary residence permits], who, every time they have to renew a work permit, there's this period of time when their current work permit has expired, even though they're within the timeline they should apply for their next one, and their MSP expires.

A small number of clinics in the lower mainland provide services to people without medical coverage, including both migrants and others without provincial medical cards, but this is based on charity rather than entitlement. One participant had used such a clinic: "When I didn't have any status, once I got sick and I was lucky that there are clinics that offer you service without asking what is your status in Canada." Apart from the occasional charitable clinic, people without status are unable to obtain state-funded health care at all, including for childbirth and HIV-related medical concerns.[12]

Although emergency services were available on a private-fee basis, some migrants reported their reluctance to use such services because they feared deportation. Indeed, in one reported case, immigration enforcement did arrive at a migrant's house to initiate deportation shortly after an emergency room visit. Another bar to accessing such fee-based service was the inability to bear the costs of treatment. One participant described paying $5,000 for basic childbirth services in the 1990s, and another reported a more recent figure of $12,000. In the latter case, a woman made alternate, lower-cost arrangements to give birth at home with a midwife. An agency worker recounted her situation:

> Her visa expired; she was still pregnant, of course, and then the information given to them was that they had to pay almost $12,000 in the labour if they want service. Then we ended talking about a midwife, then she got a midwife for $2,500. Then what we end up doing is that, because they don't have status, then they usually live in a building with eight, ten people, and the delivery is obviously going to be at home, then in the

case of somebody without status, we have to negotiate with the landlord [...] We have to tell the neighbours, "Don't call the police if you hear a lady screaming. It's just that there is going to be a delivery at home." Taking all these extra measures, it's ugly.

The same agency worker reported a case in which a migrant worker who had status but did not have a provincial medical card was unable to pay a $700 hospital fee for lab services – the hospital staff responded by calling the police.

Front-Line Policies

Based on migrants' experiences with regard to health care, I made Access to Information requests to the provincial Ministry of Health as well as to hospitals to find out more about the role of migration status in their policies. While the *Regulations* describe who is a resident and a "deemed" resident for the purposes of health care eligibility, the front-line decisions about access are made by Ministry representatives and hospital administrators as part of day-to-day operations. The Ministry of Health policymakers decide who is eligible for provincial health care coverage, and regional health authorities and hospitals provide or deny access to their medical services directly, including decisions about the provision of medical services to people without provincial coverage.

The Ministry of Health's policy manual excludes visitors to Canada as well as refugee claimants from provincial coverage. All temporary migrants who are covered need to be able to show an immigration document (work permit, study permit, or temporary resident permit) that is valid for at least six months. People who have applied to extend their temporary migration status can have their health coverage extended if they have applied for and obtained a new permit before the last one expires. However, as discussed in previous chapters, delays in processing time make this unlikely. The policy gives two different instructions for situations like this. According to one section of the manual, if the migrant applied to immigration authorities for a new permit before the expiry of the old one but has not received it because of processing delays, he or she is entitled to continuous coverage.[13] However, another section of the same manual states that continuous coverage is allowed only if the new permit is issued before the end of the month during which the old one expired.[14] Thus, migrants waiting for new immigration documents may lose health care, even where they are considered to have legal status.[15] People who have lost status entirely and then have it restored are required to go through the six-month waiting period again before they are eligible for health care coverage.

In its policies, the regional health authority Vancouver Coastal Health (VCH) states that "residents of Canada should have access to full services of the Canadian health care system. This encompasses Canadian citizens, landed immigrants, and visitors on work or student visas." Emergency care "should be available to everyone," but people who are not covered must pay back the cost. For urgent care, the policy for migrants is "to stabilize and repatriate the patient." Non-emergency care is not available to "foreign patients" unless they have the right kind of status,[16] doctors have agreed to treat the patient, and the treatment is either extremely specialized or required for survival or reasonable quality of life.[17] According to this policy, treatment should not be offered if the person could access health services elsewhere. It would also not be offered on the basis of "social criteria," such as "marital status, social status, dependents [...] contributions to society, squeaky wheel considerations."[18] The policy allows for some discretion to waive costs: "On occasion, the patient's extreme need for treatment, or some other benefit accruing to VHHSC [the Vancouver Hospital and Health Sciences Centre] (e.g. improved public relations), may justify treating them on a charitable basis."[19]

To help the health authority interpret the provincial regulations governing health care, Vancouver Coastal Health provides a chart listing immigration status in order to clarify who is considered a "resident." People are considered residents when they have a work permit, study permit, or confirmation of permanent residence after the first three months of residence in Canada, and if they can obtain Medical Services Plan coverage. Refugee claimants are eligible for care, but only as long as they have valid Interim Federal Health documents. Those with working holiday visas are not eligible for coverage as residents. Immigration and MSP documents are required upon request prior to obtaining health or hospital services. Those who are unable to provide the required immigration documents must pay for health services.[20]

In its policy documents, the regional health authority Fraser Health defines non-residents of Canada as those who are:

- From outside of Canada either with or without a visitor visa
- Unable to provide proof of valid residency status (i.e., Landed immigration papers or permanent residency cards or student or work visas issued for 6 or more months)
- Refugee claimants without valid Interim Federal Health Coverage on the date of the service
- Returning Canadians who are not permanent residents of Canada (not physically present in Canada at least 6 months in a calendar year)[21]

This list uses the vocabulary of federal immigration law, but Fraser Health policy also activates those definitions in ways that diverge from the federal immigration regime. For example, this policy has built in a residency determination that is stricter than that required under federal law: while the *Immigration and Refugee Protection Act* requires permanent residents to maintain physical presence in Canada for two out of five years (and citizens have no such requirement at all), the Fraser Health policy requires residence for six months out of every year.[22]

Like Vancouver Coastal Health, Fraser Health uses a definition of "uninsured" patients to exclude from care those residents without insurance and those who are waiting for provincial medical coverage. In order to have access to emergency services, these patients are required to provide a deposit on admission. Fees for treatment are similar in both regional health authorities.[23] Fraser Health records the expiry dates of migrants' immigration status, as well as their work or school information, when they are admitted to hospital.[24] Physicians are directed to discuss with non-residents and uninsured persons "their earliest possible discharge or transfer back to their home country or province as soon as possible after their admission."[25]

Several study participants mentioned debts and costs associated with health care. Such costs were usually borne by workers without authorization, but health care fees also applied in the case of one worker who had a work permit but had not yet met the requirements of "residency" for the purposes of obtaining medical coverage.

Migration status is a complex mediating factor in the state's provision of health care. The provincial health care statute does not name status as a requirement for receiving care; rather, exclusion occurs as a result of residency requirements in the regulations. The federal taxonomy of migration status is imported into these laws to create a category of "deemed residents," under which migrants are excluded if they do not fall within the listed categories. The determination of status and residency come to life in the policies of health authorities and hospitals. These policies reveal not only the relevance of migration status, but also the variety of ways in which it may be interpreted at the front-line service level. Such interpretations are made in tandem with residency determinations, manifested in one hospital's troublingly broad definition of a "non-resident" as anyone "from outside of Canada." This front-line use of migration status has real effects on non-permanent migrants, with both health and financial consequences. Local institutional practices vary in determining who gets care, and the documents they need, but hospital and health district policies tend to be more restrictive in their application of status requirements than is the health care legislation itself. Furthermore, confusion between federal and provincial coverage and/or delays in processing immigration permits can result in migrants' losing access to care. Thus, migration status functions as a barrier not only though exclusion in the law but also through particular institutional practices, including practices that may work to exclude even those who are legally entitled to coverage.

Education

Alongside health care, basic public education for children has a long-standing association with membership in Canadian society.[26] Although only a minority of migrants who participated in this study had children with them in Canada, these children's access to public education was affected by their migration status. Access to education for migrants with uncertain status has moved toward inclusion in some Canadian cities. The Toronto District School Board has adopted a "don't ask, don't tell" policy that enables schools to enrol and teach students independently of their migration status, as well as to commit to the non-disclosure of immigration status information to Canadian immigration authorities.[27] Advocacy toward a similar goal is underway in Montreal.[28]

In British Columbia, laws and school board policies include requirements that, like those concerning health care, are associated with the definition of a "resident" but that turn on migration status directly or through their effect. The provincial Ministry of Education publishes a policy guideline on how to determine residency through immigration status. At the local level, school districts disclosed a variety of practices concerning the screening of students and their families on the basis of migration status. In ways similar to practices in the health care system, lack of migration status justified restriction and exclusion, and increasingly so from the level of statute to that of policies and practices.

Legislation

Education is a matter of provincial jurisdiction, but it is also mentioned specifically in section 30(2) of the federal *Immigration and Refugee Protection Act,* which states, "Every minor child in Canada, other than a child of a temporary resident not authorized to work or study, is authorized to study at the pre-school, primary or secondary level."[29] This section does not guarantee enrolment of students, which is a provincial responsibility, but it does confirm that all minor children except those whose parents are not allowed to study or work under the *Immigration and Refugee Protection Act* are not breaking immigration law by attending school. At the time of writing, this section has not been considered by courts, so it is unclear whether a "temporary resident not authorized to work or study" refers only to a visitor, or whether it also excludes temporary resident permit holders or persons with no status. Read together with section 22 of the same *Act,* which defines temporary residents as those who have obtained a document after meeting requirements, this section could be construed narrowly to exclude only those who have a document other than a work or study permit. This interpretation would put children without status, and those of parents without status, within the sphere of authorization to study. However, because this *Act* does not govern provinces, it cannot be used to advocate for students' enrolment within the provincial public education systems.

The British Columbia *School Act* requires children residing in the province to enrol in school by age five and remain in school until age sixteen,[30] it mandates the provincial government to provide education for "residents" in British Columbia free of charge, and it specifies that a student is a resident if "the student and the student's guardian are ordinarily resident in British Columbia."[31] The *Act* does not define "ordinarily resident," nor is this term interpreted in case law. The Ministry's guidelines, however, set out specific indicators that it will consider as aspects of "ordinary residence" based on case law from other fields. If a student is found to be part of a family "ordinarily resident," the student will be able to enrol without cost. If not, they are required to pay private fees.

Participants reported cases in which children's migration status resulted in enrolment problems when the students came to the attention of their school. One agency participant described this happening when a student became ill and required medical attention, at which point the school noticed the lack of medical plan card and other Canadian identification. A migrant family told me that a school refused to enrol their children without sufficient proof of status; in another case, parents were afraid to enrol their children in school because they wished to avoid having their immigration situation made more visible. One refugee claimant family said they knew they couldn't enrol their children until they had started the refugee claim process.

It is not only the child's migration status that can determine access to school, but their parents' status. A foreign worker parent of a child who is a Canadian citizen described what he called an "interrogation" by a school on the basis of his status:

Interviewee: The school interrogated me about my status; if I lose my status, my child won't be able to continue studying.

Interviewer: So you said they interrogated you. Can you tell me a bit more about how that happened or what they asked you for?

Interviewee: The school itself, they weren't, they didn't ask very directly, but the board of education, the school board, they interrogated me about that.

Interviewer: Your child is a Canadian citizen; how did they come to know that your status is something they want to talk to you about?

Interviewee: I am not sure exactly how they were able to identify me, but I guess it was because when enrolling my child into school, I submitted information about my personal status.

Interviewer: So when did they, did they ask you for a meeting, or did they talk to you when you dropped your son off? How did they talk to you?

Interviewee: They had a meeting with me in the school board.
Interviewer: So what sort of things did they ask you?
Interviewee: So they basically let me know that had my visa expired, if it wasn't granted extension, that my child would have to leave or pay over $10,000 as an international student.
Interviewer: Are they aware that your child is a Canadian citizen?
Interviewee: They knew because we had his passport and his identification.
Interviewer: So since that time, have you had any interactions with the school board about that same issue?
Interviewee: Just a little bit prior to when my visa expires, they contact me every year.
Interviewer: Do they phone you or do they send you a letter?
Interviewee: The school board gives a letter to the principal of the child's school. The principal gives it to my son's teacher. My kid brings it home to me.

In this case, the school and board kept track of the parents' status as an aspect of their own records in order to determine eligibility for enrolment of a child who is a Canadian citizen. This practice is consistent with both the Ministry of Education policy on fee assessment for foreign students and the policies of some schools, which base their decision on the parents' migration status, regardless of the status of the children.

Front-Line Policies

In 2011, British Columbia's Ministry of Education issued a policy statement, to be applied by all school districts, with regard to which students are provincially funded and which are not. The policy describes its purpose as follows: "Boards of education are entitled to scrutinize the purpose for which the person or family has established its residence in the community to prevent an abuse of the system under which higher fees may lawfully be charged for out of province/international students."[32] This policy gives a list of indicia of "ordinarily resident" that does not refer directly to immigration status:

Ownership of dwelling or long-term lease or rental of dwelling,
Residence of spouse, children and other dependent family members in the dwelling,
Legal documents indicating British Columbia residence,

Provincial driver's licence,
Employment within the community,
Parent or guardian filing income tax returns as a BC resident,
Provincial registration of automobile,
Canadian bank accounts or credit cards,
Links to community through religious organizations, recreational and social clubs, unions and professional organizations,
Subscriptions for life or health insurance, such as MSP coverage, and
Business relationships within the community.

The policy refers specifically to immigration status in a later section: "Immigration status is relevant but not determinative of ordinary residence. The determination of whether a person is ordinarily resident should never be based solely on the person's immigration status. A person need not be a Canadian citizen or permanent resident to be 'ordinarily resident' in BC for the purposes of s. 82."[33] Although the policy states that immigration status is not determinative of residency, it also includes a list of immigration statuses that do indicate residency. The use of a list itself invites exclusion for those who are not listed, and muddles the role of immigration status in this policy.

The children of temporary residents who have a valid study or work permit are covered by this policy as long as the parents have sufficient documentation. They are less likely to have access to funded enrolment if their parents fall within a variety of other status situations, including parents who hold a temporary resident permit, who cannot be removed to their countries of origin, and who are undocumented, as well as pre-removal risk assessment applicants and humanitarian and compassionate applicants. Furthermore, this policy bases children's access to education solely on the status of their parents, which means that children who are Canadian citizens and permanent residents can be denied access to funded education on the basis of their parents' status, as was the situation with the child described above. Families in such a situation may well fit the indicators of ordinary residence as described in the law, but they would have a more difficult time enrolling without fees, as they are not specifically mentioned in the policy document.

Specific school boards reported a variety of operational policies that exclude children on the basis of their immigration status, or that of their parents. To learn more about these policies, I made Freedom of Information requests to both the Ministry and to school boards across British Columbia. The Ministry itself referred me to its online "Decision Aid" for schools. It is clear from this document that, where the child "entered Canada with parent or legal guardian," only the parent's or guardian's status is considered when determining funding eligibility. According to this document, the following categories are eligible to have their children's education funded: citizens, permanent residents, refugees, protected persons, people with Minister's Permits,[34] those who have applied for landed status, and those with work or study permits valid for a year or longer.[35] Ineligible are individuals with visitor visas and temporary resident permits.[36] While these categories capture some status situations, many are not mentioned, including a person who has implied status, whose status is expired, or who has entered Canada without authorization.

Actual decisions to admit or refuse a student are made at the level of local schools, so their specific policies as well as the practices used by specific districts are vital in determining who can enrol. In response to Access to Information requests, I received responses from school districts outside the lower mainland of British Columbia, but I have included here only the school boards in the areas in which I interviewed participants. School districts provided a variety of written policies and information about practices, which fall into two categories: measures to screen students initially, and measures to confirm ongoing eligibility.

Screening and Status Determination by School Districts

Some school boards referred specifically to Ministry policy, indicating that they had adopted it and applied it directly. The Chilliwack School District, for example, indicated that it had adopted Ministry policy, but also confirmed that, in its interpretation of the policy, migration status was a necessary consideration: "If the family has no official status in Canada (illegal), we would not register the children."[37]

More often, though, school boards disclosed written policies of their own, which diverge to a greater or lesser degree from Ministry policy. The Surrey School District, for example, classifies certain "international" students as being exempt from yearly tuition fees of $12,000. This category includes students who are refugees or claimants, and students whose parents or guardians are permanent residents, are applicants for permanent residence, or have work or study permits valid for a year or longer. This policy allows discretion to admit those "whose parents or custodians satisfy, through an administrative review, [...] that there are special circumstances which warrant a tuition free education."[38] Vancouver School District disclosed a similar list of exemptions from payment.[39]

These policies are fairly similar in content to the list in the Ministry policy described above, with an important exception. Unlike the Ministry policy, there is nothing to indicate to front-line decision makers that those who are not on the list of included students may meet the definition of "residents" under the *School Act*. Furthermore, the power of the list is augmented by the explicit allowance of discretion for "special circumstances." The use of a list plus discretion for "exceptions" to it underscores the importance of migration status and diminishes the likelihood of establishing residence for people who are not listed, even though this is clearly a possibility under the legislation and the Ministry's policy.

The Coquitlam School District disclosed a checklist for registration that includes separate requirements for "Status in Canada" and "Residency." To demonstrate "Status in Canada," parents/guardians are required to provide one of the following documents:

- Canadian birth certificate, passport or citizenship card
- confirmation of landing documents plus passport
- permanent resident card or Status Indian documentation, or
- work/study permits valid for one year plus proof of work of 20 hours or more per week or postsecondary enrolment.[40]

As a part of registration, both citizenship status and documentation of ordinary residence are verified and recorded in school computer systems.[41]

The requirement for parents/guardians to have status, regardless of the status of their children, was universal in the policies I reviewed. For example, the Vancouver School Board interprets section 82 of the *School Act* to mean that both the student and the parent/guardian must be "ordinarily resident." This policy explicitly confirms that "if a student is ordinarily resident in British Columbia, but their guardian is not, the student is not entitled to a publicly-funded educational program."[42] The wording of this policy describes a residency requirement, not an immigration requirement, which excludes students from funded education. But it is clear that lack of immigration status alone can result in exclusion from state-funded education, regardless of other indicia of attachment. The application of this policy also distinguishes between different categories of people, apparently on behavioural grounds: the "unsuccessful refugee claimant" is entitled to enrol his or her children, whereas children of "parents caught overstaying" would be excluded, although these two phrases could describe the same family.[43] Furthermore, the child's status seems to be irrelevant in screening measures, which confirms that children who are Canadian citizens and permanent residents would be excluded on the basis of their parents' status.

The policy in North Vancouver is the most divergent from the Ministry guidelines. This district has a specific policy for non-Canadian students, separate from its residency requirements concerning Canadian non-residents (i.e., out-of-province students). For temporary residents, this policy allows funded admission only for children of parents who hold a study permit for two years or longer and on a discretionary temporary basis for visitors. There is no reference to the other allowable categories listed in the Ministry policy, including work permit holders, refugee claimants, and protected persons without permanent residence.[44] This policy also reaches further than others in its interaction with immigration law, as it actively prohibits the board from issuing documentation to support a study permit. The seeming absence of categories of temporary migrants that other jurisdictions include might be explained by this policy's interpretation of federal jurisdiction. It states that the federal government is responsible for both "the admission of non-Canadian students to Canada" and "the specification of privileges associated with such admission."[45] This interpretation is unique among school policies; other policies appear to be based on the understanding that the provinces have jurisdiction over education, which is consistent with the constitutional division of powers.

Ongoing Status Confirmation

In making Freedom of Information requests to school boards, I specifically asked for any documents or procedures concerning reporting of immigration status to Citizenship and Immigration Canada and/or the Canada Border Services Agency. None of the responding schools disclosed such a policy, and many confirmed that they had no such policy. However, multiple school boards provided information on their own ongoing verification of status and residence.

One practice common to both Vancouver and Surrey was the use of formal written declarations by parents concerning their status. Vancouver, for example, uses a "Parent Declaration" in which parents/guardians must swear that they belong to one of the following categories: citizen, permanent resident, refugee, holder of a work or study permit for a year or more, diplomatic, or "other" as confirmed with immigration authorities.[46] The Surrey School District also provides a "Parent Declaration" form for permanent residents, which requires parents to declare that they are not residing in their country of origin and "will not be taking extended vacations during the school year."[47] The policies of the Vancouver School District include recommendations for monitoring the residency of students, including monitoring ordinary residence and address, having the parent or guardian report to the office, and calling the student to appear at the window of his or her home while a staff member drives past to confirm they are present.[48] The practice of monitoring residence status by observing the student at home or requiring parents to report to the school is purely a creation of this Board's policy. Again, while "residency" is the determining factor in access to funded education, it is likely that, based on the use of inclusion lists and the treatment of status as a gatekeeper, such practices would be applied to families headed by adults with non-permanent migration status.

The Coquitlam School District explained the following about its ongoing monitoring:

> In response to your emailed questions regarding "checking in with the family at the end of the permit," in the 2011–2012 school year, there were 103 parents with work permits and 10 parents with study permits in the current database. Reminder letters are sent to parents when their work or study permit is about to expire, requesting that a copy of the new permit (or copy of the application for a new permit) be sent in.[49]

For non-permanent migrants with accompanying children, public education is another place where migration status matters. In the laws, regulations, and policies governing access to public education, migration status is associated with exclusion from this aspect of the social state. While the *School Act* itself does not mention immigration status, it requires both the parent and the child to be "ordinarily resident."[50] Policy at the provincial level states that migration status is non-determinative of whether a parent is "resident"; at the same time, the province has compiled a status list that indicates whose children should be enrolled, and such a list creates the potential to filter on the basis of status.

The policies of school boards, which illustrate a wide variation in application of this provincial policy, make it clear that migration status of the parents does in fact function as a filter. In practice, school boards require immigration documentation in addition to residency documentation. Families without sufficient status can be barred, regardless of whether they meet the other indicia of residency. In conjunction with this practice, two school boards had policies that actively monitored the status of parents on a regular basis, including in-person reporting requirements in the case of Vancouver. These requirements make distinctions on the basis of status for children who are Canadian citizens and permanent residents and allow the exclusion of children if their parents do not have permanent status. In a way similar to that in the health care system, the potential for restriction of services widens through front-line policies and practices.

In 2015, the British Columbia Teachers' Federation drafted a "Sanctuary School Policy" with the aim of welcoming all students, regardless of immigration status, and advocated for the adoption of this policy by school boards. The draft policy includes:

- non-co-operation with federal immigration enforcement
- education of school administrators, staff, and teachers in issues concerning students without status and the requirements to admit students under the British Columbia *Education Act*
- alternative verification of name, address, and date of arrival in Canada if required (such as through a lawyer's or doctor's letter)

- security and privacy of information concerning immigration status, and a commitment not to refuse access if a student does not provide immigration status information.[51]

In its response to this policy proposal, the Vancouver School Board states that both non-status and refugee families are eligible for a publicly funded education, and it emphasizes that residency, and not citizenship status, determines access to its schools. At the same time, it noted that proof of long-term residency must be provided to ensure that international student fees do not apply, and proof of status in Canada is requested for parents and children as well. The policy response states that the School Board's practice is not to turn families away, but to support them on a case-by-case basis. With regard to privacy of information, the Board states that it has to collect information on citizenship status because not doing so would result in funding not being provided for that student. With regard to disclosure of information, it notes that it does not initiate contact with federal immigration enforcement, but that it "must provide information when required by law to do so" and will centralize federal immigration requests through a district principal's office.[52]

Employment Insurance

Employment Insurance is a federally administered program of financial support for workers unemployed as a result of layoffs, maternity leave, caring for family members, or illness. All employees who are formally employed, including precarious migrant workers, contribute to the Employment Insurance fund, usually through payroll deductions.

Although they often contributed to Employment Insurance through payroll deductions, study participants identified multiple barriers to obtaining these entitlements. Of the participants who were eligible for Employment Insurance, only two had applied for and obtained benefits, and both experienced status-related barriers to receiving those benefits. For those who were eligible but did not apply, the reasons they were reluctant to claim this entitlement were intimately linked with their precarious status.

Legislation and Policy

Employment Insurance is governed by the federal *Employment Insurance Act*[53] and associated *Regulations*.[54] Nothing in this law or policy explicitly requires a specific migration status, or even that workers have status at all. But there are eligibility requirements that may have a disproportionate impact on workers without permanent status. To be eligible, workers must show a period of labour force attachment, measured by the hours of work in the year prior to an application for Employment Insurance. The number of hours varies based on regional unemployment.[55] However, workers who are "new entrants" to the Canadian workforce must show a total of 910 hours in the twelve months leading up to the termination of employment. Precarious migrants will belong to this category in their first year of Canadian employment, regardless of their previous work experience elsewhere. It is possible for them to meet the requirement if they work full time for a year, but for those who suffer layoffs earlier in their contract, this requirement is a barrier. While this requirement is intended to apply to Canadians who have no previous work experience, it also encompasses precarious migrants with work experience outside Canada and is likely to affect them differentially on this basis.

In order to be eligible for benefits, workers must show that they are "available for work," which also has a differential impact on precarious migrant workers with closed work permits.[56] Closed (employer-specific) work permits can limit the extent to which they are considered to be "available for work." Appeal decisions reveal ambivalence as to whether a person with an employer-specific work permit is "available for work." While some decisions have found that a person with a closed work permit cannot meet this requirement,[57] others have reached the opposite conclusion – namely, that a temporary foreign worker cannot be said to be unavailable for work when the circumstances are beyond the worker's control, including where worker permits are restricted within the federal immigration system.[58] A 1993 decision on this issue found that this differential effect did not amount to a breach of equality rights under the *Charter*.[59] The policy manual used to administer Employment Insurance benefits is similarly unclear: it leaves open the possibility that migrant workers would be considered available in certain circumstances but does not provide concrete requirements.[60]

One agency participant reported that many migrants without status believed that Employment Insurance was unavailable to them because they were working informally. In such cases, there would be no payroll records, no deductions, and no formal Record of Employment. Eligibility for Employment Insurance would be next to impossible to establish, because these workers would have difficulty in proving that they had worked. When workers lacked immigration status entirely, they were unable to become formal participants in the workforce, and, as such, they would effectively be barred from Employment Insurance, no matter how long their service or what the circumstances of the termination of their employment. Although the laws governing Employment Insurance do not explicitly require status, without any immigration status it is functionally impossible to obtain the required proof of labour market attachment.

As described in Chapter 2, immigration law provides for implied status, in which a person is legally authorized to remain in Canada but does not yet have a status document, often while waiting for a renewed or updated document. Agency participants reported cases of workers who had implied status but who could not obtain Employment Insurance because they were missing the physical documents:

> It's a bit challenging for them to get it [EI] if they are on implied status, because EI asks for a valid SIN number and a valid work permit, so they often get refused. And I've always thought, next time we have a client who comes because they got refused EI because they were on implied status, I'd want us to appeal it, because they should have status. It's just that they don't have the paper proving it.

If applicants cannot prove that they are available for work, including showing a work permit, they may be disentitled from receiving Employment Insurance, even where they had the required length of labour market attachment and were terminated through no fault of their own. In other words, such workers would be disentitled, whereas a permanent resident or citizen worker would be eligible for benefits.

Another situation in which precarious migrants encounter barriers to Employment Insurance is when they have a closed work permit for one employer, but are working for another employer without authorization. As explained in Chapter 2, this can happen when an employer terminates a worker prior to the expiry of the work permit and the worker must find a new employer more quickly than a permit can be issued.

When asked why she hadn't applied for Employment Insurance, one worker responded, "I didn't know that was possible and because I didn't want to have in my records that they fired [me]. And it was important that I was still working with them for immigration. Because I was lying for the immigration, government agencies, saying I was working for that person when it wasn't true." Although this worker may have been disentitled from obtaining Employment Insurance by virtue of the fact that she had been fired, if she applied, she would at least have been able to tell her side of the story and had this evidence considered within the Employment Insurance system, which is the right of all applicants. But because her permanent status hinged on the fiction of her employment with the original named employer, she was too apprehensive to even start a claim for benefits.

A caregiver described a similar situation, in which maintaining employment on paper was paramount to maintaining status:

> I can't apply for EI because my employer did not release me. The situation was, I was still under the name [of that employer]. So because I was able to apply for permanent residence after the twenty-four months, so I was supposed to be twenty-four months by June 2011, but since I went home for a holiday for two months, I need to make up for that two months. Since my employer is so nice, they want my papers to be moving.

In addition to barriers endemic to the Employment Insurance system itself, migrants also reported that they were reluctant to avail themselves of benefits. Such reluctance was reported not only by workers without authorization, but also by those who were clearly authorized and who were working formally and within the conditions of their permits. Migrant participants, and particularly live-in caregivers, were concerned that applying for EI would detrimentally affect their permanent residence applications. Although they were aware that they could apply for Employment Insurance when they were laid off, they were unwilling to do so on the basis of perceived risk. In one case, a worker did not apply for EI when she needed it, even after she had met the requirements for permanent residence by working for two years as a caregiver. She said this was because she was concerned that if the government knew she had been unemployed, this would have negative consequences for her permanent residence application.

Caregiver participants connected their perceptions of disentitlement and risk with the idea that they would be perceived as a burden to Canadian society and therefore deemed unsuitable for permanent residence. Four different caregivers revealed similar concerns:

> [W]hen applying for immigration, the government may believe that you are coming here and you are already taking without providing for society.

> I ask for the ROE [record of employment] from my employer and I got that, but people say it might affect your application and because you get the social welfare from the government, some people say that it is a burden to society and it might not be good for your application. I think don't try that.

> But if you don't have PR [permanent resident] status and you only have a work permit, I feel that applying for EI assistance isn't that easy. Because I'm young and I don't have a PR status and with this situation of me receiving money from the government, would that affect my PR application?

> I knew that EI existed, but I heard it would be unfavourable for my application had I tried to apply, and I didn't understand about the actual application procedure either.

There is nothing in immigration law or policy to indicate that receipt of Employment Insurance is a factor in assessing permanent residence applications.[61] Workers' responses, however, showed a perception of the Canadian state as a unified whole and, particularly, that taking entitlements from one area of state authority (Employment Insurance) would lead to consequences in another (immigration), regardless of the lack of formal links between these two. The immense fear of doing anything that might endanger their potential for permanent status prevented workers from applying for EI, even though they had paid into it. Migrant participants described an acute awareness of the need to present themselves as only giving to Canada, and never taking from it, even when the legal entitlement to benefits does not overtly make distinctions on the basis of status. These migrants appeared to view themselves as undeserving of the benefit and as required to work without respite. The construction of migrants as economically efficient by avoiding EI may function as a manner of appearing "less illegal" though compliance with ideas of deservingness,[62] and in this way serves as a disciplining feature.

Precarious migration status mattered not only as an impediment to the initial availability of benefits, but also to the process of obtaining them. One worker who did apply for Employment Insurance after a layoff described being required to provide additional paperwork and information after she became medically unable to work:

Interviewee: After fifteen days, they called me – and I don't know if that's normal, it never happened to me before – but they were like, "I need your work permit because I have to see your status." So I sent three work permits, and then after they were like, "I don't understand; I never have that happen before. Why do you have three work permits?" "I apply and apply and apply and I get three different work permits in the whole time." I don't know if they didn't believe me; I faxed everything [...] then he [the EI representative] was really rude. He was like, "Why are you applying for this?" "Because I have this happen." "Yeah, but you're not Canadian."
Interviewer: Someone from Service Canada said this to you?
Interviewee: I said, "Yeah, I'm not Canadian, but I still pay for it, so it's my money." "Yeah, but usually it's for Canadians." "I don't think so, because every paycheque they take off money and I didn't use this since I started. I should get something." [...]
Interviewer: Did they ask for your passport or birth certificate?
Interviewee: Just the work permit ... oh, and the passport copy.
Interviewer: Was it just that one guy?
Interviewee: It was the same guy all the time. If that's just for Canadians, why do they take money from me? Imagine if I go back to Mexico now; I'm not gonna get that money back.

In this instance, the worker did not fear losing status on the basis of making her claim, and felt entitled to be treated similarly to other workers, but the distinction between Canadian and non-Canadian workers defined the officer's approach to her file. Multiple work permits are not uncommon, as workers are often required by immigration law to obtain new work permits to change jobs or employers. The association of her status as a "non-Canadian" with a lack of entitlement to Employment Insurance evokes a notion of precarious migrants as morally disentitled from taking, much like that described by the caregiver workers quoted above.

Case Law and the Doctrine of Illegality

Courts and tribunals have considered whether Employment Insurance is available to workers working without authorization. Whether work undertaken by a migrant worker without status renders work non-insurable for the purposes of Employment Insurance has occasionally been the subject of judicial consideration. In the case of *Still v M.N.R.*,[63] the Federal Court of Appeal considered the traditional doctrine of illegality in the situation of a foreign worker working without a permit. In *Still*, the trial judge had upheld the denial of Employment Insurance benefits to a housekeeper who was working without status while she waited for her permanent residence application to be processed. The trial decision turned on the fact that the worker had contravened immigration laws in working without status, and, while the decision recognized exceptions to the doctrine of illegality, the trial judge found social utility in the denial of benefits, specifically, in the protection of the Employment Insurance fund. This decision was overturned on appeal to the Federal Court of Appeal, which found that the worker was entitled to benefits regardless of the fact that she had worked without status. In applying a modern approach to the doctrine of illegality, the Court found that simple illegality of a contract does not preclude a worker's entitlement to benefits, and that the particular objects of the statute in question should be considered. The Court held that "where a contract is expressly or impliedly prohibited by statute, a court may refuse to grant relief to a party when, in all of the circumstances of the case, including regard to the objects and purposes of the statutory prohibition, it would be contrary to public policy, reflected in the relief claimed, to do so."[64] The Court of Appeal considered both the Employment Insurance and immigration laws in its policy analysis: "while on the one hand we have to consider the policy behind the legislation being violated, the *Immigration Act*, we must also consider the policy behind the legislation which gives rise to the benefits that have been denied, the Unemployment Insurance Act."[65]

The Court of Appeal distinguished between those acting in good faith, like Still, and "those cases where a person gains entry to this country through stealth or deception."[66] It also held that, while "moral disapprobation of employment obtained in flagrant disregard of Canadian laws is not an unreasonable policy consideration, this sentiment should not be permitted to degenerate into the belief that everyone who gains employment in Canada without a work permit should be so judged."[67] The Court found that Still was acting in good faith and was not "an illegal immigrant," and that the denial of Employment Insurance benefits would constitute a de facto penalty for non-compliance with immigration law, disproportionate to the statutory breach.[68] The Court distinguished Still's case on policy grounds from other cases in which migrant workers were seen as more purposefully remiss, including where a worker was seeking to work for a new employer for whom he was not already authorized,[69] where a worker had started work prior to the issuance of a delayed work permit,[70] and where a worker continued working after being turned down for a work permit.[71] However, the line between "good" and "bad" migrant behaviour in a policy benefits analysis may not always be clear, and inaction can sometimes tip the analysis in favour of denying benefits. For example, in the case of *Mia v M.N.R.*,[72] a refugee claimant who had failed to renew his work permit was disentitled from obtaining Employment Insurance benefits on the basis that he knew, or should have known, he was required to obtain a new work permit.

In terms of practical access to benefits, precarious migrants may be subject to differential requirements as "new entrants" to the labour force, or may be unable to demonstrate sufficient work experience, if they have been working informally or beyond the authorization of their permits. Furthermore, even when precarious migrants are entitled to Employment Insurance, they may be deterred from applying because of the fear of its preventing them from obtaining permanent status. Migrant participants tied this fear to the idea of being perceived as a "burden" or taking something they did not deserve from Canadian society. While case law does not mirror this sentiment, it does include an element of moral sanction and division of migrants into the "good" and the "bad." Although being out of status itself is not sufficient to render a contract illegal for the purposes of EI determination, court and tribunal decisions about entitlement consider the individual migrant's behaviour vis-à-vis his or her own migration status as a factor.

Unlike other aspects of the social state, Employment Insurance includes a gesture of inclusivity developed through case law. The cases cited in this section identify as a matter of public policy the desirability of including workers regardless of status, which stands in stark contrast to the complete rejection of an analogous policy aim with regard to health. This gesture of inclusion is not the entire basis for determination of entitlement, though: the cases also describe a limit to entitlement, determined on the basis of the migrant's compliance with immigration law and on the level of culpability associated with it. Employment Insurance benefits may be available to workers without status, but in the case law, these workers are subject to a standard of "good faith" behaviour with regard to their status and to the potential for an assessment of whether a restrictive interpretation is appropriate given the moral content of their conduct, with specific reference to immigration law and status. This creates a dimension of assessment and a prerequisite associated with migration status that would not apply to workers who are permanent residents or citizens. Some of these cases explicitly consider the purpose of immigration law, and the construct of status imported from it seems to function in a manner paramount to, rather than alongside, the federal power to regulate Employment Insurance for all workers. Migration status and the assessment of deservingness thus act to create categorical barriers for precarious migrants who would otherwise be entitled to benefits. It is clear that judicial and tribunal decision making contribute to the "moral economy of deservingness" in determining migrants' entitlement to benefits commonly associated with membership.[73]

Welfare

Income assistance, or "welfare" as it is more colloquially known, is a system of basic minimum income support, which, like health care, is within provincial jurisdiction. As for health care and education, applicants must meet residency requirements, and like health care, they must prove their immigration status. While not as deeply entrenched as an aspect of Canadian society as education and health care, welfare is nonetheless a social benefit across Canadian jurisdictions. It is funded through taxpayer revenue, and it is more strongly associated with stigma and moral scrutiny than other aspects of the social state – for Canadians as well as non-citizens.[74] For example, in 2012, the federal Immigration Minister (as he then was) referred to migrants' use as a way of constructing them as undesirable takers from Canada, although data on migrants' use of welfare were not included with this press release.[75]

Legislation and Policy

In order to receive welfare or disability benefits, a person must be a citizen, permanent resident, refugee or claimant, temporary resident permit holder, or subject to an unenforceable removal order.[76] A family will receive benefits only for those members who fall into one of these categories, plus any dependent children, regardless of the children's status.[77] For mixed status families, while one person's lack of status or documentation would not disqualify the entire family, it would receive a lower amount based on the subtraction of that adult from the determination of the rate payable to the family. In an interesting bifurcation, adults without sufficient status are included as family members for the purpose of income contribution (which would reduce eligibility and rate of benefits) but are excluded for the purpose of determining family need (which would increase the level of benefits).[78]

In law and policy, some precarious migrants are excluded from benefits; these include work and study permit holders, visitors, migrants without status, those who have applied for permanent residence but not yet received it (e.g., spousal sponsorship, humanitarian and compassionate applicants), and all children, including citizens, who do not have a qualifying parent.[79] In a response to a Freedom of Information request, the Ministry of Social Development confirmed that it denied benefits to applicants when they do not meet its immigration requirements. Furthermore, they explained that their policy is to deny benefits to migrants, even when they met immigration requirements, if they had been sponsored by a family member and were still within an immigration sponsorship period. In the latter situation, the Ministry considered the sponsor(s) to be financially responsible for the applicant in such a manner as to pre-empt benefit entitlement, even where the applicant otherwise met eligibility criteria. The number of such refusals was usually under 100 per year from 2005 to 2011.[80]

Case Law and Eligibility

The role of migration status in welfare eligibility has not been judicially considered, but there are several relevant decisions of the Employment and Assistance Appeal Tribunal, which hears welfare appeals in British Columbia. The Tribunal's decisions are not binding, but they provide examples of the way migration status is considered at the level of administrative appeal.

In some of its decisions, the Tribunal made eligibility findings based on migration status and, in so doing, considered information which welfare authorities had apparently obtained from federal immigration. In a 2010 decision, for example, the Tribunal refused the eligibility appeal of a person who had made a refugee claim. The Immigration and Refugee Board had declared that the individual had abandoned the refugee claim, but then the person had sought legal counsel and was in the process of making an application to re-open it. The Tribunal noted that the Ministry of Social Development had "confirmed with Immigration the appellant had no status in Canada."[81] The Tribunal rested its denial of benefits on information shared between the Ministry and Citizenship and Immigration Canada. Similarly, in a 2007 decision, an appellant claimed to have current temporary migration status.[82] The Tribunal, however, preferred the Ministry's contrasting evidence, which included a computer search provided by the Canada Border Services Agency showing the applicant's lack of status. A 2011 case considered the situation of a failed refugee claimant who had a child who was a Canadian citizen in provincial care. In that case, the Tribunal found that neither the mother nor the child qualified under the citizenship requirements of the *Regulations* and they were both declared ineligible for income assistance.[83]

In one example of a positive decision, the Tribunal considered the case of a person on disability benefits whose temporary resident permit had expired. The person had made an application to extend his status with Citizenship and Immigration Canada but had not yet received a decision.

The Tribunal reviewed section 183(5) of the *Immigration and Refugee Protection Regulation,* which gives "implied status" to people once they have applied to extend temporary status (and until a decision is made). The Tribunal found that this person was eligible for benefits because he had status under immigration law, and it found that he was in fact "authorized to take up permanent residence in Canada" under section 7(1)(b) of the *Employment and Assistance Regulation* because he held a temporary residence permit.[84] In this example, the interpretation of migration status is consistent with federal immigration law; it stands out, as well, in its integration of the federal construct of "implied status," which is otherwise not well incorporated in the application of other provincial laws.

In other cases, though, the Tribunal used migration status in ways that were inconsistent with immigration law. In case 09-310, for example, the Tribunal refused eligibility to a person who had received a negative refugee decision but was subject to an unenforceable removal order.[85] The applicant had an expired work permit and Interim Federal Health Certificate. The Tribunal relied on the fact that his work permit and IFH Certificate stated, "this document does not confer status" and "this document does not authorize re-entry." At the time, a person who had a failed refugee claim but who had not yet been given the opportunity to file a pre-removal risk assessment was considered to have a non-enforceable removal order. According to the Ministry of Social Development's own policy, this person should have been eligible for benefits. Furthermore, every work permit issued by Citizenship and Immigration Canada states "this document does not authorize re-entry," and no work permit issued to a refugee claimant confers status. This case gives one example of exclusion from provincial benefits on the basis of a tribunal's own interpretation of federal law. While the federal language of status is used in decision making, it is applied in institutionally specific ways, which can diverge from federal laws governing status.

Although many study participants were aware of the existence of welfare benefits, very few applied for or received them. Of the migrant participants, only two referred to having been on welfare while they had precarious migration status, and both of these were refugee claimants at the time they applied for benefits. One participant noted that the only reason she needed to apply for welfare was because the family was waiting for a work permit. Where applicants did receive benefits, they described welfare as inadequate to provide for the basics of life. Participants also identified several barriers to applying for benefits, most of which referred in some way to migration status. For example, an agency participant reported that his clients assumed they were not eligible for welfare: "They are not going to apply to welfare. They know they are not allowed to apply; they are illegal workers."

For others, the desire to be seen as "working" people made applying for welfare undesirable, similar to the reluctance described above with regard to Employment Insurance. Also comparable is the fear of potential loss of status based on the application for welfare benefits: "Our clients typically don't apply for welfare, not because they don't need it but because they are very afraid it's going to affect their immigration status." Although they are two different benefit schemes at law, and are in separate jurisdictions, some workers associated income assistance and Employment Insurance together as barriers to permanent residence: "I have a concern that if I applied for Employment Insurance or social benefits, the immigration services would know and they wouldn't support my application for immigration because I would be without work."

One participant who had applied for income assistance after obtaining her permanent residence reported a welfare officer's comment to her during the welfare application process, which she attributed to the "refugee" designation on the back of her permanent resident card:

Interviewee: Just two months while I find another job, and then they refused me at the beginning; they were saying, like, "No, you're only trying to take advantage. You just want to take advantage of the system."
Interviewer: Do you think it was because of your status?
Interviewee: Because of my status, yes, because all they seen the back of card, it's like your mark, you know, your mark, like, forever.

Another agency participant described a case in which the federal immigration system interacted with provincial welfare law to deprive a disabled woman of her benefits. The woman had applied for permanent residence on humanitarian and compassionate [H&C] grounds, but when she obtained approval, the provincial government removed her benefits:

> She had applied for an H&C five years ago. I think at some point it was approved in principle, and once it was, the provincial social assistance

program cut her off because it said she was then eligible for a work permit. It had something to do with even though the H&C was still being processed, because one part of it was approved in principle they didn't think they were financially responsible for her anymore. She has a child that was born in Canada, she has serious health costs and health issues, and she is not someone who was able to have a job, and she was suddenly cut off her disability.

The legal regime governing welfare benefits specifically lists migration status as a necessary component of eligibility. But this was not the only way in which migration status mediated access to welfare. As with Employment Insurance, study participants were reluctant to apply for welfare on the basis that it could interfere with their eventual permanent residence. Unlike EI, however, use of welfare benefits could result in a determination of financial inadmissibility under federal immigration law, which would be a legal barrier to permanent and temporary residence.[86] Specific institutional practices in this area use federal concepts of migration status. In both the determination of initial eligibility and in welfare appeals, migration status and information gathered from immigration authorities were used to allocate benefits, with varying degrees of adherence to federal interpretations of immigration law.

Compared to other aspects of the social state, income assistance or "welfare" laws and policies in British Columbia are more explicit in their use of migration status as a qualifying requirement, using the language of status from federal immigration law. Like other aspects of the social state, however, the devolution of law to policy tended to increase the exclusion of people from benefits. Most study participants indicated that they had not applied for benefits, as they were aware that they would be ineligible, and some associated welfare with Employment Insurance as "taking" from the state, which would potentially endanger their status. Yet, most non-permanent workers would not be eligible for welfare benefits at law. Of the categories of migrants considered in this study, work permit holders, non-status workers, and those waiting for status would be ineligible for welfare benefits on the basis of status, while refugee claimants would be eligible. Children of non-status parents are also ineligible in many circumstances, regardless of the children's own status. This aspect of the social state is the most restrictive of those considered in this chapter: although welfare is available as a basic entitlement for permanent members when no other source of income is available, people seen as temporary are, for the most part, excluded.

Conclusion

Migration status shapes social state entitlements in areas of the law on which people rely for access to health care, education, and a minimum income both within and outside the workforce. Laws governing the distribution of social benefits sometimes use migration status explicitly as a determining factor in assessing entitlement, but status also becomes relevant through interpretation of other requirements, such as residency. These social state entitlements are administered primarily under provincial law, with the exception of Employment Insurance, which is federal. Even for the three areas of provincial responsibility, there does not appear to be any purposeful harmonization of status and residency requirements, either in law or in practice. While there are themes and patterns of exclusion and legitimation, they are most visible through particular institutional practices, rather than in the text of the law.

Migration status is not an explicit requirement in provincial laws governing health care and education. Rather, it has been incorporated as an indicator of residency, which *is* explicitly a requirement. Employment Insurance does not mention migration status at all, but it becomes relevant through other requirements. The provincial welfare regime is unique among those canvassed, as it specifically uses migration status as a requirement in the legislation. Yet, whether or not it was explicitly mentioned, migration status was deployed in the application of all of the regulations discussed in this chapter, through effects, policies, and practices, and application tended to become more restrictive as it devolved from law to practice. Furthermore, migration status played a role in access to benefits through migrants' adoption of a discourse that associated benefits with the risk of loss of status – in tension with their feelings of expectation and entitlement to basic equality. Court jurisprudence is most robust the area of Employment Insurance, where it tied the receipt of benefits to "good" behaviour and adherence to migration laws. This reasoning incorporates the discourse of deserving and undeserving migrants as an additive aspect of the law. Although there is nothing in statute to indicate that benefits should be denied on a punitive basis or as an aspect of enforcement and deterrence vis-à-vis immigration law, this logic was applied as a primary basis of decision making at the judicial and quasi-judicial level. This is consonant with policy across the social state, in which the idea of disentitlement is framed by an understanding of the social state as a provider of "free" benefits, a treasure chest of generosity to be carefully allotted and guarded.

Relative to the laws governing workplaces, migration status tends to be deployed in a more restrictive and exclusive manner in the context of the social state. Migrants' participation as workers is disjointed from the benefits of the social state; Canadian society accepts migrants as workers and contributors to the social state, but not as beneficiaries of social state entitlements. This is effected through the incorporation into laws, policies, and practices of a notion of membership in which moral scrutiny is applied to those determined to be outsiders, even while they are within the state physically, socially, and economically. Such a stance not only justifies the exclusion of migrants from equal benefit from the social state, but also, in the case of Employment Insurance, the deprivation of benefits as a punitive measure ancillary to immigration law. The application of the criterion of migration status forges a link between immigration laws, which are intended to create closure and restrict entry to the state, and social benefits laws, which are intended to apply to those who reside within its territory. The result is a hierarchy of membership, in which migration status means that some become more equal than others. In the case of the social state, however, the interaction of migration status with the laws governing benefits takes on more active features: beyond deprivation, the framing of status justifies moral scrutiny and the monitoring of status continuity by local authorities. Moral scrutiny informs judicial and quasi-judicial reasoning to augment the legal relationship between immigration laws and those that govern social benefits. Exclusion on the basis of status is thus consonant with particular constructions of precarious migrants as "illegal," greedy, undeserving, or, at the very least, as a group whose potential for malfeasance is ubiquitous and related to their very presence within the state.

As detailed in Chapter 3, the law recognizes precarious migrants as workers. The laws and policies of the social state, for the most part, fail to include the same migrants in basic social entitlements. When precarious migrants are commodified as labour through participation in paid work, differential access to workplace protections is more a failure of the law to adequately account for precarious migration than direct exclusion. In the case of the social state, the connection between the person and their labour is less evident, and institutional practices include direct exclusion and moral surveillance. In this sense, the state is fragmented: the law creates demarcations that function differently in different locations. While the overall effect certainly results in subordination of precarious migrants, the lack of consistent treatment between these two spheres supports the characterization of the assemblage of state institutions to include tensions that "cut simultaneously through law, policy, and practice" rather than as a binary conflict between formal law and practice.[87]

The state institutions described here operate separately from each other in terms of jurisdiction and have specific functions and concerns, but migration status is relevant in all of them, particularly from the perspective of precarious migrants. Local institutions act as agents of sovereign power, but their activities are "far more suggestive of a highly fragmented system of governance than a coherent and systematic sovereign logic."[88] In effect, these laws and policies coalesce in the lives and experiences of migrants even in the absence of intentional cohesion on the part of state institutions. This recognition invites a closer examination of the role of state institutions in maintaining inequality, to which I turn in the following chapter.

5

Multi-Sited Enforcement

MAINTAINING SUBORDINATE MEMBERSHIP

Redefining Enforcement

In the popular imagination, immigration enforcement often encompasses dramatic scenes of immigration police, workplace raids, and physical coercion, but direct immigration enforcement is just one aspect of a multi-sited enforcement regime that functions to structure the subordinate membership of migrants who have precarious status. In this chapter, I propose an expansive understanding of the notion of enforcement as an appropriate way to view the mechanisms that exclude precarious migrants. Formal immigration enforcement is defined by law in discrete terms and pertains primarily to the revoking of status, the removal of people, and other punitive measures for those who contravene the conditions of their status. Based on data from migrants whom I interviewed and from institutions, however, I would argue that precarious status seems to catalyze coercive power within state and non-state relations across multiple sites, most of which do not involve direct interactions with immigration authorities. Instead of using the definitions of enforcement in the federal immigration regime, I use the criterion of coercive power when considering whether an interaction can be considered enforcement, and I explore the role of status in legitimizing this coercive function across various sites.

Federal immigration authorities enforce closure of the state by physical and territorial means – that is, through the physical removal of individuals and by revoking status. Other forms of enforcement also create closure, but, unlike direct immigration enforcement, they are affected non-territorially. Through interactions in working life and with the state, individuals are not ejected from Canada's territory, but they are effectively excluded from social state benefits and are limited in their access to employment rights, even when their entitlement is clear. Like territorial closure, this social and economic exclusion relies on the construct of status. However, its boundaries are not national borders; rather, they are apparent in daily life and in multiple local sites, impairing participation even while migrants live and work in Canada. Although legally governed by statutes and regulations that stand apart from the federal immigration regime, and that often exist entirely outside federal jurisdiction, migrants' interactions with the worksite and social state demonstrate that these sites function not only as sites of exclusion but also as sites of enforcement that help to maintain social and economic stratification.

For the migrants who participated in this study, direct immigration enforcement was rare, yet migration status was relevant in their interactions with community members, employers, and multiple state agencies. The intricate relationships between migration status and various aspects of life bear directly on social inclusion or marginalization and provide insight into the ways in which exclusion happens, even in the absence of direct enforcement by immigration authorities. Studies, including the present one, have linked uncertain status to limitations on the ability to reside or work in Canada, inadequate or exploitative working conditions, reluctance to claim rights and entitlements, and circumscription of social life. I propose here that the use of migration status as a differentiating factor across multiple sites serves to create and actively maintain social and economic stratification in which full membership is denied to significant numbers of migrants in the Canadian workforce. In place of full membership, migrants are not completely excluded. Rather, they are offered a form of membership in which their labour is commodified and accepted as necessary, but in which they are also disciplined to accept substandard conditions of labour and to construct themselves as more "deserving" through both state- and self-exclusion from social benefits associated with higher tiers of membership in Canadian society.

Direct immigration enforcement limits the capacity of migrants to reside, work, or study legally in Canada. The federal immigration authorities have the power to issue removal orders, arrest and detain non-compliant individuals, remove people from Canada, and impose terms and conditions of stay. Insofar as precarious or temporary migration is constructed as a problem from the perspective of the federal state, the idea of enforcement or exclusion is readily enlisted as the solution. In the Canadian context, however, direct immigration enforcement appears to function primarily on a symbolic level. At the time of this study, the number of prosecutions and deportations of unauthorized migrants was small in comparison to the likely number of migrants without status or with improper documentation, and enforcement against employers of precarious migrants has also been ineffective at best.[1]

Talk of the dangers of large-scale incursions of migrants, both workers and refugees, persists in policy discourse.[2] In practice, large-scale enforcement has not been actively pursued by the state, but the idea of enforcement is entrenched in the context of precarious migration through the conflation of border control and migrant control.[3] The former refers to controlling the entry of persons into a state, and the latter to the regulation of persons who are already within the state's territory and whose presence gives rise to specific normative claims to membership that do not exist for those outside the state's borders.[4] In other words, while living in Canada, precarious migrants are socially and politically excluded on the basis of sovereignty, even while they participate in economic and social communities inside the country's borders. Marginalization of precarious migrants within a territory is justified by a logic that appeals to sovereignty, borders, and national integrity, but the boundaries are constructed *within* rather than outside the state, in what Catherine Dauvergne has called "the reciprocity of sovereignty and illegality."[5]

Beyond the federal immigration authority, non-immigration state agencies and local authorities (e.g., schools, hospitals, transit officers) and non-state actors such as employers and community members all functioned as sites of enforcement for the precarious migrants who participated in this study. Interactions ranged from surveillance and document scrutiny to questioning, threats of deportation, and informing. Migrants also described an indirect disciplining effect: often, even when they had no direct interaction with these actors, they modified their actions and behaviours based on the potential for enforcement. Migrants often reported weighing the perceived potential for enforcement action against the advantages of accessing services and social benefits, demanding basic employment rights, or being active in social life. This was the case for many participants even when there were clear and significant consequences, such as forgoing medical assistance or basic income security.

For the migrants in this study, the fact of legal entitlement to benefits did not appear to mitigate the perceived danger of enforcement or the disciplining effect of enforcement/illegality dialogues. As a result, migrants experienced a lack of access to membership benefits even where entitlements were clear in the text of the law. Although distinct from law's written dictates, disciplining features are an intimate part of law in a broader sense, and they flow from status distinctions that originate in law. These distinctions are integrated in relationships between migrants and both state and non-state actors. The effects of legal and policy exclusions on the basis of status, as well as the function of deportability, are pervasive in multiple sites outside the federal immigration authority. I argue that these diverse sites are best understood as part of the phenomenon and enforcement of stratified social relations. Through examples and themes which emerged in migrant and agency interviews, this section will offer a broad depiction of enforcement, as defined by its coercive or disciplining effects rather than by the traditional understanding of immigration authorities as the primary mechanism of enforcement.

Federal Enforcement – Deportation and Removal

Federal immigration law empowers the state to enforce status-based distinctions in a direct and physical manner, by way of removal orders. The federal immigration regime has recourse to different types of removal, depending on the nature of the migrant's situation. There are three types of order that a peace officer is empowered to issue (although these are almost always enforced by the Canada Border Services Agency).[6] In terms of consequences for migrants, the departure order is the least serious of the three. It is an order requiring the person to leave Canada, but is not immediately enforceable and may be issued on a conditional basis.[7] An exclusion order is an order prohibiting a person from re-entering Canada for a specified period of time (one or two years, depending on the basis for issuing the order).[8] A deportation order is a complete bar to re-entry to Canada without specific authorization and is more likely to result in actual expulsion from Canada.[9] For the latter two categories, persons who wish to return to Canada during their exclusion must make an application for authorization to return on the basis of "compelling reasons" to re-enter; the decision to allow re-entry is a discretionary determination on the part of the Minister of Immigration (or their delegate).[10] Deportation orders represent the greatest likelihood of actual enforcement action, as well as the most serious consequences in terms of re-entry prohibition.

In response to an Access to Information Request, the Canada Border Services Agency (CBSA) provided data on removal orders issued in British Columbia from 2003 to 2012. In issuing removal orders, the Agency records the status of the individuals to whom it issues removal orders, specifying whether they entered without authorization, entered with authorization, or are permanent residents.[11] Among these categories, those who are not permanent residents constitute a large majority of removal orders (78–93 percent). The reason for removal is also tracked, using the following categories: Criminality–Lesser, Criminality–Serious, Financial, Health, Human Rights Violations, Misrepresentation, Non-Compliance with the *Immigration and Refugee Protection Act*, Organized Crime, and Security Grounds. Of these, non-compliance is by far the most frequent category, constituting the basis for at least 80 percent of tracked cases in each year.

The Canada Border Services Agency reported that it had issued 249–449 deportation orders annually in British Columbia between 2003 and 2012, with no noticeable pattern of increase or decrease over that time period. Deportation orders represent a small share (10–20 percent) of total removal orders issued in the province.[12] The majority of removal orders (50–70 percent) are departure orders. Pursuant to the *Immigration and Refugee Protection Act*, departure orders become deportation orders if a person does not leave Canada,[13] but on the basis of the above numbers, it is reasonable to assume that most departure orders do not result in deportation orders.

Another measure of direct enforcement is the number of offences investigated under the *Immigration and Refugee Protection Act*. In response to a further Access to Information request, the CBSA provided data on the processing of offences under the *Act*. I requested data on investigations across Canada since 2006 that resulted in a charge and for which the initial investigation was commenced under sections of the *Act* that would be most relevant to the question of enforcement against persons without status or with irregular status,[14] namely, contravention of a section of the *Act* or failing to comply with a requirement of the *Act*,[15] with specific reference to staying, working, or studying in Canada without authorization;[16] employing a person without authorization;[17] aiding entry of persons without authorization;[18] and organizing entry through fraud or deception.[19] The results of this request showed several charges pursuant to aiding entry (N=14, of which 2 were in Vancouver) and for employing a foreign national without authorization (N=33, of which 4 were in Vancouver). The Canada Border Services Agency does not record charges with regard to staying, working, or studying in Canada without authorization specifically, but it did disclose more than 800 investigations for failing to comply with the *Act* (which would encompass a wide variety of potential reasons for investigation), of which at least 90 took place in Vancouver.[20] Most of these resulted in a guilty verdict and subsequent incarceration. Annually, the numbers of criminal investigations under the *Act* in Vancouver ranged from 16 to 44, with no clear pattern of increase or decrease during the period under consideration.[21]

Based on this brief sketch of data on removal orders, several tentative observations can be made. First, although there are no firm data on the number of people lacking status or with irregular status, the number of deportations is very small compared to even the most conservative estimates of the number of irregular or undocumented migrants in Canada. Second, non-permanent residents constitute a large majority of those for whom removal orders are issued. At the same time, the number of actual deportation orders issued for all groups is much smaller than the number of removal orders. In other words, non-permanent residents are clearly a target group of initial enforcement action; however, because most removal orders do not appear to result in deportation orders, we can assume that most of the enforcement situations of non-permanent residents do not result in actual deportation. While the reasons for this are difficult to surmise in the absence of exit data, possibilities include the persistence of removal orders that are not enforceable legally or practically, voluntary departure, individuals "going underground" or otherwise losing contact with immigration authorities, and lack of enforcement activity on the part of the Canada Border Services Agency. The data on offences indicate that offence investigation is relatively common, although given limits in federal data classification, it is not possible to determine the frequency with which foreign nationals are actually charged with an offence on the basis of overstaying or working or studying without authorization.

The policy of the CBSA is to prioritize enforcement cases to determine the urgency of enforcement action. The five priority levels are as follows: 1) Security Threat; 2) Organized Crime or Crimes against Humanity; 3) Serious Criminality or Health (i.e., serious risk to their own or others' health); 4) Criminality; and 5) Non-Criminal.[22] Immigration offences and irregular status are categorized separately from criminality and are identified as the lowest priority for enforcement action. This does not indicate a lack of actual enforcement, but it does support an assumption that, for those with irregular status who are not seen as posing a risk on criminal or health grounds, enforcement is not as vigorously pursued as it is for higher-priority categories.[23]

Direct Enforcement in the Community

Although only a small minority of migrant participants had experienced enforcement action directly, one case merits description as an example of direct enforcement at the workplace. The participant in question entered Canada as a live-in caregiver, but her initial employer decided she no longer needed the caregiver's services part way through the two-year contract. The employer advised the caregiver that she wished to "help" – she agreed to keep her as an employee "on paper" in order to facilitate her permanent residence application but did not continue to pay her. Instead, the employer offered to connect the caregiver with other employers (for whom she was not authorized to work), to do cleaning work in their homes for cash on an informal basis. After some months of this work, the worker was approached in her initial employer's home by Canada Border Services Agency officers:

> So around ten o'clock, someone rang the bell, because in my part-time home there's a monitor that you can see who is outside the gate, and you just press the button open and then the gate open. So I did it twice. I saw two lady outside the gate [...] I went out and open the gate and it's the people from CBSA [...] I did ask them what's going on, and they say, "No, you don't need to ask," like, "Show me your ID." They were asking for my

ID, so I gave them my ID. They were interrogating already, and I did ask them "Oh, can you just tell me what's going on" and the lady said, "Maybe now you can think what's going on" and then they ask me, "What are you doing here" [...] They did search the whole house like "Okay, it's positive she is alone" [...] At first I was just trying to collect all my thoughts, and she said, "Have you ever been handcuffed before" [...] I was so scared [...] like there was no way out.

This participant was quite distressed while recounting her experience. It was clear that part of the force of this encounter was associated with her deportability. She mentioned that "they have a plane ticket" to send her back to the Philippines as an aspect of the initial enforcement encounter, although it was unclear in the interview whether the officers actually threatened deportation. The officers advised her that they had received a tip but did not identify their source. She suspected it had been one of her family members, with whom she had had a disagreement and who had learned of her situation by way of social media. This situation echoes a case documented in Geraldine Pratt's work with live-in caregivers, in which the employer practice of "sharing" or subcontracting a caregiver led to the caregiver's deportation.[24]

Many migrants referred to actual or potential interactions with the immigration enforcement authorities as an influential factor governing their own lives. In their descriptions of immigration authorities, migrants spoke first of their expectation that immigration authorities would make decisions against them and of their resulting preoccupation with the thought of deportation, whether or not it was actually imminent. In the words of one agency representative, "Whenever they get something [i.e., letters from immigration authorities] that's uncertain or that doesn't look too positive, the first question is 'Am I going to get deported?'" Thus, although direct enforcement by the CBSA is infrequent relative to the number of people with irregular status, enforcement was influential not just in terms of both face-to-face interactions but also its potential, what Bosniak calls the "specter of deportation."[25] The risk of actual enforcement action by immigration authorities for precarious migrants is real, but alongside direct enforcement action is the pervasive force of the potential for deportation, often invoked through reference to or the implication of enforcement. For many people for whom the only basis for enforcement is irregularity of status or lack of status, the "specter of deportation" may never be actualized, but it is potent nonetheless.

In some cases, social acquaintances of migrants acted as connectors or informers to immigration authorities. Direct contact with immigration officials that resulted in enforcement action was reported by agencies and migrants in various sites in social life: on the street, on re-entry to Canada, and at social gatherings. Migrants reported that various people in their personal lives – friends, co-workers, classmates, and family members – played the role of informant or potential informant. Although many of these potential informants were distant from physical state authority, for uncertain migrants, they evoked a tone of surveillance. For example, one migrant participant recounted the manner in which a roommate took on an authoritative, scrutinizing role:

> I used to have a roommate, Canadian, and he was like ... like a cop. He always asked me, "Your friends are legal, your friends are not" or "What are you doing, why you came here, show me your work permit," like that. He was like crazy. When I say I'm legal, and I have this – he changed his mind about me, you know what I mean? It was more friendly, but when I say my friend doesn't have ... he didn't want to talk to them, or he was rude.

In response to such situations, migrant participants described curtailing their social lives, limiting social activities, not going out of the house, or actively hiding their status when interacting with others. One agency representative also commented on the high frequency of enforcement action following anonymous tips or "poison pen" letters from community members concerning unauthorized employment. Canada Border Services Agency's data disclosure did not include information on the sources of information leading to enforcement action.

Fear of enforcement was described as an aspect of community information sharing, and the potential for enforcement had a disciplining effect. For those without documents, in particular, the feeling of scrutiny was pervasive: "You feel worried, like, oh, the police, like, you have to do everything perfect, or just worried about immigration, all the time ... I never had it happen, but some of my friends got deported like that." The amplification and internalization of the fear of enforcement contributes to the framing of irregular migrants as "lawbreakers" despite the minor nature of immigration infractions themselves.[26]

Although deportation and prosecution are infrequent relative to the number of migrants in Canada who have precarious status, direct enforcement is nonetheless a fundamental pillar of the enforcement regime. The fact of deportability flows from federal law, and its potency is established through actual deportations but also their potential– a potential that exists for migrants regardless of the number of actual deportations or prosecutions carried out. It is the possibility, rather than the statistical likelihood, that influences the lives of migrants and that interacts with other areas of working life and the social state to create diverse sites of enforcement.

Sites of Enforcement in Working Life

In this study, both agency workers and migrants referred to workplaces as a major site of enforcement. Worksites serve as an interface for direct contact with Canada Border Service Agency officers and regular police, but deportability also arose as a primary feature of the relationship between employers and employees, even where direct enforcement had not occurred. Furthermore, although it is not a part of the worksite, many participants relied on public transportation in order to get to work (as many workers do), and I have included here a discussion of the role of transit authorities as part of the matrix of enforcement encountered by precarious migrants.

Migrants reported direct or community knowledge of immigration visits, regular police, and fear of "checking papers" at construction sites, farms, restaurants, private households where domestic workers were employed, massage parlours, and "cash corners" where workers in informal sectors wait to meet potential employers. Participants did not always make the distinction between regular police and immigration police, but they certainly connected the presence of any type of police at worksites to the risk of losing status, deportation, or criminal sanction. Even the possibility of police presence, in conjunction with uncertain migration status, led to a heightened awareness of risk. As described in detail in Chapter 3, migrants were often reluctant to complain about workplace abuses, unpaid work, and health and safety concerns, and they experienced an exaggerated power disparity within employment relationships as a result of their status. Although employment relationships are governed by laws unrelated to the federal employment regime that determines status, and those laws are in principle inclusive of all workers, status functions as a barrier to equal treatment through those regimes. The combination of deportability and the unequal employment relationship associated with precarious status means that the workplace functions as a site of enforcement both through employer actions and through workers' reluctance to claim rights.

The most poignant instance of status-based enforcement by an employer in this study was described by a worker who had received a performance complaint from her employer. The employer's disciplinary letter to the worker cited an alleged failure by the employee and threatened immediate termination for further infractions, as many disciplinary letters do. However, this letter also stated that the employer would inform immigration authorities that the worker was not authorized to work and that, consequently, she would be unable to work legally in Canada; it also pointed out that it might be difficult for the employee to obtain another work permit (further details cannot be provided here without risking identification of the worker). The worker disputed the facts alleged by the employer but felt she could not speak up because of the link with her migration status.

In this letter, the use of legalistic language such as "offences" and "infraction," and reference to inside legal expertise, are combined with a direct threat to contact immigration enforcement. The employer invokes power not only through its willingness to activate immigration enforcement if the worker does not comply with demands, but also by substituting itself directly as the arbiter of legal migration status for that worker. Employers are able to enlarge the power disparity in situations like these because the legal structure surrounding migration status places the employment relationship in a pivotal role with respect to obtaining and maintaining status. Thus, while no employer has direct immigration authority, the deportability and illegality of migrants are reproduced and enlarged specifically in worksites, which function as a site of enforcement in one aspect of what Villegas calls "surveillant assemblages of illegalization."[27] Employers and work-related institutions do not collect data in the same sense as the federal immigration authority, but they nonetheless perform a surveillance function by leveraging migration status to obtain conditions of labour beneficial to the employer.

Another work-related site of enforcement reported by migrants and agency representatives was the public transit system in Greater Vancouver, specifically interactions with transit police. Such interactions were of concern specifically where migrants did not have legal documents establishing status, as transit police were reported to have turned over such migrants to the Canada Border Services Agency for enforcement and deportation. Two agencies reported transit ticket checks as a regular site of enforcement and counselled their clients to "be careful" and ensure they rode with a ticket. Moreover, one Mexican migrant reported community knowledge of "immigration on the Skytrain." One agency worker gave the following example:

> Lately, most of the illegal workers from Latin America, they get caught on the Skytrain. A guy who was living in the country for two years [...] he was caught a few weeks later when the security was re-enforcing the transportation, especially on Skytrain. One of the police officers got him and told him, "You know, you're getting checked." But he was so nervous and they see something is wrong about this guy. They didn't know why he was nervous and they said, "Can we have an ID?" He didn't have any ID. That's when they call the police or, after, immigration. Sometimes, they call straight to immigration. They show up to pick the guys. I think that has been really successful for immigration, catching the illegal ones.

In British Columbia, the public transit service has a distinct police force formally known as the South Coast British Columbia Transportation Authority Police Service. As police, its members are "peace officers" within the meaning in the *Criminal Code of Canada*[28] and thus are legally empowered to take enforcement action with regard to acts of Parliament, including the offence provisions of the *Immigration and Refugee Protection Act* and *Regulations* described above, in relation to migration status in Canada. Transit police are guided by their own *Policies and Procedures Manual*,[29] which contains a specific section concerning immigration arrests and includes an interpretation of the offence provisions of the *Act*. Rather than directly importing categories articulated by the *Act*, the policy casts a broader net, including the suspicion on "reasonable grounds" that a person is "in Canada by fraudulent or improper means" or is "no longer a visitor," or for "not leaving Canada as specified in a departure order."[30] Each of these categories may include individuals who could be in Canada with authorization. For example, the broad language of "improper means" may capture a refugee claimant who used inauthentic documents to travel to Canada, but this is specifically considered under immigration law to be non-punishable.[31] A person may be "no longer a visitor" because he or she has obtained a study permit, has applied for permanent residence, or has implied status. In addition, as described above, a departure order is often stayed or otherwise considered to be non-enforceable under the *Immigration and Refugee Protection Act*.

Pursuant to a Freedom of Information request, the Greater Vancouver South Coast Transportation Authority provided information about actions taken by its members relating to immigration status or the *Immigration and Refugee Protection Act* and *Regulations*. The data showed between 27 and 103 recorded transit enforcement interactions annually from 2006 to 2012 that were pursuant to immigration offences.[32] Many of these interactions are coded as an "assist," likely to the Canada Border Services Agency. Some represented interactions initiated by transit police to directly enforce their interpretation of the *Act*. In an email, a representative from the transit police noted that, "the majority of our contacts made is as a result of fare checks on the sky train system. Our members place themselves in the Fare Paid Zone at the stations, check for fares and if a fare cannot be produced a check of identification is done which results in the incidents that are listed here."[33] The act of boarding a transit vehicle without the requisite proof of payment is normally a minor offence attracting only a fine. For precarious migrants, it serves as a venue for enforcement of immigration laws, either through transit workers' assisting the immigration authorities or through the transit police's particular policy derivative of the terms contained in the federal immigration regime.

In December 2013, after I had conducted the participant interviews, Lucía Vega Jiménez was arrested by transit police in Vancouver subsequent to a fare infraction and handed over to the Canada Border Services Agency. As recorded in the subsequent coroner's inquest verdict:

> She could not produce proof of payment of her fare and offered identification in two different names. As part of their investigation the transit

police contacted the Canada Border Services Agency (CBSA) who advised them that if she was the person identified on one of the pieces of ID, she had been deported previously and was in Canada illegally. A CBSA agent attended to the station and Ms. Vega Jimenez admitted that she had come across the border illegally. She explained that she was working in BC for cash and was afraid to return to Mexico because of a violent boyfriend.[34]

Vega Jimenez committed suicide while in the custody of the Canada Border Services Agency, drawing attention to holding security shortfalls and accountability gaps within the Agency, including the lack of independent review of CBSA action, and giving rise to a number of specific recommendations in a coroner's inquest verdict.[35] That verdict did not address the issue of transit police enforcement, but, in 2015, the transit police force reportedly ended its policy of handing over those it suspected of immigration infractions to the CBSA.[36]

Through the data provided by participants in this study, places of employment and activities peripheral to employment emerge as sites of enforcement in which status provides a catalyst for the enactment of power in several ways. Direct enforcement and surveillance by immigration authorities at worksites is a straightforward example of the way in which status may interact with state authority to create situations of control and coercion. One step removed, status-based arrests created through the adoption of migration status as an aspect of transit fare infraction policy create an additional site of enforcement in a space of daily living often ancillary to work. In the workplace itself, even in the absence of a federal removal order or investigation, the possibility of losing status is invoked by employers to control the activities of employees and provide a strong disincentive to dissent or complaint in the workplace. While working life can potentially be subject to unfairness for any worker, in the case of workers with precarious migration status, these enforcement features in the workplace create categorical exclusion from particular spheres.

Sites of Enforcement in the Social State

Along with the workplace, areas such as health care, education, and income security also become visible as sites of enforcement. Within the social state, migration status is deployed in policies and practices to exclude precarious migrants, as described in detail in Chapter 4. The persistence and potency of this exclusion flows not from the mere exercise of bureaucratic discretion, but also from the coercive function of the potential for punitive measures on the basis of status, which, as with working life, provides a categorical disincentive to claim benefits and contributes to the maintenance of a subordinate membership group within Canadian society. When discretion is imbued with patterns of denial based on migration status, surveillance, or the perceived potential for punitive measures such as status removal, it creates both disciplining and self-disciplining features through which power disparity is maintained and reproduced in these sites to the disadvantage of precarious migrants as a class. Although they are legally distinct from the enforcement apparatus under federal immigration law, institutions within the social state also, therefore, emerge as sites of enforcement. When laws, policies, and practices deploy migration status as a determining factor in front-line decision making, migrants' interactions with the social state are never only about the benefit or service in question, but are enmeshed with deportability and illegality. As with working life, the construct of status is actively deployed by state actors with the actual capacity to enforce differential access and is internalized by migrants in terms of self-discipline that arises from a fear of losing status.

In terms of health care, both agency representatives and migrant participants reported that seeking medical assistance was associated with the fear of having irregular status discovered and of facing immigration enforcement, whether directly enacted or not. One agency worker related the following situation of a worker without status:

> There was a lady who worked in washing dishes. She fell on the kitchen floor and she spent one night before coming to the office with a broken, open wound. The bone had broken and got out of the skin. She was in pain and with a towel covering that, and the only thing I told her was, "Okay, we're going to the hospital." And she told me, "I have no papers. They are going to deport me" [...] And I took her to the hospital, and they treated her in the hospital. She spent quite a long time in the hospital, probably two or three weeks. After they left her to go home, immigration showed up and told her her status. She was more worried [about] the way she was going to pay the hospital than the deportation.

This example shows not only the initial reluctance of the migrant to obtain what was clearly essential emergency care because of fear of deportation, but also that the power of the hospital to collect on a debt seemed to persist even once the course of immigration enforcement was already decided. Another migrant participant mentioned health care as a site of enforcement in association with status distinction, explaining that, once you had a work permit, "any problem, you can go to the doctor, you're not like, 'Oh, they're going to catch me at the doctor.'" While none of the health authorities that I contacted disclosed specific policies of reporting to the Canada Border Services Agency, subsequent to the closure of the present study, the *Georgia Straight* reported that Fraser Health had made approximately five hundred calls to the CBSA in 2015 and that the majority were to confirm the migration status of patients for billing purposes. The same report noted that Vancouver Coastal Health updated its policies in 2015 to state that it will ask permission of patients before contacting the CBSA.[37]

Interactions with health services can lead to police involvement, although this is unusual. One agency described a situation wherein a migrant worker (with migration status, but not yet covered by provincial health care due to residency requirements) who was treated at a hospital was asked to pay $700 for lab work and a physician's time. The worker had not anticipated the cost, and, when he said that he didn't have the money, the administrative staff at the hospital called the police. Although the police did not detain the worker and took no further action, the hospital's readiness to ask for police assistance to settle a debt could have profound consequences for status and non-status temporary migrants. The message that hospital interactions may result in direct enforcement is confirmed by this example, and such incidents – however rare – are likely to further entrench the enforcement effect. This case shows the multiple levels of enforcement and exclusion that are at work: the migrant is excluded from state-funded medical care despite his legal status and economic participation, and the interaction arising from the demand for payment in conjunction with lack of status created a situation in which the police were involved, although the police would not under normal circumstances attend to enforce payment of a debt.[38]

Migrants, particularly those without any legal status, faced barriers to medical care because of lack of coverage, but also because of the fear of being discovered without status as a result of their trying to access the health care system. Some migrants specifically cited status as a reason for avoiding necessary medical care. One agency worker described having contact with a number of women who required prenatal medical care and medical care during childbirth, but who did not seek this care from doctors or hospitals due to fear associated with their immigration status. This invocation of authority creates a strong disincentive to obtain necessary medical care and contributes to the maintenance of a class of migrants whose labour is readily accepted, but for whom access to health care comes with undue risk. As such, health care is one point within the social state in which subordinate membership is enforced through specific policies and practices.

As in health care, public education is a site of both disciplining and self-disciplining functions related to precarious migration status. In Chapter 4, I described a situation in which the parents held work permits and were required by school administrators to report regularly to provide updates on migration status, though the child in question was a Canadian citizen. Furthermore, policy documents disclosed by the Vancouver School Board encouraged physical surveillance of children's homes to determine residency, which may be a proxy for status. Status may deter participation in education, even in the absence of direct exclusion on the part of the educational institution or school board: one family reported choosing not to enrol their child in school when they thought that it would not be possible because of their status. Yet, keeping children out of school could draw enforcement attention from neighbours: one agency reported cases where neighbours noticed migrant children not in school and contacted the Ministry of Child and Family Services, who then investigated the family. In other cases, children without status were enrolled in school for years, and were identified as non-status children only when health care needs arose. While education laws and policies have no direct or formally delegated authority over issues pertaining to migration status, they contribute as a site of enforcement: as with health care, both formal distinctions on the basis of status and migrants' unwillingness to participate in education due to fear of loss of status render an entire class of families subordinate in this aspect of social membership. As detailed in Chapter 4, this site of enforcement applies not only to precarious migrants, but also to their children, who may be Canadian citizens.

In terms of income security, migrants regularly reported that they would never apply for welfare because they knew they were ineligible. This understanding is consonant with provincial law, which categorically excludes those with less than permanent residence from obtaining welfare benefits. However, participants also avoided applying for Employment Insurance, even though, unlike welfare, many workers would have been eligible for it upon layoff. This response was consistent across the interviews. When I asked participants who had experienced non-voluntary work stoppage or layoff if they had applied for Employment Insurance, I found that none had applied for it. Many gave the reason that they were afraid that such an application would in some way affect their potential to obtain permanent resident status. Some precarious migrants may in fact be excluded from Employment Insurance on the basis of lack of "availability for work," but my research did not disclose any evidence that applying for Employment Insurance would result in immigration enforcement activity. For those who would be eligible for Employment Insurance but for their status (i.e., those working without authorization), courts and tribunals have, as discussed in Chapter 4, applied a liberal version of the doctrine of illegality in which the conduct of the migrant was a factor to be determined in considering eligibility. The bifold operation of migration status is evident in these sites as well: some precarious migrants are categorically excluded, or subject to virtue assessment before receipt of benefits. But even for those who would not be excluded, there was a very strong perception among migrants that requesting income assistance of any type would endanger their immigration status. Thus, these sites, too, contribute to the social and economic subordination of precarious migrants to positions in which their entitlement is contingent on good behaviour – and for some migrants, state recognition of "deservingness" – and the entitlement to benefits is entirely out of reach in the absence of permanent status. Through this exclusion, subordinate status is enforced.

6

Rights and Membership

TOWARD INCLUSION?

Migration status operates as an organizing social force in the lives of migrants. Through a spectrum of precarious migration status situations that involve various degrees of authorization, participants in this study described the destabilizing and marginalizing nature of status. As I have shown in the preceding chapters, while legal authorization of migration status is granted and enforced by federal state institutions, the experience of the lack of status or fear of its removal gains potency through exclusion of precarious migrants in multiple sites beyond the federal state. Within employment contexts, precarious migration status served to exacerbate the power differential between employer and employee and to reduce labour security and mobility. Study participants described shortfalls in basic employment rights, as well as physical and mental health concerns and the impact of their status situation on family relationships. Yet, as a group, precarious migrants are less likely to obtain remedies in such situations. Provincial laws governing standards and workplace safety do not exclude workers on the basis of migration status, but status nonetheless played a major role in determining access to the protection afforded by these laws. With regard to the social state, migration status was often integrated into the allocation of entitlements both explicitly and through institutional practices of exclusion, but migrant participants were also reluctant to claim benefits on the basis of their status for fear of being presumed undeserving of status regularization. Moreover, in determining allocation of benefits, formal decision making in judicial and quasi-judicial venues related to the social state often relied on concepts of deservingness concerning migrants' status situations.

In the spheres of working life and the social state, I have identified multiple sites in which the boundaries between precarious migrants and permanent residents/citizens are maintained through sites of enforcement beyond the federal immigration authority. This returns us to the main problematic underlying this work, namely, the tension between the presence of precarious migrants within the Canadian state and their concurrent subjection to categorical forms of exclusion on the basis of status. Liberal, egalitarian values provide a strong argument in support of formal membership allocation to precarious migrants, or at least equal inclusion in basic employment and safety standards and necessary social benefits.

As articulated by Linda Bosniak, the tension between egalitarianism and exclusion is easier for liberal states to navigate when closure is activated at the border of a state's territory, and equal rights are assumed to apply to all of those "inside."[1] But, in practice, territory and national community are not so neatly parallel; through both authorized and unauthorized channels, workers enter the national territory to live and work, often at the behest and to the benefit of both employers and the state. This enmeshment of territory and precarity represents a greater challenge to equality and raises fundamental questions: At what point should the federal determination of closure cease to affect those who are physically present within a society? At what point do such individuals become part of the "everyone"? At what point does their presence, work, or connection to Canada justify treatment on par with permanent residents and citizens?

For many scholars who have considered these questions, the answers hinge on the degree of connection and participation. Social connections, length of residence in Canada, and participation in paid and unpaid labour have all been suggested as the basis for assignment of membership on a moral basis, consistent with the principles of liberalism.[2] Another set of scholars answer these questions from a different angle. Rather than premising their work on the eventual goal of liberal egalitarianism, they explore the particular function of having separate classes of workers, and challenge the assumption of liberal values as guiding forces in the organization of capitalist states. Robin Cohen, for example, points out that capitalist economic systems consistently rely on a mix of free and unfree labour.[3] Precarious migrants may thus be treated as necessary on an economic basis, but framed as outsiders for the purposes of distribution of membership entitlements. This latter interpretation is consistent with the patterns observed in this study, in which migrant workers' labour was readily accepted, and migrants were theoretically included in workplace standards but explicitly excluded from social state entitlements.

I have argued that across working life and the social state are multiple sites in which boundaries are drawn around entitlements, creating a subordinate category of membership in Canada. Although legally governed by statutes and regulations that stand apart from the federal immigration regime and beyond federal jurisdiction, these data cast worksite and social state interactions not only as sites of exclusion, but as sites of enforcement which help to maintain social and economic stratification.[4] The way exclusion is carried out goes beyond simple denial at points of access, isolated from the context of migrants' lives. Rather, practices within the social state, including surveillance, mandatory reporting, and police involvement, often pivoting on migration status, function to enforce exclusion through both explicit denial and indirect exclusion. Furthermore, even in the absence of actual enforcement action, it is clear that such practices have a disciplining effect on migrants: the potential presence of any level of observation and control within the social state in conjunction with the potential to lose status or be deported also functions to entrench exclusion. The fact of enforceability is integral to the nature of law and its corollaries, whether direct or indirect:

> [T]here is no such thing as law that doesn't imply in itself, a priori, in the analytic structure of its concept, the possibility of being "enforced," applied by force. There are, to be sure, laws that are not enforced, but there is no law without enforceability, and no applicability or enforceability of the law without force, whether this force be direct or indirect, physical or symbolic, exterior or interior, brutal or subtly discursive and hermeneutic, coercive or regulative.[5]

While there is no singular state agency through which governance occurs, the sites described in the preceding chapters are unified through diverse laws, policies, and practices that all deploy the construct of migration status. In organizing all of these interactions under the rubric of enforcement, their function in reproducing exclusion inside Canada's physical territory against those who are already present within it becomes clear. This highlights the problematic of migrants' simultaneous presence in, and exclusion from, Canada, and invites examination of potential rights-based responses as well as of the basis on which membership within the Canadian state and society can be determined and contested.

Migration theorists and activists focus on the potential allocation of permanent membership status at the federal level through the provision of legal immigration status via amnesty and regularization programs, for example. Migrant participants in this study pointed to the capacity to obtain formal permanent residence as a major concern, and there is little doubt that obtaining such residence would be beneficial for the people who spoke with me, and others like them. With permanent residence would come a degree of security in which the threat of deportation would be greatly reduced, as would its corollaries of fear of reprisal from employers and access to the social state. Strong moral arguments can be made on the basis of liberal equality to include precarious migrants as full members of the state on the basis of their presence, family connections, work, and identification with communities within Canada. Arguments to exclude migrants mistakenly elide the question of border control with the question of migrant control, attempting to create analogies to the territorial border within Canada but without a territorial basis, which often result in the direct or indirect promotion of social and economic hierarchies. On the premise of equality arising from territorial presence, it is straightforward to argue that liberal values demand formal inclusion of those who are already present and have a connection to Canada. Within an ostensibly liberal state, the most potent way in which to claim permanent membership on an egalitarian basis is through human rights claims, which can be made in three primary types of jurisdictions: national, transnational, and subnational.

National Rights

The *Charter of Rights and Freedoms,* which forms part of Canada's Constitution, facilitates judicial review of legislative provisions on the basis of the rights it guarantees. Courts of competent jurisdiction are enabled by the *Charter* to provide such remedies as they find "appropriate and just in the circumstances."[6] Judicial remedies for *Charter* breaches include "striking down" offending provisions and "reading down" to modify the explicit content of a provision.[7] Provincial, territorial, and federal governments are subject to the provisions of the *Charter*. As such, it plays a unique and dynamic role in Canadian law, empowering the judiciary to refigure legislation on the basis of specific challenges. In terms of the equality provisions of section 15 of the *Charter*, such challenges often flow from situations of individuals or groups who wish to contest a distinction made in law. Section 15 jurisprudence addresses distinctions and exclusions pertaining to individuals on the basis of belonging to an identifiable group, precarious migrants or non-citizens may constitute a group for these purposes.

The Supreme Court of Canada has made it clear that "[t]he most fundamental principle of immigration law is that noncitizens do not have an unqualified right to enter or remain in Canada."[8] However, once they are in Canada, such individuals are subject to *Charter* protection, including section 15.[9] The Supreme Court of Canada has considered the claims of non-citizens under the *Charter*, but a majority of those cases dealt with situations of deportation or deprivation of status rather than access to state-based entitlements for non-citizens within Canada.[10] The most notable exception to this pattern is the *Andrews* case, which I consider in detail below.

Section 15 of the *Charter* provides the following guarantee:

(1) Every individual is equal before and under the law and has the right to the equal protection and equal benefit of the law without discrimination and, in particular, without discrimination based on race, national or ethnic origin, colour, religion, sex, age or mental or physical disability.

This section is most commonly used to challenge provisions in statutes and regulations on the basis of their discriminatory effect, but governmental policies can also be considered part of the law for the purposes of such challenges. Protection from discrimination is not limited to the grounds enumerated in this section: grounds determined to be "analogous" to those listed in Section 15(1) are also subject to protection. Identification of an enumerated or analogous ground as the basis for distinctions in treatment is a necessary component of a successful section 15 claim, but not all distinctions made on the basis of enumerated or analogous grounds will offend section 15. In determining whether a basis for distinction constitutes an analogous ground, courts consider whether the characteristic is immutable (sexual orientation is a common example), or constructively immutable (i.e., changeable only at unacceptable personal cost – religion is a common example) and also weigh the historical disadvantage faced by a group and its status as a "discrete and insular minority."[11] Analogous grounds identified thus far in *Charter* jurisprudence include sexual orientation, off-reserve Aboriginality, marital status, and non-citizenship.[12]

In *Andrews v The Law Society of British Columbia,* the Supreme Court of Canada considered the situation of a man of British nationality, a permanent resident of Canada who was precluded from applying for admission to the Bar of British Columbia on the basis that he was not a citizen. Andrews successfully challenged the regulation in question, and the Supreme Court found that citizenship constituted an analogous ground that could attract the protection of section 15. In its finding, the Court stated:

> Relative to citizens, non-citizens are a group lacking in political power and as such vulnerable to having their interests overlooked and their rights to equal concern and respect violated. They are among "those groups in society to whose needs and wishes elected officials have no apparent interest in attending".[13] Non-citizens, to take only the most obvious example, do not have the right to vote. Their vulnerability to becoming a disadvantaged group in our society is captured by John Stuart Mill's observation in Book III of Considerations on Representative Government that "in the absence of its natural defenders, the interests of the excluded is always in danger of being overlooked ..." I would conclude therefore that non-citizens fall into an analogous category to those specifically enumerated in section 15. I emphasize, moreover, that this is a determination which is not to be made only in the context of the law which is subject to challenge but rather in the context of the place of the group in the entire social, political and legal fabric of our society. While

legislatures must inevitably draw distinctions among the governed, such distinctions should not bring about or reinforce the disadvantage of certain groups and individuals by denying them the rights freely accorded to others.[14]

The migrants in this study constituted a specific subset of non-citizens: those whose migration status in Canada is less than permanent. The decision in *Andrews* referred to non-citizens generally as compared to citizens, and the applicant in that case was a permanent resident. Although the Supreme Court has not specifically considered "migration status" itself as a potential analogous ground, the Federal Court of Appeal did so in 2011, in an appeal of the Federal Court's decision in *Toussaint v The Attorney General of Canada*. In *Toussaint*, the Federal Court considered the situation of a woman who had entered Canada as a visitor from Grenada in 1999 and then stayed in Canada without regular immigration status for more than ten years. Toussaint worked for the first seven of those years, but in 2006, she became ill and was unable to work. She obtained sporadic free health care, but the Ontario health authority refused access to publicly funded health care on the basis of her lack of immigration status in Canada. She was billed for emergency medical services and subsequently was refused medical services and medication. In her request for medical services, Toussaint provided medical reports to indicate that the refusal and delay of treatment had had a deleterious effect on her health, and that she "would be at extremely high risk of suffering severe health consequences if she does not receive health care in a timely fashion."[15]

Toussaint attempted to regularize her status by applying for permanent and temporary residence in Canada in 2009 but could not afford the processing fees of $550 and $200, respectively. She requested a waiver of the processing fees for these applications, but her request was denied and thus neither application was ever considered. As her medical situation became more serious, she applied to Citizenship and Immigration Canada to be covered under the Interim Federal Health Plan (IFHP), was refused, and sought judicial review of that decision. She argued that her exclusion from the ambit of the IFHP violated sections 7 and 15 of the *Charter* as well as international law.

The basis for the IFHP at the time was Order in Council P.C. 157-11/848, which applied to "immigrants" as described therein. Toussaint argued that she was an "immigrant" within the meaning of that word under the *Immigration Act* in force at the time the Order in Council was drafted, namely, "a person who seeks admission to Canada for permanent residence." She argued that she fit within this definition as soon as she applied for permanent residence. The Federal Court noted that no application had actually been filed, as Citizenship and Immigration Canada had refused to process the application without the requisite fees.

Toussaint argued that section 15 of the *Charter* was infringed by her exclusion from the IFH program on the basis of disability and citizenship. The Court rejected this argument, stating:

> [T]he applicant was not excluded from IFHP coverage on the basis of her lack of Canadian citizenship. The applicant was excluded from coverage because of her illegal status in Canada. Only if "immigration status" is an analogous ground could the applicant's exclusion from IFHP coverage be said to violate section 15(1) of the *Charter*.
>
> The applicant did not argue that "immigration status" was such an analogous ground. It is not for the Court in *Charter* cases to construct arguments for the parties or advance them on their behalf. Given the applicant's failure to argue that "immigration status" was an analogous ground, the applicant's section 15(1) argument must fail.[16]

Although it identified the potential basis of the applicant's section 15 claim as "migration status," the Court did not assess the merits of an argument that migration status could constitute an analogous ground, because the applicant had not made this argument.

Toussaint appealed to the Federal Court of Appeal, which, in applying an equality analysis, relied heavily on the idea of individual choice. In its decision, the Court of Appeal returned to the concept of individual choice in its application of existing section 15 jurisprudence as a basis for rejecting the applicant's claim. At the outset of its section 15 analysis, the Court adopted the two-part iteration of the *Law* test that had recently been confirmed by the Supreme Court in *Kapp* and *Withler*, namely:

(1) whether the law creates a distinction that is based on an enumerated or analogous ground and
(2) whether the distinction creates a disadvantage by perpetuating prejudice or stereotyping.[17]

The Court of Appeal accepted the definition of discrimination in *Andrews*, which is quoted above, but found that, unlike citizenship status, migration status was not an analogous ground under section 15. The Court based its reasoning on several different aspects of equality jurisprudence, but, through each, it returned to the finding that Toussaint had wilfully maintained her status as an illegal resident of Canada.

Toussaint is introduced in the first paragraph of the Court of Appeal judgment as having "stayed in Canada, contrary to Canada's immigration laws." Three paragraphs later, the Court reminds us that she was "still in Canada contrary to Canada's immigration laws" at the time she tried to regularize her status by submitting both temporary and permanent residence applications.[18] After summarizing the trial court's decision, the Court of Appeal returns to the issue of Toussaint's lack of adherence to immigration laws:

> If the Federal Court accepted the appellant's request, the curiosity of some might be piqued: even though the appellant has disregarded Canada's immigration laws for the better part of a decade, she would be able to take one of Canada's immigration laws (the Order in Council), get a court to include her by extending the scope of that law, and then benefit from that extension while remaining in Canada contrary to Canada's immigration laws.[19]

In its reasoning on section 15, the Court of Appeal found that the Order in Council does not necessarily make a distinction on the basis of status, and that it is available to all persons "regardless of immigration status."[20] To support this reasoning, the Court noted that the applicant may have had access to the health program while she was a legal visitor in Canada. The Court did not explicitly mention "choice" here, but it is implied by the logic. The Court's finding on this point relies on the assumption that the range of possible legal statuses, which are not within one's control, are limited to authorized status and do not include situations where status is lacking. Moreover, there is no consideration of the domestic or global socio-economic context of temporary migration.

The Court of Appeal used a comparator group in explaining why migration status is not a basis for discrimination; in choosing a comparator group, however, the Court does not use "migrants with status" in comparison to "migrants without status." Instead, it refers to a group to which the Order in Council would not actually apply at all, namely Canadian citizens, noting that "[t]he Order in Council treats the appellant – a non-citizen who has remained in Canada contrary to Canadian immigration law – in the same way as all Canadian citizens, rich or poor, healthy or sick."[21]

The Court of Appeal went beyond the trial court's decision to specifically consider the issue of whether "immigration status" could be understood as an analogous ground. In this regard, the Court of Appeal stated:

> I do not accept that immigration status qualifies as an analogous ground under section 15 of the *Charter*, for many of the reasons set out in *Corbiere v. Canada (Minister of Indian and Northern Affairs)*, [1999] 2 S.C.R. 203 at paragraph 13, recently approved by the Supreme Court in *Withler* [...] Immigration status is not a "[characteristic] that we cannot change." It is not "immutable or changeable only at unacceptable cost to personal identity." Finally immigration status – in this case, presence in Canada illegally – is a characteristic that the government has a legitimate interest in expecting [the person] to change. Indeed, the government has a real, valid and justified interest in expecting those present in Canada to have a legal right to be in Canada. See also *Forrest v. Canada (A.G.)*, 2006 FCA 400 at paragraph 16; *Irshad (Litigation Guardian of) v. Ontario (Minister of Health)* (2001), 55 O.R. (3d) 43 (C.A.) at paragraphs 133–136.[22]

This reasoning draws on the Supreme Court of Canada's finding in *Corbiere* that a characteristic is more likely to be an analogous ground where it is a "characteristic that we cannot change, or that the government has no legitimate interest in changing." The purpose of the Court's reasoning in *Corbiere* was to make room for "constructively immutable" traits, like religion or, in the case of *Andrews*, citizenship. Such traits may have a significant impact on equal treatment but are not physically immutable in the sense of gender or race. In contrast with some Supreme Court rulings on analogous grounds – for example, in the case of social condition or poverty – the Court of Appeal makes no reference to social science or other supporting data to indicate whether "immigration status" is in fact a choice or whether it is associated with factors beyond the control of the individual within the socio-economic context. In *Toussaint*, there was evidence before the Court that Toussaint had attempted to regularize her status but was refused on the basis that she did not pay the fees. In other words, the Court did not consider the complex features of precarious status and its mediating function in the application of law and policy support. Such a consideration may well support the conclusion that status is associated with social disadvantages in ways that closely resemble other axes of discrimination.

Had the Court considered social science evidence, it may have had the opportunity to more fully evaluate the argument that the applicant did not choose her status. Perhaps more important, though, is the Court's use of the concept of individual choice in applying the reasoning in *Corbiere*. By immediately formulating immigration status as a matter of choice, the Court was able to move directly to the disjunctive second trait of analogous grounds: characteristics that the government has a legitimate interest in changing. This move allowed the Court to use the notion of individual choice to bring the government's prerogative in determining membership into the initial discrimination analysis. This is a powerful and disturbing use of the construction of choice, because it could be applied to any ground of distinction rooted in social, rather than physical, traits (e.g., sexuality, religion): as soon as something is categorized as having been "chosen," the government's prerogative is at the forefront of analysis. This approach has the potential not only to ignore the context in which ostensible "choices" are made, which is relevant to precisely those traits that are social rather than physical, but also to circumvent the purpose of the *Charter* in limiting government action where it infringes section 15 equality guarantees.

Having foregrounded the government prerogative in determining immigration status, the Court of Appeal proceeded to connect the potential to enforce membership boundaries with the provision or refusal of health care. The Court framed the relationship between immigration misconduct and health care as part of "our law," implying that refusal of medical care is an appropriate measure to discourage non-compliance with immigration laws:

> The appellant submits at paragraph 34 of her memorandum of fact and law that governments ought never to deny access to healthcare necessary to life as a means of discouraging unwanted or illegal activity, including to those who have entered or remained in a country without legal or documented status. The appellant submits that this principle is fundamental to judicial and legislative practice in Canada [...]
>
> At the root of the appellant's submission are assertions that the principles of fundamental justice under section 7 of the *Charter* require our governments to provide access to health care to everyone inside our borders, and that access cannot be denied, even to those defying our immigration laws, even if we wish to discourage defiance of our immigration laws. I reject these assertions. They are not part of our law or practice, and they never have been.[23]

The Court refers again to the relationship between compliance with immigration law and health care at the conclusion of its decision. Without referring to specific evidence, it reasons that, if an applicant such as Toussaint were successful in establishing the right to medical care "without complying with Canada's immigration laws," others might do the same, making Canada a "health care safe haven," undermining its immigration laws, and possibly causing the potential "others" to fall into the hands of smugglers, all of which might result in scrapping the IFH program entirely.

The Supreme Court of Canada's 1989 decision in *Andrews* was widely seen as a commitment to substantive equality. In the intervening time, jurisprudence considering substantive rights under section 15 of the *Charter* has taken a complicated path and has attracted considerable academic commentary on the potential of the Court's approaches to substantive equality.[24] While more decisions dealing with section 15 – notably the decisions in *Kapp*,[25] *Withler*,[26] and *Quebec v A*[27] – have proclaimed a continuing commitment to substantive equality in interpreting section 15, scholars have critiqued the Court both for its lack of clarity and consistency in the legal constructs with which it defines equality and for its failure to adequately capture the basis of substantive inequality in deciding claims under this section.[28] The Federal Court of Appeal's interpretation of section 15 in *Toussaint* not only echoes what Dauvergne has observed in the Supreme Court as a "failure of the *Charter* to deliver on its promise of human rights protections for non-citizens,"[29] but also provides a clear demonstration of the ways in which equality jurisprudence is impaired in its potential to address shortfalls in substantive equality for precarious migrants.

The Federal Court of Appeal has made it clear that immigration status cannot be treated as an analogous ground for the purposes of the anti-discrimination provisions of the *Charter,* nor can a non-status migrant rely on other provisions of the *Charter* to obtain necessary health care.[30] As understood in Canadian courts, migration status is a direct expression of the right of a state to exclude non-members as an aspect of sovereign control, and, if a person is already excluded from membership, his or her capacity to make national rights–based claims is limited.

International Rights

The present study supports the conclusion that those without full formal membership in the national state should be able, at least on an ethical basis, to make rights claims. Furthermore, the principles of universal human rights, and the identification of all individuals as rights bearing regardless of migration status, would certainly be consistent with the struggle for inclusion. Migrant workers are the subject of international rights, primarily in the context of the International Convention of the Protection of the Rights of All Migrant Workers and Members of Their Families (the Migrant Worker Convention).[31]

Canada has not ratified the Migrant Worker Convention, and it is among the majority of states that have not done so: the United Nations reports that 132 countries have not signed the convention, 18 have signed it, and 48 have ratified it. Of those who have ratified it, a vast majority are countries of the global South that are more likely to be the source country than the host country of migrant workers. The lack of ratification means that the Convention cannot be used directly for the assertion of rights in Canada; in fact, it has been mentioned briefly only three times in Canadian case law, and one of these was in the *Toussaint* case. Nonetheless, because it represents the structure of an international framework for the rights of precarious migrants such as those included in this study, the Convention is worth considering as a normative response to the issue.

The Convention enshrines basic political and civil rights, such as the right to life, to freedom from slavery, and to the freedom to leave a country, as well as freedom of thought and religion, liberty, and security of the person, as well as equality before the law in terms of criminal process. It also specifically allows for the removal of a residence permit on the basis of failing to fulfil an employment obligation where that contract is tied to the person's authorization to enter the state (such as in the case of closed work permits in the Canadian system). It also stipulates that the Convention does not affect the right of a state to establish criteria governing admission of migrant workers.[32]

In terms of the regulation of working life, the Convention provides for wage parity with citizens, as well as equality with respect to conditions of work, holidays, overtime, and so on, with the specific proviso that these standards apply even if the worker's status is irregular. The right to join and participate in trade unions is protected. With regard to the social state, the rights are more limited: while education for children is to be granted on par with citizens, equal treatment in the realm of social security is subject to fulfilling the host state's legislative requirements, and the right to medical treatment is limited to that which is urgently required for preservation of life or the avoidance of irreparable harm. All of these rights are applicable without regard to status, but the Convention also includes a number of rights specifically for workers whose status is "documented" or "in a regular situation." These include voting rights and access to vocational training, housing, and social and health services more generally (though, again, with the proviso that the state's requirements must be met).[33] As noted by Judy Fudge, certain categories of workers, such as seasonal workers, are excluded from particular provisions of the Convention, including those pertaining to labour mobility.[34]

Fudge also highlights the International Labour Organization's Multilateral Framework on Labour Migration, which sets out non-binding principles and guidelines. That Framework is, in some regards, an improvement over the Convention, particularly with regard to positive steps states should take in terms of protecting vulnerable groups and establishing enforcement mechanisms.[35] Fudge notes that neither the Convention nor the Framework prohibits restrictions on labour mobility for migrant workers (e.g., by the creation of work permits that are tied to a single employer), which serves to "reinforce the status of these workers as commodities."[36] Her conclusion that migrant workers are denied basic labour standards and rights despite their formal inclusion in the law is corroborated by the present study, as is her concern with the lack of labour mobility for migrant workers.

While international standards for migrant workers have not been subject to judicial interpretation in Canada, their limitations are similar to those of national rights. Like national rights claims under the *Charter*, the status of migrants as bearers of rights in international law is subject to admission and membership granted by a sovereign state. This contingency is due to the entrenchment of the absolute right of states to determine both admissions criteria and conditions thereupon. The rights that follow do not challenge this sovereign right, but rather are subordinate to it. The persistence and acceptance of temporary work programs in which overt contraventions of the international standards are tolerated is evidenced by the recognition of Canada's Seasonal Agricultural Worker Program as a positive example within global migration policy communities, despite Canada's failure to ratify the Convention or otherwise entrench its standards.[37] In international law, as in national law, the issue of membership remains embedded as a precursor to consideration of rights claims. Particularly in claims where social and economic entitlements are at stake, state institutions retain "very substantial latitude."[38] The potential for international law to respond directly to migrants' concerns is also limited by practical considerations: Canada, along with a vast majority of migrant-receiving nations, has not signed the main international convention aiming to protect the rights of migrant workers. Even if it had done so, the application of the Convention would, in the absence of explicit incorporation into domestic law, be limited to persuasive value in Canadian jurisprudence.

Subnational Rights

All Canadian provinces and territories have their own human rights codes, which apply more broadly than those enshrined in the *Charter*. While there are some regional variations, in general these statutes prohibit discrimination in services available to the public, employment, and housing. Discrimination is prohibited on the basis of such things as race, ethnic origin, gender, nationality, age, family status, and sexual orientation. In British Columbia, complaints under the provincial *Human Rights Code* are heard by a quasi-judicial tribunal that has the capacity to award damages for injury to dignity and for lost wages and out-of-pocket costs and can order the cessation of the conduct in question.

None of the provincial human rights codes include migration status as a protected ground, although it may overlap with race and nationality, and, in some cases, migrant workers have been able to base claims in provincial laws where there has been a clear distinction on the basis of nationality. Unlike the *Charter,* provincial human rights codes are applied for the most part by statutory tribunals and thus are not subject to judicial expansion through such concepts as "analogous grounds." Such protections thus tend to be restricted to the grounds of protection actually enumerated in the legislation. Provincial human rights legislation in all jurisdictions of Canada includes protection on the basis of grounds that may overlap with precarious migration status, including, in British Columbia's *Human Rights Code,* for example, race, colour, ancestry, and place of origin.[39] All Canadian jurisdictions contain similar grounds of protection, but none include protection on the basis of immigration status or non-permanent residence.

There are two main provisions in the BC *Human Rights Code* that could potentially address the barriers described by precarious migrants if "immigration status" were to be added to the list of protected grounds. Section 13 of the *Code* deals with employment. It prohibits the refusal to employ a person on the basis of protected grounds and also includes a general prohibition on discrimination in "employment or any term or condition of employment" unless such discrimination is demonstrably a "bona fide occupational requirement."[40] Workers regularly use this section to dispute differential pay and hours, biased hiring practices, and discriminatory comments. If precarious migrants as a group were subject to protection under the *Code,* many of the difficulties encountered in the sphere of work would likely fall within the ambit of this section. The types of problems they describe are well within the normal operation of the *Code* in terms of its scope, but, without the recognition of immigration status or non-permanent status as a protected ground, the *Code* is not available unless a potential claimant is able to make a case on one of the existing grounds of discrimination. It is impossible to determine whether precarious migrants have made claims under the *Code* on other grounds unless they are specifically identified as such in the text of the decision; however, it is possible to view those cases in which workers were specifically identified in terms of temporary migration status.

The rights of precarious migrants have been considered by the British Columbia Human Rights Tribunal in several cases. In *SELI*, the Tribunal considered a case in which an employer on a construction site provided differential wages and working conditions for two different groups of foreign workers, one of Eastern European origin and one of Latin American origin. In that case, the employer argued that differential wage policies constituted a "bona fide occupational requirement" because the wages offered had to be better than local wages in a particular country of origin, which, of course, varied on the basis of the economic position of the country in question. Thus, it argued, higher wages were required to recruit workers from European countries in which wages were higher than in Latin America. The Tribunal rejected this argument, finding as follows:

> In effect, the application of SELI's actual international compensation practices to the Latin Americans employed by them on the Canada Line project was to take advantage of the existing disadvantaged position of these workers, who are from poorer countries, and to perpetuate that disadvantage, and to do so while they were living and working within the province of British Columbia. As such, the application of those practices in British Columbia perpetuated, compounded and entrenched existing patterns of inequality.[41]

The Latin American workers in *SELI* were successful in their complaint and obtained a remedy from the Tribunal that included orders for the cessation of the employer's practices, back wages to compensate for the wage differential, and damages for injury to dignity.

In the current configuration of the *Code*, remedies were available to the workers in *SELI* only on the basis of their race and place of origin as compared to other workers. While the fact of temporary migrant status was implicitly considered in the Tribunal's analysis, the workers would not have been able to pursue their claim on this basis alone. If, for example, an employer's practice was to underpay all foreign workers regardless of race or place of origin, this practice would not likely fit within existing grounds of protection. Study participants recounted situations in which a workplace employed a mix of permanent residents, foreign workers, and non-status workers whose race, place of origin, and nationality were the same. In such a situation, if the non-status or temporary workers were treated differentially, they would currently have no recourse under the *Code*, despite the potential for exploitation similar to that described in *SELI*.

In 2014, a group of Mexican citizens employed by Tim Hortons restaurants filed a human rights complaint, alleging discrimination in conditions of employment and in housing (they allege they were forced to live in substandard housing under the control of the employer), and subjection to disparaging racist remarks based on race, colour, place of origin, and ancestry.[42] At the time of writing, this case had not yet gone to hearing.

The Ontario Human Rights Tribunal has recently made a large award to two female foreign workers on the basis of sexual harassment, sexual assault, and discrimination in the workplace – the amount of the award is unprecedented for that Tribunal. Although the claim in *O.P.T. v Presteve Foods Ltd.* was not alleged or heard on the basis of migration status specifically (this is not possible under the relevant legislation), the Tribunal considered expert evidence with regard to the impact of precarious status and lack of labour mobility in rendering its award:

> A very significant award of compensation for injury to dignity, feelings and self-respect [...] is justified, in my view, on the basis of O.P.T.'s particular vulnerability as a migrant worker, as part of the analysis of the impact of the respondents' conduct on the applicant referenced in *Arunachalam v. Best Buy Canada*, 2010 HTRO 1880 (CanLII) [...] O.P.T. was 30 years old when she came to Canada. Her husband had been tragically killed, and she was left to support her two children. As a temporary foreign worker in Canada, O.P.T. was put in the position of being totally reliant upon her employer. As Dr. Preibisch testified, temporary

foreign worker programs in Canada operate on the basis of closed work permits, which only entitle a migrant worker to employment with one designated employer. While theoretically possible to transfer employment to another employer while in Canada, there are significant barriers that make this practically impossible or at least very difficult. As a result, a migrant worker like O.P.T. tends to be reliant upon the employment relationship with the designated employer to a degree that is not experienced by Canadian workers. Migrant workers like O.P.T. live under the ever-present threat of having their designated employer decide to end the employment relationship, for which they require no reason and for which there is no appeal or review, and being "repatriated" to their home country and thereby losing the significant economic and financial advantages of their Canadian employment upon which they and their families depend. In O.P.T.'s case, the personal respondent was repeatedly explicit about this threat to send her back to Mexico if she did not comply with his demands and had demonstrated that he was capable of doing so by repatriating other Mexican women.[43]

Based on the information compiled in this study and similar work documenting the impact of non-permanent or precarious status, there is a strong argument to be made that immigration status on its own functions in a manner similar to race, gender, and other protected grounds. The evidence would support the inclusion of immigration status as a protected ground under both constitutional and statutory rights structures. This would resolve the problem that, while it is sometimes associated with place of origin or racialization, status does not always overlap with these grounds. Furthermore, it would address the fact that, in this study, individuals who were from various places of origin and who would be racialized differentially experienced similar impacts. If a measure does not distinguish on the basis of race or origin per se, because it is equally detrimental to Chinese and Mexican workers, for example, it would be difficult to challenge on the basis of race or place of origin. Because it is politically unlikely that immigration status will be enshrined as a protected ground in Canada, an alternative would be developing advocacy to continue to promote analysis similar to that used by the Tribunal in the *O.P.T.* case, in which immigration status is considered as part of the remedial stage of a complaint.

In terms of section 15 of the *Charter*, using non-permanent migration status as a potential analogous ground allows an analysis in which the relevant comparator group is people with permanent residence, or citizens of Canada, rather than other groups affected by a particular legal provision or policy. However, through examination of the decision in *Toussaint*, it is clear that distinctions between non-permanent and permanent residents are not judicially constructed in the same manner as the distinction between permanent residents and citizens in *Andrews*. In *Toussaint*, membership considerations and moral sanction of the applicant's very presence in Canada as "illegal" precluded any serious consideration of immigration status as an analogous ground. Furthermore, as this possible ground was proactively addressed by the Court of Appeal, rather than argued by the applicant herself, it is unlikely that either level of court had access to social science or other data in support of the contention that the impact of status should be understood similarly to that of other enumerated and analogous grounds. It is unclear whether there will be an opportunity to have such information judicially considered in support of this argument in the future. For such an argument to be viable, however, it would require more than data establishing the impact of status and its constructive immutability. It would also require a shift in the construction of membership.

Based on the logic in *Toussaint* as well as previous jurisprudence, membership distinctions are framed as an *a priori* aspect of sovereign discretion – anything that is contingent on a membership decision, even as applied to those already within Canada, can thus be shielded from human rights scrutiny. Asking a court to decide that the very distinction on which people are excluded from the "everyone" is itself subject to analysis with respect to discrimination is effectively asking it to reframe the basis of membership in terms of factors such as presence, identity, and belonging through social and economic participation. Protection on the basis of status challenges the basic closure assumed by the liberal state, and the subordination of non-permanent members within the labour force, by framing the question of exclusion as a potential source of discrimination rather than as simply an expression of sovereign discretion. Such a conceptual shift seems unlikely on the basis of current jurisprudence. *Charter* litigation to this end is worth pursuing and is well supported in some ways by data such as those presented in this study, but is unlikely to provide a practical remedy to the marginalizing features of status documented here.

The legal role of provincial human rights regimes is distinct from that of the *Charter;* while human rights codes often contain clauses by which other provincial laws need to be interpreted consistently, they do not have the power associated with constitutional status. Furthermore, they are applied for the most part by tribunals, whose role is much more constrained than that of courts, as they are limited to the considerations and remedies listed in the enabling statute. There is no legal equivalent to an argument on "analogous grounds" within provincial human rights regimes – if a basis for discrimination is not listed in the enabling statute, a tribunal cannot consider it. Thus, the addition of immigration status as a specific protected ground would require legislative change. While such a change could be justified on the basis of data documenting the situation of precarious migrants, it would also likely require a conceptual shift on the part of lawmakers similar to that described above with regard to *Charter* jurisprudence. Even short of such a change, however, provincial human rights regimes hold potential for the amelioration of some of the problems associated with precarious migration status. Human rights tribunals may be willing to consider the inequality faced by foreign workers. While in the *SELI* decision, the decision was based on place of origin and not status, the analysis specifically considered the lack of status and mobility of workers in a way that *Charter* jurisprudence has not. This type of reasoning employed in *SELI* would not provide a remedy for all precarious migrants, but it does show promise as an avenue through which the impact of status may be considered as an aspect of "place of origin," "nationality," or "race." The *O.P.T.* case represents a significant advance, both in terms of remedy and in terms of analysis and active engagement with evidence concerning the particular vulnerabilities of precarious migrants; although it has no binding effects on other tribunals or courts, it may influence the consideration of similar claims by other human rights tribunals.

While it is the domestic state with which migrants interact and which still serves as the primary arbiter of membership and entitlements, the context in which migration occurs is inevitably also subject to transnational realities. The fact that the impact of foreign economic conditions as a precursor to inequality was considered in a provincial rights determination shows promise in terms of the essential work of contextualizing local rights struggles within globalizing conditions, as does the consideration of the lack of labour mobility and categorically greater vulnerability in the *O.P.T.* case. In deciding these cases, provincial human rights tribunals did not seem to be impeded by membership and sovereignty considerations in the same manner as the Court of Appeal in *Toussaint*, but the facts were also quite different: the workers in the tribunal cases had status and were demanding parity in working conditions, rather than access to the social state. Whether membership constructs, like those employed in *Toussaint*, would eventually impair the potential of human rights claims like those in *SELI* and *O.P.T.* is impossible to determine, but the use of human rights legislation in this manner is certainly worth exploring. Furthermore, human rights tribunals have a broad scope of application, as seen through the example of the British Columbia Human Rights Tribunal, which already functions as a venue for challenging decisions in all of the local sites which this study has identified. The remedies are concrete, and while they may be limited by statute rather than the judicial imagination, insofar as they include such possibilities as wage compensation, cessations orders, and compensation for injury to dignity, they have the potential to be meaningful in the lives of individuals in concrete ways. Finally, provincial human rights regimes are much more accessible to individuals, both practically and legally. Unlike *Charter* litigation, applicants can make claims without legal counsel or the need to meet legal tests for "standing," and they can expect decisions within a reasonable period of time.

There is some potential for precarious migrants to find meaningful remedy in formal human rights structures at multiple levels. In the case of international rights, there is a normative function that may be persuasive to courts, or at least can serve for a venue for the articulation of rights principles that may be deployed in more local forms of advocacy, even in the absence of ratification of the Migrant Workers' Convention by migrant-receiving states. In the case of *Charter* arguments, current jurisprudence has rejected immigration status as a ground on which individuals can be protected from discrimination, yet further advocacy may result in the ability to put forth status as a ground for consideration, using the increasing body of social science evidence detailing the genesis, nature, and long-standing effects of precarious status. Such evidence has now been considered by provincial human rights tribunals, which also do not recognize immigration status as a potential basis for discriminatory action but which have showed some promise in being able to integrate the context of precarious migration into decision making on existing protected grounds such as race, national origin, and sex.

A limitation common to all three levels of human rights protections is the prevalence of membership over rights – in all of them, there is no dispute that the state's determination of admission to permanent membership is not the type of decision that can be challenged using human rights–based arguments. This is expressed overtly in the UN Convention as well as in *Charter* jurisprudence. And, while it is not explicitly stated in the provincial human rights decisions, provincial tribunals have no jurisdiction to consider immigration status without a legislative change, which would undoubtedly falter on the basis of the federal expression of membership sovereignty, even if the political will to make such a change were present at the provincial level. While a human rights analysis may provide one way in which to measure the detrimental impact of non-permanent migration status, and to frame the obligations of the state, the options in terms of enforceable rights are limited to those that do not pose a challenge to the nature and expression of sovereign power over membership determination. Thus, addressing the issue of membership directly is a necessary component of any strategy aimed at the full inclusion of precarious migrants.

Membership: National, Transnational, Local

The issue of membership arises as a necessary precursor in the analytical framing of rights, and in the lived realities of migrants. While expanding rights for migrants is certainly a desirable aim, it is incomplete without considering the question of membership because, in the context of sovereign states, memberships determine who bears rights. Thus, the question of membership, rather than rights, is the necessary starting point to address the marginalization faced by precarious migrants. It is "outsider status," rather than any particular race, religion, or culture, that tends to result in marginalization,[44] although "outsider status" is often assigned on the basis of particular social and political contexts.

In order to formulate membership in a way that is meaningful to precarious migrants such as those who participated in this study, it is necessary not only to consider the basis on which membership should be allotted, but also the ways in which it can be effectively pursued in such a way as to challenge underlying divisions and barriers. Enforcement occurs directly through federal immigration authorities, empowered by federal immigration legislation, but, as earlier chapters have demonstrated, much of the power of status is in the way it colours everyday life for precarious migrants. The effect of status pervades people's lives through surveillance and control on the part of state and non-state entities through law, policy, and practice, generating interactions that serve to discipline migrants. Thus, while migrants identify their own belonging and connection to Canada, the risk of having their status reported or otherwise attracting negative state attention is sufficient to discourage participation in many aspects of life, including those entitlements to which they have formal access.

The data in this study establish a clear line between permanent membership and the less complete, less inclusive forms of membership associated with precarious migration status. From an analysis of both interview responses and legislative texts and policies, it is beyond question that regularization by way of granting permanent residence would work to reverse the subordination of precarious migrants. Moreover, while both transnational and local membership are considered below, the national level is determinative in terms of the allocation of formal membership in the Canadian state; and it is this formal membership, or migration status, which is so deeply influential on the policies and practices in which subordinate membership is enforced.

Membership claims are often justified on the basis of presence with the territory of a state, but they must also account for the role of migration in capitalism. Territorial logic is only one force operating within migration policy. Moreover, the liberal paradigm does not provide a complete and accurate depiction of the Canadian state. While a gesture toward liberal egalitarianism has been present, at least on the surface, in immigration law for decades, the operation of the logic of capital as a strong force in migration policy must also be considered.[45] Understanding the logic of capital as a separate, non-derivative force helps to explain the difficulty in obtaining material equality for those categorized as migrant "others," as well as the persistence of barriers where formal equality is present in law but is substantively ineffective, as is the case with employment standards. Temporary residence through labour migration – whether through legal channels or otherwise – becomes an integral part of the national economic system as a result of the demand for cheap, flexible labour. In the case of temporary work permits, federal law often mandates a closed work permit, with the concomitant loss of labour mobility and bargaining power on the part of workers. Under conditions of globalization, this governance of migrant workers also plays a part in maintaining the global economic order, which relies on the exploitation of migrant labour.[46]

The production and maintenance of precarious status helps maintain a supply of workers who are available on request for low pay, or even no pay, in dangerous or deleterious conditions, and who face barriers to both employment protection and in meeting basic needs through interactions with the state in areas such as education, health care, and income security. The double bind faced by workers in which they struggle to increase their "civic capital" through functioning as good workers while simultaneously increasing their risk of illegality (by working without authorization) gives rise to a structure of "contradictory symbolic framings,"[47] which functions to serve the interests of capital and diminish those of workers. Thus, while liberal theory provides a strong argument to justify the formal inclusion of precarious migrants, it is limited in terms of its capacity to actually unsettle the socio-economic structures of which precarious migration status is an integral part. Furthermore, while both desirable and justified from an equality-based perspective, allotment of permanent resident status through federal structures is unlikely: the maintenance of a population of non-permanent residents serves both political and economic ends in Canada. The multi-sited enforcement regime described in the chapters above supports this national system insofar as it underscores the limits of membership for precarious migrants through the proliferation of migration status as a determinative factor in access even to those benefits that are not administered directly by the national state.

Furthermore, even if national membership became more feasible for precarious migrants, it is worth noting that permanent residence and citizenship themselves are also subject to erosion and degrees of non-permanence. In the Canadian immigration regime, permanent residents have the right to enter and remain in Canada, but they can lose their permanent residence rights on the basis of, for example, serious criminality. Citizenship does not guarantee full access to services, such as in the case of children who are Canadian citizens but who may be refused eligibility to enrol in school based on their parents' lack of status. There are also, increasingly, differential rights for certain categories of citizenship in Canada, particularly for those with relatives born abroad, which are effected through the "variable extension of rights, processes of securitization, and the suppression of democratic dissent."[48]

Alternatives to National Membership

One alternative to national membership is the idea of "local" or "subnational" membership. A common example is the idea of "urban citizenship" and the concomitant organization of municipal authority to provide services, recognition, non-enforcement, advocacy, or attempted shelter from other forms of government, such as federal immigration enforcement. As noted by Chauvin, "urban citizenship seems more easily tied to the mere fact of being here than other scales of potential political members," and municipalities in some jurisdictions will actively "sabotage" national membership policies, through regional sponsorship, for example.[49] While in some jurisdictions, notably the United States, there is empirical work documenting the integration of undocumented migrants into the local institutions of their communities,[50] this was not the case for the individuals I spoke to nor was it evident in the laws and policies I examined.

This study has shown that status is much more than the formal labelling undertaken by the federal state and that marginalization is maintained through a multiplicity of sites, most of which are unrelated to the federal immigration authorities on paper, yet are tied to its structure through the application of status distinctions using their own adoption of the federal taxonomy of status. The urban citizenship approach is appealing in its ability to address those sites in which status is relevant in everyday lives, rather than the federal structure itself, as venues for the contestation of membership.

This study supports the view that municipal action and other localized policy changes could be used to strengthen entitlements and decrease barriers, contributing to forms of belonging. However, because they would never displace the role of the federal state in generating status distinctions, they are somewhat limited in their application. In this study, there was evidence of some tolerance as well as formal equality for precarious migrants, but there were also policies of active exclusion, surveillance, and control, often in localized interpretations of the statute. Localized action means that multiple sites are available in which to contest exclusive policies and practices. For example, school boards could be asked to consider completely removing immigration status from their consideration of residence, while hospitals could be requested to confirm in writing that they will not provide information to the immigration authorities or use police to enforce medical debts. The response to exclusion could thus be multifaceted, building belonging in a variety of different sites rather than relying on a decision from a centralized federal authority. Connecting multiple sites under the rubric of "access without fear" would also serve to resist the compartmentalization of migrants' lives in a disjunctive fashion in which they are accepted as labour but rejected as members. Furthermore, organizing on the basis of access provides a common venue for solidarity between groups with different status situations and cultural backgrounds, as well as solidarity with non-profit organizations, researchers, activists, and potentially members of the particular institutions subject to action, as is the case in Toronto. As these movements are new, it remains to be seen whether they hold potential for political momentum toward change at the federal level on the issue of membership determination in Canada.

Local or urban citizenship holds out the potential of establishing membership through contestations at the local level, and grounding alternative forms of status in the reality of residence and presence in a place, rather than bounded by the federal government's consent to enter and remain in a territory on the basis of an assumed political community.[51] Through this study, it is clear that, while the construct of status may originate in distinctions produced in federal legislation, it takes on multiple meanings and functions at local levels through specific practices and relationships, many of which could be contested without the necessity of satisfying federal immigration law requirements. While it is true that the force of law is invoked through local practices, and that status and enforcement are already constituted through various interactions with local institutions, local contestations of membership are more appropriate as a necessary counterpart to, and not a replacement for, the struggle for permanent regularization. This idea concurs with the comments of Monica Varsanyi that the idea of urban or local citizenship may contribute to alternate formulations of belonging but should not be taken as a solution to the exclusions of the nation-state, which is "still the hegemonic container of the citizenry"; rather, it forms part of the foundation for a critique of nation-state-based citizenship.[52] In other words, membership at the local level, while it could certainly improve conditions for precarious migrants, will inevitably be limited by its incapacity to challenge federal status determinations. Alongside disputing status within the structure of federal law, membership strategies should seek to contest and establish status throughout the diverse local sites in which it is enacted. This can involve a critical assessment of the content of citizenship and an examination of "a variety of different social practices and experiences, and then asking whether the practices and experiences named by citizenship are, in fact, confined to the national sphere."[53]

Transnational membership is another proposed alternative to national state membership. Drawing on cosmopolitan values and international human rights and labour norms, transnational formulations of membership suggest relying on a non-state entity, such as, for example, an international trade union, for membership determination.[54] The potential for migrants to maintain portable membership on the basis of labour skills is appealing and provides direct recognition of their economic contribution. Other conceptions of post-national citizenship draw on transferable social and political capital within groups present across national boundaries.[55] While there are undoubtedly benefits to transnational organizing under conditions of globalization, particularly in the labour context, this modality will also need to contend with the national state, at least in the Canadian context. As with local membership, transnational formulations of citizenship are potent in terms of their capacity to enlarge conceptions of membership and potentially to empower negotiations with national authority, but they do not replace it.

Conclusion and Recommendations

Membership alternatives are most likely to be effectively formulated if they address the complex of authority organized by status. While there are significant barriers to full inclusion of precarious migrants, particularly given the role of labour migration in globalized capitalism, it is worth examining recent urban initiatives and formulating specific recommendations on the basis of the present research.

Since the completion of this study, the City of Vancouver has taken note of the issues facing precarious migrants. The city has published a policy document entitled *Access to City Services without Fear for Residents with Uncertain or No Immigration Status*.[56] The city recognizes several key features of precarious status that are corroborated in the present study – namely, that immigration status is a social determinant of health, and that fear of harm, deportation, and detention prevents people from seeking help. The policy confirms that access to city services should not involve being asking for immigration status information (although the report notes that city services at present do not require status), and that the city should not share status information without an individual's explicit consent. In its detailed report, the city recognizes the multiple ways in which status irregularity can arise, as well as particularly vulnerable individuals such as women fleeing abuse and workers in exploitative working situations.[57] In addition to this municipal initiative, regional health authorities in Greater Vancouver have moved toward policies of non-disclosure and non-reporting of status to immigration authorities without the consent of the individuals concerned.

The City of Vancouver has specifically avoided the use of the term "Sanctuary City," in deference to national jurisdiction over status, noting that "it is not within municipal governments' jurisdictional authority to offer 'sanctuary' to people without status, or for municipal government to grant permanent status to individuals."[58] The policy is significantly milder than its counterpart in Toronto, which, in addition to recognizing the negative impacts of precarious status and amending its own policies, committed to:

- advocating with the federal government to establish a regularization program for undocumented residents
- advocating with the federal government to increase provincial nomination program levels with priority processing for undocumented workers with children
- requesting the provincial government to review health care, emergency services, and housing policies within a social determinants of health framework.[59]

The Toronto District School Board already has in place a "Don't Ask, Don't Tell" policy in order to facilitate access to education for children with precarious status. It remains to be seen whether the city's police force will implement a similar policy, which sociologist David Moffette argues will reduce the potential for racial profiling in policing.[60]

Based on the data collected in this study and the conclusions that arise from it, it is clear that there is no simple response sufficient to ameliorate the conditions of precarious migrants or their systemic subordination through the multiple sites of enforcement they are likely to encounter. While no single answer is likely to be complete, various initiatives have the potential to contribute, if not to the reformulation of the role of sovereign determination of membership, at least to the improvement of conditions for migrants, which may aim for "liberation from the blackmail of permanence."[61] Importantly, because of the multi-sited nature of the boundaries precarious migrants face, advocates should aim for a coordination of efforts in multiple sites. Rather than suggesting detailed policy plans, the present research serves to provide an initial set of considerations by which to measure policy proposals both within and beyond government. Specifically, legal and policy alternatives are more likely to be ameliorative if they:

- actively canvass the needs of precarious migrants directly prior to implementing policies
- examine not only relevant legislation, but all regulations, policies, and practices associated with that legislation to determine the effective function of the law
- for policies and laws that do expressly exclude migrants on the basis of status, use political, academic, and activist approaches to advocate for inclusion
- for policies and laws which do not exclude migrants, advocate for amendments that require active protection of the particular vulnerabilities of precarious status migrants
- create strong and direct disincentives for employers for the mistreatment of precarious migrants, including effective monitoring, accessible reporting, and meaningful enforcement

- create clear, research-based guidelines for equitable treatment of precarious status migrants within social state institutions, including enforceable guarantees of information privacy
- create regular reporting requirements for all levels of government on issues relevant to precarious migrants, including direct enforcement
- revoke policies that promote or require sharing of information with immigration enforcement authorities and replace them with ones that do not provide for the sharing of information without consent
- promote regularization of precarious status migrants at the federal level by granting permanent residence
- promote faster family reunification
- entrench international human rights standards applicable to precarious migrants
- recognize precarious migration status as a protected ground in anti-discrimination law.

Federal, international, and local institutions can be understood as sites of transformation in terms of the potential to generate a culture of inclusion: once an institution is willing to modify policies, it becomes easier for others to do the same. Working toward access in multiple sites involves a critique of the membership prerogative of the federal state; in this way, articulations of membership by precarious migrants go beyond the moral argument, becoming "generative of a political subjectivity" through the declaration of non-citizen membership.[62] By providing access to the social state and reducing barriers to parity in employment even in the absence of federal recognition of individuals with precarious status, the potency of federal status is potentially decreased, even if not displaced. Redefining membership on the basis of de facto connection allows us to put migration policy questions in a broader social context to include the reproduction of power relations and enduring inequalities, rather than simply applying a strict legal definition as a test for membership.[63] Through multiple venues, advocates can use an understanding of conditional and precarious status to

> strengthen arguments in favour of expanding the bases of rights and reducing insecurity which can be consistent with the call to liberate

temporariness. These alternatives may include strategies to link rights and membership more equitably to other bases – whether through the language and instruments of human rights, claiming equal rights and membership regardless of legal status, or focusing on employment rights regardless of legal status, for rights based on residence, rights to the city, and so forth.[64]

Finally, if localized enforcement can be unsettled though policies of active acceptance, the ability to mobilize is also strengthened. These "democratic iterations"[65] may have the potential to strengthen the role of migrants' voices in federal immigration policy, rendering membership dialogues between local policy, public discourse, and legislation more meaningful in the struggle toward inclusion.

Postscript

This study took place during a time in which Stephen Harper's Conservative government held power federally in Canada, and the rhetoric and policy of that government certainly contributed to the commodification of labour, the criminalization of migration, and the absence of meaningful remedies for migrant workers. A Liberal government was elected in 2015. That same year, it introduced regulatory changes establishing a detailed employer-compliance regime for those who employ migrant workers in Canada. The changes include the requirement for employers to abide by provincial employment standards, to uphold the terms of their contracts with migrant workers, and to take steps to ensure a workplace free of abuse. While investigations under these regulations number in the thousands annually, to this point few have resulted in penalties or suspensions of employers from hiring migrant workers.[1] The federal government publicizes the names of all employers who have faced any kind of penalty; from the introduction of this regime in 2015 to May 2018, sixty-two employers have faced penalties. Of these, twenty-six had monetary penalties under $2,000, two had penalties between $2,000 and $7,000, and one was issued a $54,000 penalty plus a one-year ban on hiring migrant workers. Thirty-three employers were issued a two-year ban on hiring migrant workers.[2] The regulatory changes offer nothing to workers whose status is negatively affected by an employer's penalty, which is very likely to deter reporting by workers. Given the low number of penalties issued relative to the widespread documentation of deleterious working conditions for migrant workers, it remains to be seen whether this change, or associated policy changes, will have a meaningful impact on working conditions or the inclusion of migrant workers in the protections generally associated with full membership in Canadian society. Any federal legislative change short of granting permanent residence is unlikely to fully address the problems of partial, subordinate membership.

May 2018

Appendix A

MIGRANT PARTICIPANT PROFILES

Nationality	Sex	Family status	Migration status (including past)	Type of work
Mexican	M	Married with children, family in Mexico	Work permit	Agricultural
Mexican	M	Common law, spouse in Canada	Visitor visa, undocumented	Construction
Mexican	M	Married with children, family in Canada	Visitor visa, refugee claimant	Painting
Colombian	M	Divorced with children, family in United States	Undocumented, refugee claimant, permanent resident	Warehouse
Chinese	F	Children in China	Work permit, but unauthorized employer	Domestic
Chinese	F	Single	Work permit, but unauthorized employer	Domestic
Chinese	F	Divorced with children in China	Work permit, but unauthorized employer	Domestic
Chinese	F	Single	Work permit	Domestic
Chinese	F	Single	Work permit, but unauthorized employer	Domestic
Chinese	F	Children in China	Work permit	Domestic
Chinese	F	Married with children, family in China	Work permit, but unauthorized employer	Domestic
Mexican	F	Married with children, family in Canada	Visitor visa, refugee claimant, undocumented	Painting
Chinese	F	Married with children, family in China	Work permit, but unauthorized employer	Domestic
Mexican	F	Single	Visitor visa, undocumented	Food service

Nationality	Sex	Family status	Migration status (including past)	Type of work
Mexican	F	Single	Visitor visa, undocumented, work permit	Food service, live-out domestic
Chinese	F	Married with children, family in Canada	Work permit	Domestic
Mexican	F	Married, spouse in Canada	Work permit, refugee claimant	Administrative
Colombian	F	Married with children, family in Canada	Undocumented, refugee claimant, post-claim overstay	Sales
Guatemalan	M	Children in Mexico	Undocumented	Construction
Mexican	M	Married with children, family in Mexico	Work permit, but unauthorized employer	Construction
Chinese	F	Married with children, family in China	Work permit	Construction, massage therapy
Chinese	M	Married with children, family in Canada	Work permit	Management
Filipina	F	Unknown/not identified	Work permit, permanent resident	Administrative
Filipina	F	Single	Work permit, unauthorized employment, permanent resident	Domestic
Bolivian	F	Single	Work permit, study permit	Research, academic
Korean	F	Single	Work permit, study permit, unauthorized employment	Food preparation
Mexican	F	Married with children, family in Canada	Undocumented, permanent resident	Construction
Filipina	F	Unknown/not identified	Work permit, unauthorized employment	Domestic

Appendix B

SAMPLE INTERVIEW SCRIPT

1. Have you/your clients experienced times where you/they had uncertain status or lack of status?
2. What were the factors that contributed to the uncertain status or lack of status?
3. Do you/your clients have family members in Canada, and if so, was their status uncertain or lacking as well?
4. What were the impacts of uncertain status or lack of status?
5. Did you/your client change anything in your/their life because of uncertain status or lack of status?
6. Did you/your client have any interactions with the law when you/they had uncertain status or lack of status?
7. Did you/your client have any health care needs when you/they had uncertain status or lack of status? If so, did you/they seek treatment, and was this affected by lack of status/uncertain status?
8. Did you/your client have any interaction with the education system when you/they had uncertain status or lack of status? If so, how was this affected by lack of status/uncertain status?
9. Did you/your client have any need of welfare or other social benefits when you/they had uncertain status or lack of status? If so, was this affected by lack of status/uncertain status?
10. Did you/your client seek employment or work while you/they had uncertain status or lack of status? If so, was your/their working life affected by lack of status/uncertain status?
11. Did you/your client have interactions with immigration authorities while you/they had uncertain or lack of status?

12. Did you/your client have interactions with other authorities while you/they had uncertain or lack of status?
13. Did you/your client attempt to regularize status? If so, what were the factors that affected this decision and the process of trying to obtain status?
14. Are there any other ways you/your client and your/their family have been affected by uncertain status or lack of status?

April 2011

Notes

Introduction

1. See e.g. Luin Goldring & Patricia Landolt, *Producing and Negotiating Non-citizenship: Precarious Legal Status in Canada* (Toronto: University of Toronto Press, 2013); Patti Lenard & Christine Straehle, *Legislated Inequality: Temporary Labour Migration in Canada* (Montreal & Kingston: McGill-Queen's University Press, 2012); IU Syed, "Labor Exploitation and Health Inequities among Market Migrants: A Political Economy Perspective" (2016) 17:2 J Intl Migration & Integration 449.
2. See e.g. Malcolm Sargeant & Eric Tucker, "Layers of Vulnerability in Occupational Safety and Health for Migrant Workers: Case Studies from Canada and the UK" (2009) 2 Policy & Practice in Health and Safety 51; Kerry Preibisch, "Pick-Your-Own-Labor: Migrant Workers and Flexibility in Canadian Agriculture" (2010) 44:2 Intl Migration Rev 404; Leigh Binford, "From Fields of Power to Fields of Sweat: The Dual Process of Constructing Temporary Migrant Labour in Mexico and Canada" (2009) 30:3 Third World Q 503; Ping-Chun Hsiung & Katherine Nichol, "Policies on and Experiences of Foreign Domestic Workers in Canada" (2010) 4:9 Sociology Compass 766; Amy Cohen, "'Slavery Hasn't Ended, It Has Just Become Modernized': Border Imperialism and the Lived Experiences of Migrant Farmworkers in British Columbia, Canada" (2017) ACME: An International Journal for Critical Geographies, online: <https://www.acme-journal.org/index.php/acme/article/view/1430/1308>; Kendra Strauss & Siobhán McGrath, "Temporary Migration, Precarious Employment and Unfree Labour Relations: Exploring the 'Continuum of Exploitation' in Canada's Temporary Foreign Worker Program" (2017) 78 Geoforum 199.

Chapter 1

1. For a detailed treatment of the history of Canadian migration policy, see Ninette Kelley & Michael Trebilcock, *The Making of the Mosaic: A History of Canadian Immigration Policy* (Toronto: University of Toronto Press, 2010).
2. Nandita Sharma, "On Being Not Canadian: The Social Organization of 'Migrant Workers' in Canada" (2001) 38:4 Can Rev Sociology 415 at 425.

3 Salimah Valiani, "The Shifting Landscape of Contemporary Canadian Immigration Policy: The Rise of Temporary Migration and Employer-Driven Immigration" in Luin Goldring & Patricia Landolt, eds, *Producing and Negotiating Non-citizenship: Precarious Legal Status in Canada* (Toronto: University of Toronto Press, 2013) 55.
4 WG Robinson, "Illegal Immigrants in Canada: Recent Developments" (1984) 18:3 Intl Migration Rev 474 at 475.
5 Norm Buchignani, "Vanishing Acts: Illegal Immigration in Canada as a Sometime Social Issue" in David Haines & Karen Rosenblum, eds, *Illegal Immigration in America: A Reference Handbook* (Westport, CT: Greenwood Press, 1999) 415 at 430.
6 *Ibid* at 434.
7 Citizenship and Immigration Canada, "Speaking Notes – Remarks by the Honourable Jason Kenney, P.C., M.P. Minister of Citizenship, Immigration and Multiculturalism" (30 March 2010), online: <https://www.canada.ca/en/immigration-refugees-citizenship/news/archives/speeches-2010/jason-kenney-minister-balanced-refugee-reform.html>; Citizenship and Immigration Canada, "Speaking Notes for The Honourable Jason Kenney, P.C., M.P. Minister of Citizenship, Immigration and Multiculturalism" (16 February 2012), online: <https://www.canada.ca/en/immigration-refugees-citizenship/news/archives/speeches-2012/jason-kenney-minister-2012-02-16.html>.
8 Sébastien Chauvin & Blanca Garcés-Mascareñas, "Becoming Less Illegal: Deservingness Frames and Undocumented Migrant Incorporation" (2014) 8:4 Sociology Compass 422.
9 Bridget Anderson, *Us and Them? The Dangerous Politics of Immigration Control* (Oxford: Oxford University Press, 2013) at 6.
10 Buchignani, *supra* note 5 at 434.
11 *Singh v Minister of Employment and Immigration*, [1985] 1 SCR 177.
12 W.G. Robinson, *Illegal Migrants in Canada: A Report to the Honourable Lloyd Axworthy* (Hull: Minister of Supply and Services Canada, 1983) at xi.
13 Donald Galloway, "Noncitizens and Discrimination: Redefining Rights in the Face of Complexity" in Oliver Schmidke & Saime Ozcurumez, eds, *Of States, Rights, and Social Closure: Governing Migration and Citizenship* (New York: Palgrave Macmillan, 2008) 37 at 38.
14 Daiva K Stasiulis, "International Migration, Rights, and the Decline of 'Actually Existing Liberal Democracy'" (1997) 23:2 J Ethnic & Migration Studies 197 at 199.
15 Luin Goldring, Carolina Berinstein & Judith K Bernhard, "Institutionalizing Precarious Migratory Status in Canada" (2009) 13:3 Citizenship Studies 239 at 240.

16 At the time of the study, spousal permanent residence was granted on a conditional basis, requiring applicants to continue to show the genuineness of their relationship for a period of two years in total after obtaining permanent residence. This requirement was repealed in 2017.

17 Deepa Rajkumar et al, "At the Temporary-Permanent Divide: How Canada Produces Temporariness and Makes Citizens through Its Security, Work, and Settlement Policies" (2012) 16:3–4 Citizenship Studies 483 at 506; Aihwa Ong, *Flexible Citizenship: The Cultural Logics of Transnationality* (Durham, NC: Duke University Press, 1999); Matthew Sparke, "A Neoliberal Nexus: Citizenship, Security and the Future of the Border" (2006) 25:2 Political Geography 151.

18 Parvati Raghuram, "Brain Circulation or Precarious Labour? Conceptualising Temporariness in the UK's National Health Service" in Leah Vosko et al, *Liberating Temporariness? Migration, Work, and Citizenship in an Age of Insecurity* (Montreal & Kingston: McGill-Queen's University Press, 2014) 177 at 196.

19 Rajkumar et al, *supra* note 17 at 505.

20 Sébastien Chauvin & Blanca Garcés-Mascareñas, "Beyond Informal Citizenship: The New Moral Economy of Migrant Illegality" (2012) 6:3 Intl Political Sociology 241 at 242.

21 Citizenship and Immigration Canada, *Canada Facts and Figures, 2014: Immigrant Overview Temporary Residents* (2015), online: Citizenship and Immigration Canada, Research and Statistics <http://www.cic.gc.ca/english/pdf/2014-Facts-Figures-Temporary.pdf>.

22 Judy Fudge & Fiona MacPhail, "The Temporary Foreign Worker Program in Canada: Low-Skilled Workers as an Extreme Form of Flexible Labour" (2009) 31 Comp Lab L & Pol'y J 5 at 11.

23 Patricia Landolt & Luin Goldring "The Impact of Precarious Legal Status on Immigrants' Economic Outcomes" (2012) 35 IRPP Study 1 at 30.

24 Immigration, Refugees, and Citizenship Canada, "Statistics and Open Data" (2017), online: <https://www.canada.ca/en/immigration-refugees-citizenship/corporate/reports-statistics/statistics-open-data.html>, compiled from the combined number of unique persons reported in Tables 7 ("Temporary Foreign Worker Program"), 4 ("international mobility"), and 30 ("other purposes"). Subsequent to 2012, the federal government did not publish entries of foreign workers but just the number of foreign workers present with a valid permit, which in 2013 numbered 444,913 (104,125 in the Temporary Foreign Worker Program and 236,663 in the International Mobility Program) and in 2014 numbered 353,448 (94,109 in the Temporary Foreign Worker Program and 259,339 in the

International Mobility Program). Citizenship and Immigration Canada, *supra* note 21.

25 In 2014, the federal government introduced changes to extend eligibility for permanent residence to full-time live-out caregivers under the Caring for Children or Caring for People with High Medical Needs programs. Live-in caregivers continue to be eligible for permanent residence. See Government of Canada, "Live-in Caregiver Program" (2017), online: <http://www.cic.gc.ca/english/work/caregiver/index.asp>.

26 Sandra Elgersma, *Temporary Foreign Workers* (Ottawa: Political and Social Affairs Division, Library of Parliament, 2007) at 4.

27 Citizenship and Immigration Canada, Canada – Refugee Claimants Present on December 1 by Top Source Country (table) in Citizenship and Immigration Canada, *Facts and Figures, 2012: Immigration Overview – Permanent and Temporary Residents,* online: Citizenship and Immigration Canada, Research and Statistics <https://web.archive.org/web/20140619051203/http://www.cic.gc.ca/english/resources/statistics/facts2012/temporary/26.asp>. The federal government no longer publishes the number of refugee claimants living in Canada; instead, it tracks the number of new claims per year. These are available in Citizenship and Immigration Canada, *Canada Facts and Figures, 2014: Immigrant Overview Temporary Residents* (2015), online: Citizenship and Immigration Canada, Research and Statistics <http://www.cic.gc.ca/english/pdf/2014-Facts-Figures-Temporary.pdf>. The numbers for 2013–15 were significantly smaller than for 2012.

28 Citizenship and Immigration Canada, "Interim Federal Health Program: Summary of Coverage" (2012), online: <https://web.archive.org/web/20121227071233/http://www.cic.gc.ca/english/refugees/outside/summary-ifhp.asp>.

29 *Canadian Doctors for Refugee Care v Canada (Attorney General),* 2014 FC 651.

30 Immigration, Refugees, and Citizenship Canada, "Interim Federal Health Program: Summary of Coverage" (2017), online: <https://www.canada.ca/en/immigration-refugees-citizenship/services/refugees/help-within-canada/health-care/interim-federal-health-program/coverage-summary.html>.

31 *Immigration Refugee Protection Regulations,* SOR 2002/227, ss 228(3) and 206(a).

32 David Tilson, chair, *Temporary Foreign Workers and Non-status Workers: Report of the Standing Committee on Citizenship and Immigration* (Ottawa: Library of Parliament, 2009) at 65.

33 Zeina Bou-Zeid, *Unwelcome but Tolerated: Irregular Migrants in Canada* (PhD dissertation, Osgoode Hall Law School, York University, 2007) [unpublished].
34 Confidentiality was of primary concern to migrant participants; it was carefully protected, given the risk that they might be identified as unauthorized migrants. Migrants engaged in any unauthorized activity could face detention, deportation, and charges under the *Immigration and Refugee Protection Act*. Such activity could also result in loss of work and have a detrimental impact on social entitlements. Confidentiality concerns were also relevant to agency representatives, who could be perceived as being complicit in providing assistance to unauthorized migrants. In transcripts and all other documents, participants were identified only by a number and by the group to which they belonged. Participants were never asked to provide names or other identifying information, and if any such information was given, it was permanently redacted from the interview transcripts. Any potentially identifying information has been generalized beyond the point of recognition in this book.
35 Herbert J Rubin & Irene S Rubin, *Qualitative Interviewing: The Art of Hearing Data* (Thousand Oaks, CA: Sage Publications, 2005).
36 *Ibid* at 7.
37 *Ibid* at 15.
38 Vikki Reynolds, "Fluid and Imperfect Ally Positioning: Some Gifts from Queer Theory," *Context* (October 2010) 13 at 15.
39 *Ibid*.
40 Dorothy E Smith, *Institutional Ethnography: A Sociology for People* (Lanham, MD: Altamira Press, 2005) at 29.
41 *Ibid*.
42 *Ibid* at 31.
43 *Ibid* at 38.
44 Marie L Campbell & Frances Gregor, *Mapping Social Relations: A Primer in Doing Institutional Ethnography* (Aurora, ON: Garamond Press, 2006) at 68.
45 Smith, *supra* note 40 at 165.
46 *Ibid* at 88.
47 *Ibid* at 113.
48 *Ibid* at 225.
49 Luin Goldring, "Resituating Temporariness as the Precarity and Conditionality of Non-Citizenship" in Vosko et al, *Liberating Temporariness*, *supra* note 18 at 240.
50 Ron Ellis, *Unjust by Design: Canada's Administrative Justice System* (Vancouver: UBC Press, 2013) at 2.

51 See e.g. Michael Lipsky, *Street-Level Bureaucracy: Dilemmas of the Individual in Public Service*, 30th anniversary ed (New York: Russell Sage Foundation, 2010), and, for an updated take on this topic, see Peter Hupe et al, *Understanding Street-Level Bureaucracy* (Bristol: Policy Press, 2015).

52 Ellis, *supra* note 50.

53 For a full review of administrative law in Canada, see e.g. Lorne Sossin & Colleen Flood, eds, *Administrative Law in Context* (Toronto: Emond Montgomery Publications, 2013); Sara Blake, *Administrative Law in Canada*, 5th ed (Markham, ON: LexisNexis Canada, 2011).

54 Steve Wexler, "Discretion: The Unacknowledged Side of Law" (1975) UTLJ 25:120 at 125. See also JH Grey, "Discretion in Administrative Law" (1979) Osgoode Hall LJ 17.

55 Such requests were made under the *Freedom of Information and Protection of Privacy Act*, RSBC 1996, c 165. Requests asked for 1) any decisions unavailable on the website in which the person's migration status was a relevant issue (i.e., anything to do with refugee claimants, foreign visitors, foreign students, foreign workers, or people without immigration documents, etc.), and 2) any statistics, manuals, or other information relevant to any type of benefits available to persons without full citizenship or permanent residence.

56 The most obvious example of this is the Federal Court's use of the "doctrine of illegality" in interpreting the *Employment Insurance Act*, which I examine in detail in Chapter 4.

57 E.g., "Numbers of non-resident students for whom fees are requested from 2000 to the present date, including all available information concerning immigration status of the students and parents, year, basis of fee assessment, grade, and any other information collected."

58 For a typology of information-controlling behaviours by governments, see Martial Pasquier & Jean-Patrick Villeneuve, "Organizational Barriers to Transparency: A Typology and Analysis of Organizational Behaviour Tending to Prevent or Restrict Access to Information" (2007) 73 Intl Rev Administrative Sciences 147.

59 Michael Walzer, *Spheres of Justice: A Defense of Pluralism and Equality* (New York: Basic Books, 1983) at 39.

60 Linda Bosniak, *The Citizen and the Alien: Dilemmas of Contemporary Membership* (Princeton, NJ: Princeton University Press, 2006) at 16.

61 Seyla Benhabib, *The Rights of Others: Aliens, Residents, and Citizens* (Cambridge, UK: Cambridge University Press, 2004) at 43.

62 Chauvin & Garcés-Mascareñas, *supra* note 8.

63 Nigel Harris, *The New Untouchables: Immigration and the New World Worker* (London: IB Tauris, 1995) at 110.
64 See e.g. Yasmin Soysal Nohuglu, *Limits of Citizenship: Migrants and Postnational Membership in Europe* (Chicago: University of Chicago Press, 1994); Benhabib, *supra* note 61.
65 See e.g. Joseph Carens, "The Rights of Irregular Migrants" (2008) 22:2 Ethics & Intl Affairs 163.

Chapter 2

1 *Constitution Act, 1867* (UK), 30 & 31 Vict, c 3, reprinted in RSC 1985, App II, No 5, s 95.
2 The text of s 95 states:

> [i]n each Province the Legislature may make Laws in relation to Agriculture in the Province, and to Immigration into the Province; and it is hereby declared that the Parliament of Canada may from Time to Time make Laws in relation to Agriculture in all or any of the Provinces, and to Immigration into all or any of the Provinces; and any Law of the Legislature of a Province relative to Agriculture or to Immigration shall have effect in and for the Province as long and as far only as it is not repugnant to any Act of the Parliament of Canada.

3 *Immigration and Refugee Protection Act*, SC 2001, c 27 [*IRPA*].
4 *Immigration and Refugee Protection Regulations*, SOR/2002-227 [*IRPR*].
5 *IRPA*, *supra* note 3 at s 2(1).
6 *Citizenship Act*, RSC 1985, c C-29, ss 3(1), 5(1)(c).
7 *IRPA*, *supra* note 3 at ss 34(1), 35(1), 36(1), 37(1).
8 *Ibid*, s 40(1).
9 *Ibid*, s 41.
10 *IRPR*, *supra* note 4 at s 98(1).
11 *Ibid*, s 72.1. This section, introduced in 2012, required those permanent residents sponsored by their spouses to maintain a conjugal relationship for two years, and provide evidence of this, except in the case of abuse or the death of the sponsor. It was repealed in 2017.
12 The *Act* also refers specifically to "Indians," as defined by the *Indian Act*, who have the right to enter and remain in Canada, regardless of whether or not they are a citizen or permanent resident of Canada. *IRPA*, *supra* note 3 at s 19.

13 *Ibid*, s 2(1).
14 Exceptional categories of foreign nationals have effective ongoing legal residence in Canada even if they do not qualify for temporary or permanent residence. This applies primarily to foreign nationals of countries to which Canada will not deport persons, due to extreme risk or political instability; those who have been recognized as protected persons but have not obtained permanent residence; and those whose removal is stayed on the basis of humanitarian and compassionate or public policy considerations. Such individuals are often granted work permits and become eligible for social entitlements on an interim basis, but the stability and duration of their authorization is contingent on the temporary situations listed above. *IRPR, supra* note 4 at s 230(1) and 233; *IRPA, supra* note 3 at s 95.
15 *IRPR, supra* note 4 at s 181.
16 Nandita Sharma, *Home Economics: Nationalism and the Making of "Migrant Workers" in Canada* (Toronto: University of Toronto Press, 2006).
17 *IRPR, supra* note 4 at s 204.
18 *Ibid*, s 203(3).
19 *Ibid*, s 87.1(1).
20 *Ibid*, s 72(1).
21 *Ibid*, s 113. Recent policy changes have made permanent residence available under live-out caregiving programs as well. Immigration, Refugee, and Citizenship Canada (2017), online: <http://www.cic.gc.ca/english/immigrate/caregivers/index.asp>.
22 *IRPR, supra* note 4 at s 183.
23 *Ibid*, s 124(1)(a). Refugee claimants are excluded from this section.
24 *IRPA, supra* note 3 at s 124(1)(c).
25 *Ibid*, s 125.
26 *IRPR, supra* note 4 at s 183(5).
27 Robin Cohen, *Migration and Its Enemies: Global Capital, Migrant Labour, and the Nation-State* (Aldershot, UK: Ashgate, 2006).
28 Sébastien Chauvin & Blanca Garcés-Mascareñas, "Becoming Less Illegal: Deservingness Frames and Undocumented Migrant Incorporation" (2014) 8:4 Sociology Compass 422.
29 Read "because of my status." The wording reflects the participant's literal translation of the Spanish "por."
30 Patricia Landolt & Luin Goldring, "The Impact of Precarious Legal Status on Immigrants' Economic Outcomes" (2012) 35 IRPP Study 1.
31 Nicholas De Genova, "Migrant 'Illegality' and Deportability in Everyday Life" (2002) 31 Annual Rev of Anthropology 419 at 439.

32 Linda Bosniak, *The Citizen and the Alien: Dilemmas of Contemporary Membership* (Princeton, NJ: Princeton University Press, 2006) at 47.

33 Jurisdiction is traditionally associated with geographic delimitation, but can also be understood in terms of qualitative governing features: see e.g. Mariana Valverde, "Jurisdiction and Scale: Legal 'Technicalities' as Resources for Theory" (2009) 18:2 Soc & Leg Stud 139.

Chapter 3

1 See e.g. Patti Tamara Lenard & Christine Straehle, "Temporary Labour Migration, Global Redistribution, and Democratic Justice" (2012) 11:2 Politics, Philosophy & Economics 206.

2 Sylvia Fuller & Leah Vosko, "Temporary Employment and Social Inequality in Canada: Exploring Intersections of Gender, Race, and Migration" (2008) 88:1 Social Indicators Research 31; Martha MacDonald, "Income Security for Women: What about Employment Insurance?" in Marjorie Griffin Cohen & Jane Pulkingham, eds, *Public Policy for Women in Canada: The State, Income Security and Labour Market Issues* (Toronto: University of Toronto Press, 2009) at 251; Leah Vosko, *Managing the Margins: Gender, Citizenship and the International Regulation of Precarious Employment* (London: Oxford University Press, 2009); Guy Standing, "The Precariat: From Denizens to Citizens?" (2012) 44:4 Polity 588.

3 Leah Vosko et al, *Liberating Temporariness? Migration, Work, and Citizenship in an Age of Insecurity* (Montreal & Kingston: McGill-Queen's University Press, 2014) at 8.

4 Judy Fudge & Fiona MacPhail, "The Temporary Foreign Worker Program in Canada: Low-Skilled Workers as an Extreme Form of Flexible Labour" (2009) 31 Comp Lab L & Pol'y J 5. The article deals specifically with the low-skilled worker program in Canada, but the observations therein are confirmed by present studies with regard to workers with precarious migration status.

5 The Live-in Caregiver Program required applicants to have completed the equivalent of a Canadian secondary education. *Immigration and Refugee Protection Regulations*, SOR/2002-227 s 112 [*IRPR*].

6 Geraldine Pratt, "From Registered Nurse to Registered Nanny: Discursive Geographies of Filipina Domestic Workers in Vancouver, B.C." (1999) 75:3 Economic Geography 215 at 227; Philip Kelly, "Filipinos in Canada: Economic Dimensions of Immigration and Settlement" CERIS Working Paper No. 48 (2006) at 17.

7 See e.g. Daniel Hiebert, Silvia D'Addario & Kathy Sherrell, *The Profile of Absolute and Relative Homelessness among Immigrants, Refugees, and Refugee Claimants in the GVRD: Final Report* (Vancouver: MOSAIC, 2005).
8 See e.g. Abigail Bakan & Daiva Stasiulis "Marginalized Dissident Non-Citizens: Foreign Domestic Workers" in Barrington Walker, ed, *The History of Immigration and Racism in Canada: Essential Readings* (Toronto: Canadian Scholars' Press, 2008) 264 at 267.
9 Nandita Sharma, *Home Economics: Nationalism and the Making of "Migrant Workers" in Canada* (Toronto: University of Toronto Press, 2006).
10 Citizenship and Immigration Canada, *Facts and Figures, 2011: Immigration Overview – Permanent and Temporary Residents*, online: <https://web.archive.org/web/20130622055839/http://www.cic.gc.ca/english/resources/statistics/facts2011/temporary/11.asp> [CIC *Facts & Figures* 2011].
11 Human Resources and Skills Development Canada, "Temporary Foreign Worker Program: Labour Market Opinion (LMO) Statistics, Annual Statistics, 2008–2011" (30 April 2012), online: <https://web.archive.org/web/20130405052342/http://www.hrsdc.gc.ca/eng/workplaceskills/foreign_workers/stats/annual/table7aa.shtml>.
12 CIC *Facts & Figures* 2011, *supra* note 10.
13 Sarah Marsden, "Assessing the Regulation of Temporary Foreign Workers in Canada" (2011) 49:1 Osgoode Hall LJ 39 at 48.
14 Basic Security Training, for work as a security guard.
15 Jobwave, a temporary employment agency in Vancouver.
16 Patricia Landolt & Luin Goldring, "The Social Production of Non-citizenship: The Consequences of Intersecting Trajectories of Precarious Legal Status and Precarious Work" in Luin Goldring & Patricia Landolt, eds, *Producing and Negotiating Non-citizenship: Precarious Legal Status in Canada* (Toronto: University of Toronto Press, 2013) 154.
17 *Employment Standards Act*, RSBC 1996, c 113, s 1(1).
18 *Ibid*, ss 32, 36.
19 *Ibid*, s 26.
20 *Employment Standards Regulation*, BC Reg 396/95, s 15.
21 *Ibid*, s 18(3).
22 Human Resources and Skills Development Canada, "Temporary Foreign Worker Program: National Commodity List – Agricultural Stream and the Seasonal Agricultural Worker Program" (2013), online: <https://web.archive.org/web/20130313102223/http://www.hrsdc.gc.ca/eng/workplaceskills/foreign_workers/vegetables.shtml>.
23 *Employment Standards Act*, *supra* note 17 at ss 35, 40.
24 *Ibid*, s 39.

25 *Ibid*, s 14.
26 *Ibid*, s 17.
27 Geraldine Pratt, *Working Feminism* (Philadelphia: Temple University Press, 2004) at 39.
28 *Workers Compensation Act*, RSBC 1996, c 492, s 1.
29 Terrance J Bogyo, *WorkSafeBC's Policy, Legislation and Responses to OHS and Newcomer Workers* (2009), online: Institute for Work and Health, accessed May 2016 <http://www.iwh.on.ca/system/files/documents/iw-forum-2009/bogyo_worksafebc_ohs_newcomer_policy_2009.pdf>.
30 *Workers' Compensation Act*, supra note 28, s 5(1).
31 *Ibid*, s 5.1.
32 *Ibid*, s 53(1).
33 *Ibid*, s 54(1).
34 *Occupational Health and Safety Regulation*, BC Reg 296/97, s 4.1.
35 *Ibid*, ss 5.27, 4.28.
36 Mandana Vahabi & Josephine Pui-Hing Wong, "Caught Between a Rock and a Hard Place: Mental Health of Migrant Live-in Caregivers in Canada" (2017) 17:1 BMC Public Health 498; Samia Saad, "The Cost of Invisibility: The Psychosocial Impact of Falling Out of Status" in Luin Goldring & Patricia Landolt, eds, *Producing and Negotiating Non-citizenship: Precarious Legal Status in Canada* (Toronto: University of Toronto Press, 2013) 137; Luin Goldring & Patricia Landolt, "The Social Production of Non-citizenship: The Consequences of Intersecting Trajectories of Precarious Legal Status and Precarious Work" in *ibid*, 154.
37 See e.g. Kerry Preibisch and Jenna Hennebry, "Temporary Migration, Chronic Effects: The Health of International Migrant Workers in Canada" (2011) 183:9 CMAJ 1033; Bukola Salami, Salima Meharali & Azeez Salami, "The Health of Temporary Foreign Workers in Canada: A Scoping Review" (2015) 106:8 Can J of Public Health e546.
38 While a comprehensive review of the use of court-based litigation is beyond the scope of this book (and in general less likely to be available as an option due to lack of access to legal counsel), one recent case bears mentioning here: In 2011, a group of temporary foreign workers filed a class action suit in the Supreme Court of British Columbia against Northland Properties, which operates Denny's restaurants, claiming unpaid wages, compensation for recruitment fees, injury to dignity, and airfare. The case was settled before trial in March 2013.
39 *Employment Standards Act*, supra note 17 at ss 98, 92, 91.
40 *Ibid*, s 102.
41 *Employment Standards Act Self-Help Kit* (2017), online: British Columbia Ministry of Labour <https://www2.gov.bc.ca/assets/gov/employment-

business-and-economic-development/employment-standards-work
place-safety/employment-standards/self-help/self_help_kit.pdf>.
42 *Employment Standards Act, supra* note 17 at s 75.
43 Data provided by Helen Miller, British Columbia Employment Standards Branch, 7 July 2011, in response to a request under the *Freedom of Information and Protection of Privacy Act,* RSBC 1996, c 165.
44 *Ibid; Employment Standards Regulation, supra* note 20 at s 29(1) (a) and (b).
45 Now called a Labour Market Impact Assessment (LMIA).
46 BC Employment Standards Tribunal [BC EST] # D121/09.
47 BC EST # D008/13, BC EST # D009/13.
48 BC EST # D094/09.
49 But see *Koo v 5220459 Manitoba Inc.*, 2010 MBQB 132, in which the Court found that the terms of a Labour Market Opinion cannot be enforced as terms of the contract.
50 BC EST # D061/12.
51 BC EST # D094/07.
52 Sébastien Chauvin & Blanca Garcés-Mascareñas, "Beyond Informal Citizenship: The New Moral Economy of Migrant Illegality" (2012) 6:3 Intl Political Sociology 241 at 245.
53 Delphine Nakache, "The Canadian Temporary Foreign Worker Program: Regulations, Practices and Protection Gaps" in Goldring & Landolt, eds, *supra* note 36 at 91.
54 *Workers Compensation Act, supra* note 28 at s 153.
55 Data from spreadsheet provided by Deanna Hamburg, the Workers' Compensation Board (25 August 2011) in response to a written Freedom of Information request.
56 Case 2010-01513 (1 June 2010), online: WCAT <http://www.wcat.bc.ca/search/decision_search.aspx>.
57 Case 2009-03264 (17 December 2009), online: WCAT <http://www.wcat.bc.ca/search/decision_search.aspx>. For further cases concerning foreign workers, see e.g. 2003-02365 (4 September 2013), 2006-02437 (7 June 2006), 2009-02956 (16 November 2009), online: WCAT <http://www.wcat.bc.ca/search/decision_search.aspx>.
58 *Employment Standards Act, supra* note 17 at s 63. At common law, employees are often entitled to compensation beyond the statutory minimum, but here my focus is limited to the statutory regime, for two reasons. First, it is a much more accessible venue, and thus much more likely to be relevant to precarious migrants. Unlike civil lawsuits for employment matters, which require obtaining a lawyer at one's own cost and thus are utilized by workers with above-average pay, the Employment Standards Branch is designed for public

access and self-representation. Second, the *Employment Standards Act* represents the minimum to which workers are entitled and thus functions as a part of the basic rights framework for workers.

59 Luin Goldring, Carolina Berinstein & Judith K Bernhard, "Institutionalizing Precarious Migratory Status in Canada" (2009) 13:3 Citizenship Studies 239.

60 Klara Öberg, "The Production of Deportability" in Erica Righard, Magnus Johansson & Tapio Salonen, *Social Transformations in Scandinavian Cities: Nordic Perspectives on Urban Marginalisation and Social Sustainability* (Lund, Sweden: Nordic Academic Press, 2015) at 165.

61 Leah Vosko, "Blacklisting as a Modality of Deportability: Mexico's Response to Circular Migrant Agricultural Workers' Pursuit of Collective Bargaining Rights in British Columbia, Canada" (2015) 42:8 J Ethnic and Migration Studies: 1. While Vosko's study deals with control of a worker pool in the more contained structure of the Seasonal Agricultural Worker Program, employers' removal of support can have a similar effect, where the worker is left with no alternative but to work without authorization.

Chapter 4

1 See e.g. Gillian Crease & Veronica Strong-Boag, *Losing Ground: The Effects of Government Cutbacks on Women in British Columbia, 2001–2005* (Vancouver: BC Federation of Labour, 2005); Shauna Butterwick, *Meaningful Training Programs for BC Welfare Recipients with Multiple Barriers* (Vancouver: Canadian Centre for Policy Alternatives, 2010), online: <https://www.policyalternatives.ca/publications/reports/meaningful-training-programs>.

2 See e.g. Susan Hardwick & Ginger Mansfield, "Discourse, Identity, and 'Homeland as Other' at the Borderlands" (2009) 99:2 Annals of the Assoc of American Geographers 383.

3 *Canada Health Act*, RSC 1985, c C-6. The *Act* doesn't specify permanent membership but refers instead to "residents" in section 3, which states: "It is hereby declared that the primary objective of Canadian health care policy is to protect, promote and restore the physical and mental well-being of residents of Canada and to facilitate reasonable access to health services without financial or other barriers."

4 See e.g. "Reform of the Interim Federal Health Program Ensures Fairness, Protects Public Health and Safety" (news release) (2012), online: Citizenship and Immigration Canada <https://web.archive.org/web/20130728190728/http://www.cic.gc.ca/english/department/media/releases/2012/2012-04-25.asp>, in which previous Immigration Minister Jason Kenney is quoted as

saying that Canadians are "a very generous people and [that] Canada has a generous immigration system." Kenney describes the purpose of changes with respect to removing health care benefits from refugee claimants as "taking away an incentive from people who may be considering filing an unfounded refugee claim in Canada."

5 *Canada Health Act, supra* note 3 at ss 2, 3.
6 *Ibid*, s 3. The standards established by federal law are non-mandatory, due to the division of powers in favour of provincial control of healthcare. However, because these standards function as a condition of federal financial transfers, the provision of services is roughly consistent between provinces and territories.
7 *Constitution Act, 1867*, 30 & 31 Vict, c 3.
8 *Medicare Protection Act*, RSBC 1996, c 286, s 1.
9 Although several regulations exist pursuant to the *Medicare Protection Act*, the only one relevant to this is the *Medical and Health Services Regulation*, BC Reg 426/97 [*Medical Services Regulation*].
10 *Medicare Protection Act, supra* note 9 at s 1.
11 *Medical Services Regulation, supra* note 9 at s 2. In practice, for inland spousal applicants, the provincial health authority often requires not only proof of filing an application but also a letter from Citizenship and Immigration Canada confirming that "first stage approval" has been issued (which is not usually available until several months after the date of application), or proof that the application plus a hard copy of a visitor's record of at least six months' duration.
12 A pilot project began in 2011 to provide medical care to patients with HIV/AIDS, regardless of their status or whether they had medical insurance, through the STOP AIDS program.
13 "MSP Enrolment and Account Maintenance Manual," policy manual provided by the Ministry of Health (2011) in response to a request under the *Freedom of Information and Protection of Privacy Act*, RSBC 1996, c 165.
14 *Ibid* at 61.
15 *Immigration and Refugee Protection Regulations*, SOR/2002-227, s 186(u) [*IRPR*].
16 That is, those admitted to Canada under a Minister's Permit, or other federal immigration approval (landed immigrant, study permit).
17 "AN 0500 – Non Canadian Residents as Patients," policy sheet provided by Vancouver Coastal Health (2011) in response to a request under the *Freedom of Information and Protection of Privacy Act*, RSBC 1996, c 165.
18 *Ibid* at 2.

19 *Ibid.*

20 Vancouver Coastal Health also provided examples of medical services fees that could be billed to non-resident patients: the fee for an emergency room visit is $545, a standard bed is $3,235 per day, and an MRI is $1,750. People who are residents but are uninsured also face costs, but these are considerably lower than those for non-residents. "VGH-UBCH-GFS Patient Daily Rate Sheet," policy sheet provided by Vancouver Coastal Health (2011) in response to a request under the *Freedom of Information and Protection of Privacy Act*, RSBC 1996, c 165.

21 "Admission of Non-Residents of Canada and Uninsured Residents of Canada," policy sheet provided by Fraser Health (2011) in response to a request under the *Freedom of Information and Protection of Privacy Act*, RSBC 1996, c 165 ["Admission of Non-Residents"].

22 *Immigration and Refugee Protection Act*, SC 2001, c 27, s 28 [*IRPA*].

23 "Hospital Rates Table," policy sheet provided by Fraser Health (2011) in response to a request under the *Freedom of Information and Protection of Privacy Act*, RSBC 1996, c 165.

24 The institution also records the following data for non-residents: citizenship, passport number, permanent resident card data, refugee claimant document, work or study visa number and dates of issue and expiry, as well as the name and phone number of the school or place of employment. "Admission of Non-Residents," *supra* note 21.

25 *Ibid.*

26 Although governmental sources provide funding for some postsecondary education, in this section I will consider only publicly funded primary and secondary education.

27 Toronto District School Board, "Policy P061: Students without Legal Immigration Status" (2012), online: <https://web.archive.org/web/20120417224220/http://www.tdsb.on.ca/ppf/detail.aspx?from=allDocs.aspx&id=1555>.

28 See e.g. the website of Collectif Éducation sans Frontières, online: <http://collectifeducation.org/en/>.

29 *IRPA*, *supra* note 22 at s 30(2).

30 *School Act*, RSBC 1996, c 412, s 3.

31 *Ibid*, s 82(1)–(2).

32 British Columbia Ministry of Education, "Eligibility of Students for Operating Grant Funding" (2012), online: <https://web.archive.org/web/20120507015328/http://www.bced.gov.bc.ca/policy/policies/funding_operating_grant.htm> [BC, "Eligibility of Students"].

33 *Ibid.*

34 Minister's Permits no longer exist, having been replaced by Temporary Resident Permits.

35 British Columbia Ministry of Education, "Decision Aid That Could Be Used in Determining Provincial Education Funding" (2013), online: <https://web.archive.org/web/20130203164006/www.bced.gov.bc.ca/policy/policies/international.pdf> [BC, "Decision Aid"].

36 *Ibid.* The inclusion of the temporary resident permit here is contradictory, as that permit is simply a new nomenclature for the older Minister's Permit, and the lists of eligible parties includes holders of the older permit.

37 Response provided Chilliwack School Board (2011) in response to a request under the *Freedom of Information and Protection of Privacy Act*, RSBC 1996, c 165.

38 School District No. 36 (Surrey), *Registration of International Students*, reg 9325.1 (2011), online: <https://www.surreyschools.ca/departments/SECT/PoliciesRegulations/section_9000/Documents/9325.1%20Regulation.pdf>.

39 "Entitlement to a Publically [sic] Funded Education in the Vancouver School System," policy sheet provided by Vancouver School Board (2011) in response to a request under the *Freedom of Information and Protection of Privacy Act*, RSBC 1996, c 165 [VSB, "Entitlement"].

40 "Documentation Required for Registration of All School-Age Students Funding Eligibility Checklist," policy sheet provided by Coquitlam School Board (2011) in response to a request under the *Freedom of Information and Protection of Privacy Act*, RSBC 1996, c 165.

41 "Administrative Procedure 300 – Student Registration," policy sheet provided by Coquitlam School Board (2011) in response to a request under the *Freedom of Information and Protection of Privacy Act*, RSBC 1996, c 165.

42 VSB, "Entitlement," *supra* note 39.

43 Responses provided from Vancouver School Board (2011) in response to a request under the *Freedom of Information and Protection of Privacy Act*, RSBC 1996, c 165.

44 North Vancouver School Board, "Admission of Students to School" (Policy 605) (2011), online: <https://web.archive.org/web/20111113203806/http://www.nvsd44.bc.ca/Home/Administration/PoliciesAndProcedures/Series600/Policy%20605.aspx>.

45 *Ibid.*

46 "Parent Declaration," policy sheet provided by Vancouver School Board (2011) in response to a request under the *Freedom of Information and Protection of Privacy Act*, RSBC 1996, c 165.

47 "Parent Declaration 313," policy sheet provided by Surrey School Board (2011) in response to a request under the *Freedom of Information and Protection of Privacy Act*, RSBC 1996, c 165.
48 VSB, "Entitlement," *supra* note 39.
49 Responses provided by Coquitlam School Board (2011) in response to a request under the *Freedom of Information and Protection of Privacy Act*, RSBC 1996, c 165.
50 *School Act, supra* note 30 at s 82. This section has been considered once, briefly by the BCHRT in *A obo B v School District No. C*, 2009 BCHRT 256, which found that "residency" was not an enumerated ground under the Code, and that the policy applied equally regardless of place of origin.
51 Nassim Elbardough et al, "A Sanctuary School Policy Proposal," *Social Justice Newsletter* (Winter/Spring 2015), online: British Columbia Teachers' Federation, <http://www.bctf.ca/uploadedFiles/Public/SocialJustice/Publications/SJ-NewsletterWinter2015.pdf>.
52 Vancouver School Board, Inter-office memorandum from Julie Pearce, Associate Superintendent, Re District Response to Sanctuary Schools Policy Proposal, 6 May 2016, online: <https://www.vsb.bc.ca/sites/default/files/16May11_op_commIII_agenda_item3.pdf>.
53 *Employment Insurance Act*, SC 1996, c 23.
54 *Employment Insurance Regulations*, SOR/96-332.
55 *Employment Insurance Act, supra* note 53 at s 7.
56 *Ibid*, s 18.
57 See e.g. CUB 73624 (4 November 2009), CUB 67472 (26 March 2006), CUB 73880 (15 July 2009).
58 Delphine Nakache & Paula Kinoshita, *The Canadian Temporary Foreign Worker Program: Do Short-Term Economic Needs Prevail Over Human Rights Concerns?* (Montreal: Institute for Research on Public Policy, 2010) at 19.
59 CUB 22727 (13 December 1993).
60 Employment and Social Development Canada, *Digest of Benefit Entitlement Principles* (2012), online: Service Canada <https://web.archive.org/web/20120715054748/http://www.servicecanada.gc.ca/eng/ei/digest/10_2_0.shtml#a10_2_4>.
61 While section 39 of the *Immigration and Refugee Protection Act* does create a category of inadmissibility on the basis that a person is not able to support himself or herself financially, this section refers to the receipt of social assistance (welfare, or income assistance), and not Employment Insurance. *IRPA, supra* note 22 at s 39.

62 Sébastien Chauvin & Blanca Garcés-Mascareñas, "Becoming Less Illegal: Deservingness Frames and Undocumented Migrant Incorporation" (2014) 8:4 Sociology Compass 422.
63 *Still v M.N.R.* (1998), 154 DLR (4th) 229.
64 *Ibid*, para 48.
65 *Ibid*, para 49.
66 *Ibid*, para 53.
67 *Ibid*.
68 *Ibid*, para 55.
69 *Sah v Canada (Minister of National Revenue)*, [1995] TCJ. No. 982 (QL).
70 *Polat v Canada (Minister of National Revenue)*, [1996] TCJ. No. 1667 (QL).
71 *Allendes v Canada (Minister of National Revenue)*, [1995] TCJ. No. 161 (QL).
72 *Mia v M.N.R.*, 2001 CanLII 785.
73 Sébastien Chauvin & Blanca Garcés-Mascareñas, "Beyond Informal Citizenship: The New Moral Economy of Migrant Illegality" (2012) 6:3 Intl Political Sociology 241 at 241–42.
74 See e.g. Dorothy Chunn & Shelley Gavigan, "Welfare Law, Welfare Fraud, and the Moral Regulation of the 'Never Deserving' Poor" (2004) 13:2 Social Legal Studies 219.
75 Citizenship and Immigration Canada, "Speaking Notes for The Honourable Jason Kenney, P.C., M.P. Minister of Citizenship, Immigration and Multiculturalism" (14 December 2012), online: <http://web.archive.org/web/20130104173240/http://www.cic.gc.ca/english/department/media/speeches/2012/2012-12-14.asp>.
76 *Employment and Assistance Regulation*, BC Reg 263/2002, s 7; *Employment and Assistance for Persons with Disabilities Regulation*, BC Reg 265/2002, s 6 [*Persons with Disabilities Regulation*].
77 *Employment and Assistance Regulation*, supra note 76 at s 7(2).
78 *Ibid*, s 7(3).
79 A 2012 policy change made an exception to this rule, in which mothers without legal status were able to obtain income assistance in specific circumstances, see "Exemption from Citizenship Requirements" (2013), online: British Columbia Ministry of Social Development <https://web.archive.org/web/20130118151614/http://www.gov.bc.ca/meia/online_resource/verification_and_eligibility/citreq/policy.html#3>.
80 Data on applicant numbers provided by Raymond Fieltsch, British Columbia Ministry of Social Development (15 September 2011) in response to a request under the *Freedom of Information and Protection of Privacy Act*, RSBC 1996, c 165.

81 Employment and Assistance Appeal Tribunal Decision 10-427 (2010) provided by the Tribunal in response to a request under the *Freedom of Information and Protection of Privacy Act*, RSBC 1996, c 165.
82 Decision document 20110804110455 (decision undated) provided in 2011 by the Employment and Assistance Appeal Tribunal in response to a request under the *Freedom of Information and Protection of Privacy Act*, RSBC 1996, c 165.
83 Decision document 20110804110536 (decision undated) provided in 2011 by the Employment and Assistance Appeal Tribunal in response to a request under the *Freedom of Information and Protection of Privacy Act*, RSBC 1996, c 165.
84 Decision document 20110804110650 (decision undated) provided in 2011 by the Employment and Assistance Appeal Tribunal in response to a request under the *Freedom of Information and Protection of Privacy Act*, RSBC 1996, c 165.
85 EAAT 09-310 (unpublished).
86 Section 39 states that foreign nationals may be inadmissible "if they are or will be unable or unwilling to support themselves or any other person who is dependent on them, and have not satisfied an officer that adequate arrangements for care and support, other than those that involve social assistance, have been made." *IRPA, supra* note 22 at s 39.
87 Chauvin & Garcés-Mascareñas, "Becoming Less Illegal", *supra* note 62.
88 Anne McNevin, "Ambivalence and Citizenship: Theorising the Political Claims of Irregular Migrants" (2013) 41:2 Millennium J Intl Studies 182 at 188.

Chapter 5

1 Judy Fudge, "The Precarious Migrant Status and Precarious Employment: The Paradox of International Rights for Migrant Workers," Metropolis British Columbia: Centre of Excellence for Research on Immigration and Diversity Working Paper No. 11-15 (11 October 2011).
2 For example, the following quote is reproduced from an intelligence manual aimed at educating Canada Border Services Agency officers in carrying out their duties: "In a prolonged recession and difficult labour market, Canada, which has been identified as being better positioned to weather the recession, and with its comprehensive social safety nets, will continue to be an attractive destination for displaced migrant workers and irregular migrants leaving behind social and political conflicts." Canada Border Services Agency, *The Impact of the Global Recession on*

Migration (Ottawa: Canada Border Services Agency, Intelligence Risk Assessment and Analysis Division, Intelligence Directorate, 2009) at 1; this document was provided in 2011 by the Canada Border Services Agency in response to a request under the *Access to Information Act,* RSC 1985, c A-1.

3 While it is beyond the scope of this book to provide a comprehensive review of the extensive literature on bordering practices, I do rely on the assumption that borders and bordering practices refer not only to the territorial limit of a nation-state, but also to practices determining community, social stratification, and behaviour at traditional territorial border sites as well as within states; see e.g. Gabriel Popescu, *Bordering and Ordering the Twenty-First Century: Understanding Borders* (Lanham, MD: Rowman & Littlefield, 2011); Sandro Mezzadra & Brett Neilson, *Border as Method, or, the Multiplication of Labor* (Durham, NC: Duke University Press, 2013).

4 See e.g. Joseph Carens, *Immigrants and the Right to Stay* (Cambridge, MA: MIT Press, 2010); Stephen Legomsky, "Portraits of the Undocumented Immigrant: A Dialogue" (2009) 44:65 Ga L Rev 66.

5 Catherine Dauvergne, *Making People Illegal: What Globalization Means for Migration and Law* (Cambridge, UK: Cambridge University Press, 2008) at 28.

6 *Immigration and Refugee Protection Regulations*, SOR/2002-227, s 223 [*IRPR*].

7 For example, departure orders are always issued to refugee claimants upon making their claim, but they cannot become enforceable until after the determination of the claim. *Immigration and Refugee Protection Act*, SC 2001 c 27, s 49(2) [*IRPA*].

8 *IRPR, supra* note 6, s 225.

9 *Ibid*, s 226(1).

10 *Ibid*.

11 Data provided by Daniel Kipin, Canada Border Services Agency, 2 March 2012, in response to a written request made under the *Access to Information Act,* RSC 1985, c A-1. The Canada Border Services Agency response included the following notes:

- Not all removal orders come into force, for example a removal order against a refugee claimant will not come into force if the individual is granted Protected Person status as the result of the refugee claim.
- All removal orders against an individual become void if the person becomes a permanent resident.
- Some individuals have a right to appeal their removal orders to the IRB, if their appeal is allowed the order against them may be set aside.

- Removal of an individual from Canada enforces all in force removal orders made against that individual.

12 *Ibid.*
13 *IRPR, supra* note 6, s 224(2).
14 Data provided by Daniel Kipin, Canada Border Services Agency, 3 October 2012, in response to a written request made under the *Access to Information Act*, RSC 1985, c A-1.
15 *IRPA, supra* note 7 at s 124(1)(a).
16 *IRPR, supra* note 6 at s 183(1).
17 *IRPA, supra* note 7 at s 124(1)(c).
18 *Ibid,* ss 117(1), 119.
19 *Ibid,* s 118(1).
20 Kipin, *supra* note 14.
21 *Ibid.*
22 "Operational Manual ENF 7: Investigations and Arrests," provided by Daniel Kipin, Canada Border Services Agency, 15 March 2012, in response to a written request made under the *Access to Information Act*, RSC 1985, c A-1.
23 Subsequent to the study's close, migrant workers' groups have documented and spoken out against a recent CBSA enforcement program that targets domestic workers: see "Marking International Domestic Workers Day: Stop CBSA's Project Guardian" (20 June 2016), online: Migrante BC <http://www.migrantebc.com/2016/06/20/marking-international-domestic-workers-day-stop-cbsas-project-guardian/#more-1327>.
24 Geraldine Pratt, *Working Feminism* (Philadelphia: Temple University Press, 2004) at 100.
25 Linda Bosniak, *The Citizen and the Alien: Dilemmas of Contemporary Membership* (Princeton, NJ: Princeton University Press, 2006) at 47.
26 Stephen Legomsky, "Portraits of the Undocumented Immigrant: A Dialogue" (2009) 44:65 Ga L Rev 66 at 70.
27 Paloma Villegas, "Fishing for Precarious Status Migrants: Surveillance Assemblages of Migrant Illegalization in Toronto, Canada" (2015) 42:2 JL & Soc'y 230.
28 *Criminal Code of Canada*, RSC C-34, s 2.
29 *SCBCTA Policies and Procedures Manual,* provided by Ruth Boyd, South Coast Transportation Authority (July 2012) in response to a request made under the *Freedom of Information and Protection of Privacy Act*, RSBC 1996, c 165.

30 With respect to arrests, the *SCBCTA Policies and Procedures Manual* (*ibid*) provides the following:

> Every peace officer in Canada may arrest and detain without a warrant for an inquiry or removal from Canada any person who on reasonable grounds is suspected of:
>
> 1. being a visitor who takes or continues employment without authorization
> 2. being no longer a visitor
> 3. eluding examination or inquiry
> 4. escaping custody
> 5. being in Canada by fraudulent or improper means
> 6. returning to Canada after removal without Ministerial consent
> 7. not leaving Canada as specified in a departure order
> 8. being a deserting crew member
> 9. if, in the opinion of the arresting officer, the person poses a danger to the public or is unlikely to appear for inquiry or removal.

31 *IRPA*, *supra* note 7 at s 133.

32 Data provided by Ruth Boyd, South Coast Transportation Authority, 18 June 2012, in response to a request made under the *Freedom of Information and Protection of Privacy Act*, RSBC 1996, c 165.

33 *Ibid*.

34 British Columbia Ministry of Justice, Coroners Service, *Verdict at Coroners Inquest*, 7 October 2014, file no. 2013:0380:0004, online: <https://www2.gov.bc.ca/assets/gov/birth-adoption-death-marriage-and-divorce/deaths/coroners-service/inquest/2014/vega-jimenez-lucia-dominga-2013-0380-0004-verdict.pdf>.

35 *Ibid*.

36 Tamara Baluja, "Metro Vancouver Transit Police End Controversial Agreement with CBSA," *CBC News* (20 February 2015), online: <http://www.cbc.ca/news/canada/british-columbia/metro-vancouver-transit-police-end-controversial-agreement-with-cbsa-1.2965863>.

37 Travis Lupick, "Metro Vancouver Hospitals Refer Hundreds of Immigration Cases to Border Police" *Georgia Straight* (9 December 2015), online: <https://www.straight.com/news/593441/metro-vancouver-hospitals-refer-hundreds-immigration-cases-border-police>.

38 Historian Barbara Roberts has shown that, in the first two decades of the twentieth century, doctors played a major role in the deportation of foreign nationals from Canada: "Doctors and Deports: The Role of the Medical

Profession in Canadian Deportation, 1900-20" (1986) 18:3 Can Ethnic Studies 17.

Chapter 6

1 Linda Bosniak, *The Citizen and the Alien: Dilemmas of Contemporary Membership* (Princeton, NJ: Princeton University Press, 2006) at 4.
2 See e.g. Joseph Carens, *Immigrants and the Right to Stay* (Cambridge, MA: MIT Press, 2010).
3 Robin Cohen, *Migration and Its Enemies: Global Capital, Migrant Labour, and the Nation-State* (Aldershot, UK: Ashgate, 2006).
4 See also Luin Goldring & Patricia Landolt, "The Social Production of Non-citizenship: The Consequences of Intersecting Trajectories of Precarious Legal Status and Precarious Work" in Luin Goldring & Patricia Landolt, eds, *Producing and Negotiating Non-citizenship: Precarious Legal Status in Canada* (Toronto: University of Toronto Press, 2013) 154.
5 Jacques Derrida, "Force of Law: The Mystical Foundation of Authority" (1990) 11 Cardozo L Rev 920 at 927.
6 *Canadian Charter of Rights and Freedoms*, Part I of the *Constitution Act, 1982*, being Schedule B to the *Canada Act 1982* (UK), 1982, c 11 s 24(1).
7 Aileen Kavanaugh, "Deference or Defiance? The Limits of the Judicial Role in Constitutional Adjudication" in Grant Huscroft, ed, *Expounding the Constitution: Essays in Constitutional Theory* (Cambridge, UK: Cambridge University Press, 2008) at 213.
8 *Chiarelli v Canada (Minister of Employment and Immigration)*, [1992] 1 SCR 711 at para 733.
9 In the case of s 7, "everyone" includes non-citizens physically present in Canada: *Singh v Minister of Employment and Immigration*, [1985] 1 SCR 177; in the case of s 15, the Supreme Court of Canada and other courts have used this section to determine the rights of non-citizens present in Canada: *Andrews v Law Society of British Columbia*, 1989 CanLII 2 (SCC) [*Andrews*], *Lavoie v Canada*, [2002] 1 SCR 769.
10 Catherine Dauvergne, *Making People Illegal: What Globalization Means for Migration and Law* (Cambridge, UK: Cambridge University Press, 2008) at 39.
11 *Law v Canada (M.E.I.)*, [1999] 1 SCR 497 at para 67.
12 *Corbiere v Canada (Minister of Indian and Northern Affairs)*, 1999 CanLII 687 (SCC); *Egan v Canada*, [1995] 2 SCR 513; *Miron v Trudel*, [1995] 2 SCR 418; *Andrews, supra* note 9.
13 JH Ely, *Democracy and Distrust* (Cambridge, MA: Harvard University Press, 1980) at 151.

14 *Andrews, supra* note 9 at para 32.
15 *Toussaint v the Attorney General of Canada*, 2010 FC 810 at para 12 [*Toussaint* FC].
16 *Ibid*, para 81.
17 *Toussaint v Canada (Attorney General)*, 2011 FCA 213 at para 89 [*Toussaint* FCA].
18 *Ibid*, paras 1–4.
19 *Ibid*, para 8.
20 *Ibid*, para 98.
21 The use of comparator groups in equality jurisprudence is commonly associated with a formal, rather than substantive, equality analysis. In addition to reiterating the finding that Ms. Toussaint chose her migration status, this portion of the reasoning underscores the way in which the act of framing comparator groups can shape judicial decision-making pursuant to s 15. If a law is worded to apply only to a particular group, equality concerns could arise both as a function of the law's treatment of that group relative to others and as a function of distinctions that arise between subcategories of the group to which that law applies.
22 *Toussaint* FCA, *supra* note 17 at para 99.
23 *Ibid* at para 75.
24 Jennifer Koshan & Jonnette Hamilton, "The Continual Reinvention of Section 15 of the *Charter*" (2013) 64 UNBLJ 19; Margot E Young, "Unequal to the Task: 'Kapp'ing the Substantive Potential of Section 15" (2010) 50 SCLR 183; Thomas MJ Bateman, "Human Dignity's False Start in the Supreme Court of Canada: Equality Rights and the Canadian Charter of Rights and Freedoms" (2012) 16:4 Intl JHR 577.
25 *R v Kapp*, 2008 SCC 41 (CanLII), [2008] 2 SCR 483.
26 *Withler v Canada (Attorney General)*, 2011 SCC 12, [2011] 1 SCR 396.
27 *Quebec (Attorney General) v A*, 2013 SCC 5.
28 Judith Keene, "The Supreme Court, the Law Decision, and Social Programs: The Substantive Equality Deficit" in Fay Faraday, Margaret Denike & M Kate Stephenson, eds, *Making Equality Rights Real: Securing Substantive Equality under the Charter* (Toronto: Irwin Law, 2009) at 345; Young, *supra* note 24.
29 Catherine Dauvergne, "How the Charter Has Failed Non-citizens in Canada: Reviewing Thirty Years of Supreme Court of Canada Jurisprudence," (2012) 58 McGill LJ 663 at 666.
30 *Toussaint* FC, *supra* note 15; *Toussaint* FCA, *supra* note 17.

31 *International Convention on the Protection of the Rights of All Migrant Workers and Members of Their Families*, GA res 45/158, UN GAOR, 4th Sess., Sup. No. 49A, UN Doc. A/RES/45/158 (1990) 261.
32 *Ibid*, art 63(2) s 79.
33 *Ibid*, Part IV.
34 Judy Fudge, "Precarious Migrant Status and Precarious Employment: The Paradox of International Rights for Migrant Workers" (2012) 34 Comp Lab L & Pol'y J 95.
35 *Ibid*, 127.
36 *Ibid*, 128.
37 Christina Gabriel, "Managed Migration and the Temporary Labour Fix" in Leah Vosko et al, *Liberating Temporariness? Migration, Work, and Citizenship in an Age of Insecurity* (Montreal & Kingston: McGill-Queen's University Press, 2014) at 120.
38 Brian Opeskin, "Managing International Migration in Australia: Human Rights and the 'Last Major Redoubt of Unfettered National Sovereignty'" (2012) 46:3 Intl Migration Rev 551 at 553.
39 *Human Rights Code*, RSBC 1996 c. 210, s 8(1) [BC *Human Rights Code*]. Other jurisdictions are similar. The *Ontario Human Rights Code*, RSO 1990 c H19, includes citizenship as a protected ground, but s 16(1) of that *Code* limits it: "A right under Part I to non-discrimination because of citizenship is not infringed where Canadian citizenship is a requirement, qualification or consideration imposed or authorized by law."
40 *Human Rights Code, supra* note 39 at s 13(4).
41 *CSWU Local 1611 v SELI Canada and others (No. 8)*, 2008 BCHRT 436 (CanLII) at para 489.
42 *Chein and others v Tim Hortons and others (No. 2)*, 2015 BCHRT 169 (CanLII), online: <https://www.canlii.org/t/gm113>.
43 *OPT v Presteve Foods Ltd.*, 2015 HRTO 675 (CanLII).
44 Saskia Sassen, *Guests and Aliens* (New York: New Press, 1999) at 135.
45 David Harvey, *The New Imperialism* (Oxford: Oxford University Press, 2003) at 29; Sarah Marsden, "Assessing the Regulation of Temporary Foreign Workers in Canada" (2011) 49:1 Osgoode Hall LJ 39 at 64.
46 See e.g. Stephen Castles, "Migration, Crisis, and the Global Labour Market" (2011) 8:3 Globalizations 311.
47 Sébastien Chauvin & Blanca Garcés-Mascareñas, "Beyond Informal Citizenship: The New Moral Economy of Migrant Illegality" (2012) 6:3 Intl Political Sociology 241 at 253.

48 Yasmeen Abu-Laban, "Rethinking Canadian Citizenship: The Politics of Social Exclusion in the Age of Security and Suppression" in Leah Vosko et al, *supra* note 37 at 55.
49 Chauvin & Garcés-Mascareñas, "Beyond Informal Citizenship", *supra* note 47 at 245.
50 *Ibid.*
51 Monica Varsanyi, "Interrogating 'Urban Citizenship' vis-à-vis Undocumented Migration" (2006) 19:2 Citizenship Studies 229 at 239.
52 *Ibid* at 244.
53 Linda Bosniak, "Citizenship Denationalized" (1999) 7 Ind J Global Legal Stud 447 at 488.
54 See e.g. Jennifer Gordon, "Transnational Labor Citizenship" (2007) 80 S Cal L Rev 03.
55 See e.g. Michael Peter Smith, "The Two Faces of Transnational Citizenship" (2007) 30:6 Ethnic and Racial Studies 1096.
56 City of Vancouver, Standing Committee on Policies and Strategic Priorities, *Access to City Services without Fear for Residents with Uncertain or No Immigration Status* (6 April 2016), online: <http://council.vancouver.ca/20160406/documents/pspc3presentation.pdf>.
57 City of Vancouver, "Policy Report – Social Development" (23 March 2016), online: <http://council.vancouver.ca/20160406/documents/pspc3.pdf>.
58 *Ibid* at 4.
59 City of Toronto, "Undocumented Workers in Toronto," City Council Decision, 20–21 February 2013, online: <http://app.toronto.ca/tmmis/viewAgendaItemHistory.do?item=2013.CD18.5>.
60 Nicholas Keung, "Toronto Police Urged to Stop Immigration 'Status Checks,'" *Toronto Star*, 24 November 2015, online: <https://www.thestar.com/news/investigations/2015/11/24/toronto-police-urged-to-stop-immigration-status-checks.html>.
61 Robert Latham, "Temporal Orders, Re-collective Justice and the Making of Untimely States" in Leah Vosko et al, *supra* note 37 at 339.
62 Peter Nyers, *Rethinking Refugees: Beyond States of Emergency* (London: Routledge, 2006) at 125.
63 Ayelet Shachar, *The Birthright Lottery: Citizenship and Global Inequality* (Cambridge, MA: Harvard University Press, 2009) at 167.
64 Luin Goldring, "Resituating Temporariness as the Precarity and Conditionality of Non-Citizenship" in Vosko et al, *supra* note 37 at 244.
65 Seyla Benhabib, *The Rights of Others: Aliens, Residents, and Citizens* (Cambridge, UK: Cambridge University Press, 2004) at 177.

Postscript

1 Documents provided in August 2017 by Economic and Social Development Canada in response to a request under the *Access to Information Act*, RSC 1985, c A-1.
2 Immigration and Citizenship, "Employers Who Have Been Non-compliant," online: <https://www.canada.ca/en/immigration-refugees-citizenship/services/work-canada/employers-non-compliant.html>.

Index

Note: "(t)" after a page number indicates a table; CBSA stands for Canada Border Services Agency; CIC stands for Citizenship and Immigration Canada; EI stands for Employment Insurance; IFHP stands for Interim Federal Health Program; IRPA stands for *Immigration and Refugee Protection Act*; LMO stands for Labour Market Opinion.

Access to City Services without Fear (City of Vancouver), 181
administrative delays. *See* processing delays
administrative law, 29–31. *See also* multi-sited enforcement
agricultural workers: employment standards claims, 89–90; exemption from minimum wage, 75; labour market needs, 43; study participants, 66; workers' compensation claims, 96–97. *See also* Seasonal Agricultural Worker Program
amnesty programs, 14–15, 156
Andrews v Law Society of BC (1989), 157–59, 161, 162–63, 172. See also *Charter of Rights and Freedoms*

belonging. *See* identity and belonging; membership

BNA Act. See *Constitution Act, 1867* (s 95)
Board of Referees (tribunal, BC), 32
Bolivia: study participants, 23, 188(t)
border vs migrant control, 35, 137, 156. *See also* Canada Border Services Agency (CBSA); enforcement, federal (direct); multi-sited enforcement
Bosniak, Linda, 35, 142, 154
British Columbia: *Human Rights Code*, 168–70, 173–74; labour sectors with precarious workers, 68–69. *See also entries beginning with* Vancouver
British Columbia, social benefits. *See* education of children; Employment Standards Branch; health care; welfare; Workers' Compensation Board
British North America Act. See *Constitution Act, 1867* (s 95)

Buchignani, Norm, 14
buses. *See* public transit and enforcement

Canada: historical background, 13–15; migrants' views on, 45, 47–49, 62, 121–22; motivations of migrants, 46–47; reputation for liberal values, 45, 46–47, 49, 101. *See also* laws, immigration (federal); multi-sited enforcement

Canada Border Services Agency (CBSA): about, 138–41; border vs migrant control, 35, 137, 156; confirmation of status, 150; domestic workers as targets, 141–42, 211*n*23; enforcement in worksites, 141–42, 144–48; legal research on, 139–40; lived experience, 141–42; local police interactions with, 147–48; priority levels of enforcement, 141; removal orders, 138–40, 210*n*11; statistics, 139–41. *See also* deportations and removals; enforcement, federal (direct)

Canada Health Act, 101–2, 203*n*3

capitalism, 154–55, 176–77. *See also* economic issues

caregivers: live-out caregivers, 194*n*25, 198*n*21. *See also* Live-in Caregiver Program; live-in caregivers

case law: about, 32, 124–26; class action lawsuits, 201*n*38; doctrine of illegality, 124–26, 140, 152; good behaviour, 125–26, 132–33

CBSA. *See* Canada Border Services Agency (CBSA)

charities and health services, 103, 104

Charter of Rights and Freedoms: about, 156–65; analogous grounds (s 15), 157–63, 165, 171–73, 174–75; *Andrews*, 157–59, 161–65, 172; choice vs immutable characteristics, 158, 160–63, 214*n*21; comparator groups, 172, 214*n*21; EI benefits, 119; equality provisions (s 15), 157–58, 164–65, 174–75; *Law* test for analogous grounds, 160–61; remedies, 157; *Toussaint*, 159–65, 172, 174, 214*n*21. *See also* human rights

Chauvin, Sébastien, 35, 178

children. *See* education of children; families; families, mixed status (citizen children)

Chilliwack School District, 113

China: migrant recruitment debt, 81–82; motivations for migration, 46–47; study participants, 23, 55–57, 73, 187(t)–88(t)

CIC. *See* Citizenship and Immigration Canada (CIC)

citizens, Canadian: about, 3, 40; ethnic and racial hierarchies, 17; *IRPA* category, 40–41. *See also* families, mixed status (citizen children); membership

Citizenship and Immigration Canada (CIC): pre-departure programs, 48. *See also* disclosure of status to authorities; enforcement, federal (direct); *Immigration and Refugee Protection Act (IRPA)*; status, migration

class and precarious status, 17

closed work permits: about, 20, 42–43, 50, 68, 71; barriers to asserting rights, 16, 53–54, 70–71, 73, 97–98; barriers to EI benefits, 119, 120–21;

employer needs, 53, 70; employer-employee power relations, 5–6, 16, 20, 52–54, 71, 73–74, 93, 97–98, 171; international rights, 166–67; labour sectors, 68; limited labour mobility, 16, 20, 43, 52–53, 68–73; O.P.T. (labour mobility), 170–71, 173, 174; and precarious status, 15–16, 68; social insurance numbers with "9" (temporary workers), 22, 68, 71–72; spouses with open permits, 20, 42–43; statistics, 20; uncertainty in status, 61. *See also* work permits

closed work permits, employer endorsements: about, 65, 70–74, 98–99; barriers to asserting rights, 70–71, 98, 119, 120–21; federal requirements for, 70; labour market needs, 42, 69; Labour Market Opinion (LMO), 42, 50, 65, 69, 91, 94, 202*n*49; power relations, 73–74, 98–99; processing delays, 69

Cohen, Robin, 154–55

Colombia: study participants, 23, 55–56, 187(t)–88(t)

confidentiality: illegality and legality, 58–59; of study participants, 34, 58, 195*n*34

Conservative government: Harper's policies, 185–86

Constitution Act, 1867 (s 95), 197*n*2

construction industry: deskilling, 67; health care, 6; informal economy, 68; study participants, 66; unauthorized work, 68–69, 78–79; wages and hours, 78–80; workers' compensation, 93, 95–96

contracts: doctrine of illegality, 124–26; employment standards, 76; hours of work, 76–77, 95; live-in caregivers, 76, 77–78, 82, 86, 91, 95; wages, 95

Coquitlam School District, 114, 116–17. *See also* school boards

Corbiere v Canada (1999), 162–63

Court of Appeal, Federal: *Toussaint* (status as analogous ground), 159–65, 172, 174, 214*n*21

courts: judicial review, 33; legal research on, 33. *See also* Court of Appeal, Federal; Supreme Court of Canada (SCC)

Dauvergne, Catherine, 137, 165

De Genova, Nicholas, 60

decision makers in institutions, 29–31, 33–34. *See also* multi-sited enforcement

deportations and removals: about, 60, 99, 136–41; appeals, 210*n*11; departure orders, 138–39, 147, 210*n*7; deportation orders as expulsion, 138–39; fear of deportation, 93, 95, 142–44; federal jurisdiction, 8; minimal enforcement, 22, 44, 59, 137, 140, 144; re-entry authorization, 138–39; removal orders, 136–37; statistics on, 139–41; symbolic power of, 60, 137–38, 142–44; types of removal orders, 138–40; unenforceable removal orders (refugees), 127, 129. *See also* enforcement, federal (direct); illegality and legality

deservingness: about, 14; EI benefits, 123, 125–26, 132–33; by exclusion from social benefits, 10, 132–34, 136; historical background, 14; judicial and tribunal decision making, 126;

and multi-sited enforcement, 136, 153–54
deskilling: about, 66–69, 98; of caregivers, 66, 87; education levels of migrants, 66–67, 199n5; informal economy, 67, 68–69; labour mobility, 72–73; permanent residents, 41, 67; precarious workers, 66–67, 72–73
direct enforcement. *See* enforcement, federal (direct)
disabilities and social benefits, 32, 127–29, 130–31
disclosure of status to authorities: education of children, 108, 182; health care, 150, 181; permission for disclosure, 150; recommendations for policy changes, 183; transit police, 147–48; Vancouver city policies, 181
discrimination: human rights codes, 167–68. See also *Charter of Rights and Freedoms*; human rights
doctrine of illegality, 124–26, 140, 152. *See also* illegality and legality
domestic workers: CBSA enforcement, 211n23; employment standards, 76; employment standards claims, 89–90; permanent residence, 43; study participants, 66; trends, 68. *See also* Live-in Caregiver Program; live-in caregivers

economic issues: capitalism and migrant labour, 154–55, 176–77; contributions of migrants, 13, 64, 154–55; financial needs of migrants, 59, 74–75, 80–81; historical background, 13; labour market needs, 13, 42–43, 50, 65. *See also* income inadequacy; labour; socio-economic status
Education, Ministry of: eligibility and status, 109–15; fees for non-residents, 110, 111–12, 113–14; legal research on, 33–34, 113; ongoing status confirmation, 115–18; sanctuary schools, proposal for, 117–18. *See also* education of children
education and study permits. *See* study permits
education levels of migrants, 66–67, 199n5. *See also* deskilling; skills
education of children: about, 100–1, 108–18; administrative bureaucracies, 33–34, 114; barriers to, 151–52; Canada's illiberal tendencies, 15; CIC interactions, 115–18; citizen children, 110–11, 112, 113, 114, 116, 151–52; definition of resident, 110, 111–12; disclosure of status to authorities, 108, 181, 182; eligibility and status, 108–11, 132–34; as enforcement site, 137–38, 151–52; fees for non-residents, 6, 110, 111–12, 113–14, 196n57; international rights, 166; *IRPA* provisions, 109; key questions, 7; legal research on, 31–32, 33–34, 113, 115–16; legislation, 109–11; lived experience, 6, 110–11; ongoing status confirmation, 115–18; provincial jurisdiction, 8, 109, 115; refugees, 110, 113–14; sanctuary schools, proposal for, 117–18; screening by school boards, 113–15, 151. *See also* school boards; social benefits (health, education, welfare)
EI. *See* Employment Insurance (EI)

emotional responses to precarious status: about, 39–40, 60–61; anger and despair at exclusion, 45, 47–49; fear as barrier, 51–52, 54–55, 65–66, 93, 121–23, 131, 152; fear as enforcement, 137–38, 142–44, 145; powerlessness, 57; security as permanent resident, 54; uncertainty, 39–40, 49–52, 55–58, 60; workplace stress, 84

employers: disclosure of status to authorities, 145–46, 148; *IRPA* offence to employ unauthorized workers, 137, 140; labour market needs, 13, 42–43, 50, 65; recommendations for policy changes on, 182. *See also* closed work permits, employer endorsements; power relations in workplaces; work and workplaces

employment, informal. *See* informal economy

employment, unauthorized. *See* unauthorized work (outside of work permit)

Employment and Assistance Act (2002, BC), 32, 129. *See also* welfare

Employment and Assistance Appeal Tribunal, 32, 128–32. *See also* welfare

Employment and Assistance for Persons with Disabilities Act (2002, BC), 32. *See also* disabilities and social benefits

Employment Insurance (EI): about, 118–26; availability for work, 20, 119, 120, 152; barriers to asserting rights, 20, 118–22, 131, 152; case law, 124–26; deservingness, 123, 125–26, 132–33; eligibility and status, 118–19, 132; fear of risking permanent status applications, 121–23, 131, 152; federal jurisdiction, 8, 118; good behaviour, 125–26, 132–33; lived experience, 123–24; Record of Employment (ROE), 57, 119, 120, 122; status uncertainty, 57

Employment Insurance Act (Canada): case law, 124–26; doctrine of illegality, 124–26, 140, 196n56; eligibility and status, 118–19; legal research on, 31–32

employment standards: about, 8, 75–76, 82, 92; federal regulations (2015), 185–86; labour mobility and job security not protected, 74; offences and penalties, 90, 185–86; provincial jurisdiction, 7, 63; recommendations for policy changes, 92. *See also Employment Standards Act* (1996, BC); Employment Standards Branch; hours of work; wages

Employment Standards Act (1996, BC): about, 75–76, 89–90, 202n58; application of law to workers, 63–64, 82, 89, 93, 95, 98; assumption of permanent status, 65; complaints process, 75, 89–90; hours and wages, 75–76, 78; legal research on, 31–32; offences and penalties, 90; termination without cause, 94–95; written contracts, 76

Employment Standards Branch: about, 89–92, 98–99; access by precarious migrants, 202n58; barriers to asserting rights, 64, 82, 92, 94–95; claims by precarious migrants, 64, 91–92, 94; complaints process, 89–90, 92; employee-employer power relations, 98–99; legal research on, 33–34, 64, 91

Employment Standards Tribunal: appeals and decisions, 89, 91–92; legal research on, 32–33, 91
endorsements in closed work permits. *See* closed work permits, employer endorsements
enforcement, federal (direct): about, 8, 44, 135–41, 148, 155–56; border vs migrant control, 35, 137, 156; as coercive power, 135, 136–37, 155; in the community, 141–44; deportation, 135, 138–41; disciplining power of, 143–44, 155; against employers, 137, 140; *IRPA* offences and penalties, 139–40; minimal enforcement, 22, 44, 59, 137, 140, 144; offences and penalties under *IRPA*, 44, 59, 93, 146–47; peace officers, 146, 212n30; priority levels, 141; recommendations for policy changes, 182–84; revocation of status, 135; symbolic power of, 60–62, 136–37, 142–44; types of orders, 138–41. *See also* Canada Border Services Agency (CBSA); deportations and removals
enforcement, multi-sited. *See* multi-sited enforcement
English language. *See* languages
ethical issues: about, 35–36; barriers to social entitlements, 10; Canada's illiberal tendencies, 15–17, 47–49; deservingness, 14, 125–26; good behaviour, 125–26, 132–33
exclusion and status. *See* enforcement, federal (direct); multi-sited enforcement; precarious status; status, migration

families: study participants, 187(t)–88(t); welfare benefits, 127, 208n79

families, mixed status (citizen children): differential rights, 178; education, 110–11, 112, 113, 114, 116; welfare benefits, 127, 130–31
family reunification: motivation for permanent status, 53; and processing delays, 51; by visits to country of origin, 56–57
farm workers. *See* agricultural workers; Seasonal Agricultural Worker Program
fear. *See* emotional responses to precarious status
federal immigration law. *See Immigration and Refugee Protection Act (IRPA);* laws, immigration (federal)
feminist approach to research, 27, 64
Filipinas. *See* Philippines
foreign nationals: about, 41–44, 198n14; *IRPA* category, 41; protected persons, 113, 198n14, 210n11; as residual category, 41, 43. *See also* implied status (without physical documents); study permits; visitors
foreign workers, temporary. *See* temporary foreign workers
Fraser Health, 33–34, 107, 150, 205n24
freedom of information requests, 196n55
Fudge, Judy, 66, 166–67

Garcés-Mascareñas, Blanca, 35
gender: of study participants, 23, 27, 66, 187(t)–88(t). *See also* women
global rights. *See* international rights
Goldring, Luin, 15, 56
Greater Vancouver South Coast Transportation Authority, 147–48
Guatemala: study participants, 23, 188(t)

Harper, Stephen, 185
Health, Ministry of: legal research on, 33–34, 105; regional health authorities, 105, 106–7. *See also* health care
health and safety in workplace. *See* workplace health and safety
health care: about, 30, 100–8; administrative bureaucracies, 29–31; barriers to, 101, 181; Canada's illiberal tendencies, 15, 101, 108; CBSA interactions, 150; on charitable basis, 5–6, 103, 104, 106; definition of resident and non-resident, 30, 106–8, 203*n*3, 205*n*24; disclosure of status to authorities, 150, 181; eligibility and status, 5–6, 101–8, 132–34; as enforcement site, 137–38, 149–51, 212*n*38; fear of deportation, 6, 104–5, 149–51; federal legislation, 101–2, 203*n*3; fees for non-residents, 103, 104–7, 149–50, 205*n*20; HIV/AIDS patients, 49, 103, 104, 204*n*12; implied status, 105–6; legislation, 30, 102, 108; lived experience, 5–6; medical services plan (MSP), 102–6; physical documents required, 106; police interactions, 104–5, 150; policy changes, proposal for, 178–79; pregnancy, 5–6, 104–5, 151; processing delays, 105–6, 108; provincial jurisdiction, 8, 101–2, 204*n*6; refugees (IFHP), 21, 101–2, 106–7, 203*n*4; reviews by tribunals, 30; social determinants of health, 89, 181; stereotypes of migrants, 101. *See also* Fraser Health; social benefits (health, education, welfare); Vancouver Coastal Health

history of immigration, 13–15, 42
HIV/AIDS patients, 49, 103, 104, 204*n*12
hospitals: legal research on policies of, 105; status as part of residency requirement, 101, 108. *See also* health care
hours of work: about, 75–82; eligibility for EI benefits, 119; employment standards, 75, 79, 82; excessive hours, 78–79; human rights proposal, 168–69; insufficient hours, 80; international rights, 166; overtime, 75–79; sporadic work, 70; unauthorized work, 78–79; written contracts, 76, 82, 95. *See also* employment standards; wages
human rights: about, 11–12, 35–36, 156, 165, 173–78; access to remedies, 174; administrative bureaucracies, 29–31; all people as rights bearing, 165; global citizenship, 173–74; international rights, 35–36, 165–67, 174–78; and membership, 11, 175–78, 182–84; national rights, 156–65, 175–78; provincial regimes, 7, 167–78; recommendations for policy changes, 168–69, 173–75, 182–84; roles of state institutions, 35–36; state sovereignty, 35–36; status as protected ground, proposal for, 168–71, 173–75; transnational membership, 175–76, 180; tribunals, 168, 173; UN Migrant Worker Convention, 174–75. *See also Charter of Rights and Freedoms*; Supreme Court of Canada (SCC)
Human Rights Code (BC), 168–70, 173–74

identity and belonging: about, 44–49, 64–65; economic contributions, 64; language of illegality, 58–59; long-term effects of uncertainty, 56; status as basic to identity, 38–39; status vs relationship with state, 45; and work, 64–65. *See also* membership; status, migration

IFHP. *See* Interim Federal Health Program (IFHP)

illegality and legality: about, 14–15, 58–62; barriers to accessing benefits, 59; confidentiality, 58–59; doctrine of illegality, 124–26, 140; financial needs of migrants, 59, 74–75, 80–81; IRPA offences and penalties, 59–60, 93, 139–40, 146–47; language of illegality, 58–62; lived experience, 38, 58, 62; and precarious status as analytic tool, 17–18; symbolic power of enforcement, 60–62, 137–38, 142–44. *See also* deportations and removals; enforcement, federal (direct); stereotypes; unauthorized work (outside of work permit); undocumented migrants

ILO (International Labour Organization), 166–67

Immigration and Refugee Protection Act (IRPA): about, 7–8, 40–44; appeals of removal orders, 210n11; Canadian citizens, 40; departure and deportation orders, 210n7; deportation under, 144; education of children, 109; financial self-support, 207n61, 209n86; foreign nationals, 40; implied status, 129; legal research on, 31–32; offences and penalties, 44, 59, 93, 139–40, 146–47; peace officers, 146, 212n30; permanent residents, 40–41; physical presence requirement, 107; refugee departure orders, 210n7; statistics on enforcement, 139–41; temporary resident, definition, 109; unauthorized work, 93; undocumented migrants, 43. *See also* Canada Border Services Agency (CBSA); deportations and removals; enforcement, federal (direct); implied status (without physical documents); laws, immigration (federal)

Immigration and Refugee Protection Act (IRPA), categories: about, 40–41. *See also* citizens, Canadian; foreign nationals; permanent residence (PR) status; refugees

immigration laws. *See* laws, immigration (federal)

immigration status. *See* status, migration

implied status (without physical documents): about, 41, 45, 120; barriers to EI benefits, 120; disabilities, 128–29; education of children, 113; emotional responses to, 45; health care eligibility, 103–4, 105–6; under *IRPA*, 129; need for physical document, 45; during processing delays, 50–51; in status spectrum, 16. *See also* processing delays

income from EI. *See* Employment Insurance (EI)

income from wages. *See* wages

income inadequacy: about, 80–81; debt, 63, 81–82, 107, 150; fees for

medical services, 149–50; unauthorized work due to need, 59, 74–75, 80–81
income security. *See* Employment Insurance (EI); welfare
Indian Act, 197*n*12
Indigenous peoples: labour mobility under *IRPA*, 197*n*12
informal economy: barriers to EI benefits, 119–20; barriers to workers' compensation, 95–96; "cash corners," 144; construction work, 68–69; deskilling, 67, 68–69; enforcement sites, 144; financial needs of migrants, 59, 74–75, 80–81; labour sectors, 68; precarious migrants, 22, 68–69; prevalence, 22; unauthorized work, 68–69. *See also* unauthorized work (outside of work permit)
inland refugees. *See* refugees
institutions: about, 26–31; decision makers, 29–31, 33–34; holistic approach to, 31; human rights issues, 35–36; institutional ethnography on status, 26–29; judicial and tribunal reviews, 30–31; legal research on policies of, 33–34; power relations, 27. *See also* multi-sited enforcement
Interim Federal Health Program (IFHP): eligibility for provincial services, 106, 107; for refugees, 101–2, 104, 203*n*4; welfare benefits, 129. *See also* refugees
International Convention of the Protection of the Rights of All Migrant Workers, UN (1990), 165–67, 174–75
International Labour Organization (ILO), 166–67

international rights: about, 165–67, 174–75; closed work permits (UN and ILO), 166–67; Migrant Worker Convention, UN, 165–67, 174–75. *See also* human rights; membership
IRPA. *See Immigration and Refugee Protection Act (IRPA)*
irregular status. *See* unauthorized work (outside of work permit); undocumented migrants

job security: about, 69–75, 98–99; barriers to asserting rights, 70–71; and labour mobility, 71, 74; lack of statutory protection for, 74

Kapp, R v (2008), 160, 164
Kenney, Jason, 203*n*4
Koo v 5220459 Manitoba Inc., 202*n*49
Korea: study participants, 23, 55, 188(t)

labour: historical background, 13–15; labour market needs (LMOs), 42, 50, 65, 69, 91, 94, 202*n*49; labour rights, 92; precarious work generally, 65; temporary foreign workers, 22. *See also* closed work permits; economic issues; open work permits; unauthorized work (outside of work permit); work permits
labour bargaining power. *See* power relations
Labour Market Opinion (LMO), 42, 50, 65, 69, 91, 94, 202*n*49
labour mobility: about, 52–53, 68, 69–75; bias in hiring open permit workers, 71–72; closed vs open permits, 21, 52–53, 69–72; deskilling, 72–73; employer endorsements, 65;

and job security, 71, 74; lack of statutory protection for, 74; risks to citizen workers, 75
labour rights. *See* employment standards; Workers' Compensation Board; workplace health and safety
labour sectors. *See* construction industry; Live-in Caregiver Program; restaurant industry; Seasonal Agricultural Worker Program
landed immigrant status: education of children, 113; Temporary Resident Permit, 113, 204n16, 206n34, 206n36
Landolt, Patricia, 56
languages: deskilling and limited English skills, 67; government services, 83, 89, 93; of study participants, 23
laws, immigration (federal): about, 7–8, 29–32, 37, 40–44, 60–62; administrative bureaucracies, 29–31; authorized status as discrete, limited, and well defined, 61; border vs migrant control, 35, 137, 156; Canada's illiberal tendencies, 15–17; case law, 32; concurrent jurisdiction, 40, 197n2; federal vs provincial jurisdiction, 7–8; hierarchy of status, 4–5, 35; history of immigration, 13–15; judicial review, 30–31; jurisdiction under *Constitution Act, 1867* (s 95), 197n2; legal research on, 31–32; and precarious status, 17, 37–39; primacy of federal power, 40, 197n2; uncertain status, 60–61. *See also* enforcement, federal (direct); *Immigration and Refugee Protection Act (IRPA)*; membership
legal/illegal. *See* illegality and legality

Liberal government: Trudeau's policies, 185–86
liberal values and status: about, 15–17, 154–56; Canada's illiberal tendencies, 15–17, 47–49; capitalism as separate force, 176–77; for equal inclusion, 154; separate classes of workers, 154–55; uneven effects of precarious status, 17–18; values of fairness, 49. *See also Charter of Rights and Freedoms*; human rights
lived experience of migrants, 8–9, 18, 28
Live-in Caregiver Program: about, 43, 49–51; barriers to asserting rights, 73–74; barriers to challenging employers, 94; changing needs of employers, 70; closed permits and labour mobility, 52–53, 68, 70, 73; eligibility for permanent residence, 70; family reunification, 50; LMO agreements, 91; processing delays, 49–52; return to country of origin, 48; shift to open work permits, 50; skills of workers, 66–67, 199n5; trial periods, 78; years of work for permanent status, 47, 50–51, 70
live-in caregivers: barriers to asserting rights, 70–71, 82; barriers to EI benefits, 121–22; deskilling, 66–67; employer's endorsement, 5–6; employment standards, 77–78, 82; employment standards complaints by, 94–95; enforcement site, 141–43; ethic of care, 87–88; fear of risking permanent status applications, 95, 121–22; health care, 5–6; lived experience, 5–6, 46–48, 76–78, 85–88, 122; migration as contract

with state, 48; motivation for migration, 46–47; permanent residence, 43; power relations, 73–74, 76–78, 82, 84–88, 94; recruitment debt, 81–82; resistance by, 87–88; status uncertainty, 55, 57; stress and loss of dignity, 84–87; study participants, 66–67; termination without cause, 94; unauthorized work, 141–42; wages and hours, 76–78, 91, 95; written contracts, 76, 77–78, 82, 86, 91, 95
live-out caregivers: permanent residence, 198n21; requirements, 194n25
LMO. *See* Labour Market Opinion (LMO)

MacPhail, Fiona, 66
maple card. *See* permanent residence (PR) status
Medical and Health Services Regulation (BC), 204n9
medical care. *See* health care
Medical Services Plan, BC (MSP), 102, 103–4, 106. *See also* health care
Medicare Protection Act (1996, BC) and *Regulations*: about, 30; eligibility and status, 30, 102–3, 105, 108; implied status, 103–4, 105–6; legal research on, 31–32; residency requirements in regulations, 108, 204n9
membership: about, 11–12, 35–36, 175–80; border vs migrant control, 35, 137, 156; and capitalism, 176–77; and economic contributions by migrants, 64; hierarchy of membership, 4–5, 35, 46, 133, 136, 175–76; and human rights, 172–78; and liberal values, 154–55; local membership, proposal for, 12, 178–80; and neoliberal ideas of belonging, 64; recommendations for policy changes, 182–84; and rights, 11–12, 167, 182–84; status documents as evidence, 45–46; and subordinate status, 3–4, 11–12; transnational membership, proposal for, 180. *See also* human rights; status, migration
men as study participants, 23
mental disorders: workers' compensation, 83
Mexico: as a source nation, 20, 79; study participants, 23, 47, 55, 56, 96–97, 123–24, 187(t)–88(t)
Mia v M.N.R., 125
Migrant Worker Convention, UN, 165–67, 174–75
migrant workers: recommendations for policy changes, 182–84
migration status. *See* status, migration
minimum income. *See* welfare
M.N.R., Mia v, 125
M.N.R., Still v, 124–25
mobility of labour. *See* labour mobility
Moffette, David, 182
Montreal, school policies, 108
moral issues. *See* ethical issues
moral regulation of migrants: about, 14–15. *See also* deservingness; illegality and legality; stereotypes
motivations of migrants, 18, 46–47, 52, 64–65
MSP. *See* Medical Services Plan, BC (MSP)
Multilateral Framework on Labour Migration (ILO), 166–67
multi-sited enforcement: about, 8, 11, 29, 135–38, 155–56; access without

fear, proposal for, 179; border vs migrant control, 35, 137; Canada as unified state, 62, 121–22; Canada's illiberal tendencies, 15–17, 47–49; decision makers, 29–31, 33–34; and deservingness, 136, 153–54; disciplining power of, 135, 138, 148–49, 155; education as site, 137–38, 151–52; emotional responses to exclusion, 45, 47–49; and exclusion, 136, 154–55; exclusion and status, 153–54; fear of enforcement, 137–38, 142–44, 149, 152; fear of risking permanent status applications, 95, 121–22, 130, 152; health care as site, 137–38, 149–51; holistic approach to, 31; judicial review of decisions, 30–31; legal research on, 31–33; lived experience, 37–38; power relations, 149; and precarious status, 15, 37–39, 148–49; recommendations for policy changes, 182–84; social benefits as site, 137–38, 148–52; subordinate status, 8, 11; symbolic power, 60, 137–38, 142–44; welfare as site, 152; workplace enforcement, 144–48. *See also* education of children; Employment Insurance (EI); enforcement, federal (direct); health care; welfare; Workers' Compensation Board

NAFTA agreements on foreign workers, 42
national membership. *See* membership
nationality: and precarious status, 17; study participants, 187(t)–88(t)
neoliberalism and belonging, 64

non-citizens, rights of. *See* human rights
non-permanent migrants. *See* precarious status
non-resident children. *See* education of children; families, mixed status (citizen children)
non-status migrants. *See* undocumented migrants
North Vancouver School Board, 115

objectivity, myth of, 31
occupational health and safety. *See* Workers' Compensation Board; workplace health and safety
Occupational Health and Safety Regulation, 83. *See also* workplace health and safety
offences and penalties under *IRPA*, 44, 59, 93, 139–40, 146–47
Ontario: *O.P.T.* (labour mobility), 170–71, 173, 174; *Toussaint* (status as analogous ground), 159–65, 172, 174, 214n21
Ontario Human Rights Code, 170–71, 173, 174, 215n39
open work permits: about, 42–43, 68; bias in hiring, 71–72; Labour Market Opinions, 50; labour mobility, 50, 52, 70–72; processing delays, 50–51; refugees, 21; social insurance numbers with "9," 68, 71–72; spouses with closed permits, 20, 42–43; uncertainty in status, 61
O.P.T. v Presteve Foods Ltd. (2015, ON Human Rights Tribunal), 170–71, 173, 174
organizations. *See* institutions
overstays: precarious status, 16, 19, 44. *See also* undocumented migrants

pay. *See* wages

Pension Appeal Board (tribunal, BC), 32

permanent residence (PR) status: about, 3, 40–41, 156, 177–78; benefits and rights, 40–41; deskilling, 67; detrimental effects of previous status, 19, 56; education of children, 40–41, 112–13, 114, 116; fear of risking applications for, 51–54, 95, 121–23, 130, 131, 152, 156; health care, 40–41; *IRPA* category, 40–41; and liberal values, 156; loss of status, 178; motivation for migration, 5, 19, 52–53; processing delays, 50–51; refugees, 130; skill levels and eligibility, 20, 43; spousal sponsorship, 41; stigma, 130; study participants, 23, 130; uncertainty while waiting, 51; welfare benefits, 40–41, 130, 132

Philippines: caregiver recruitment debt, 81–82; pre-departure seminars, 48; as a source nation, 20; study participants, 23, 48, 57, 66–67, 142, 188(t)

police, immigration. *See* Canada Border Services Agency (CBSA)

police, local: CBSA interactions, 147–48; enforcement in workplaces, 144–45, 148; legal research on transit police, 147; peace officers, 146, 212n30; police enforcement of debt, 150; racial profiling, 182; transit police, 146–48

policies on status, provincial: about, 3–5; and federal laws, 4–5. *See also* employment standards; social benefits (health, education, welfare)

post-national membership, 11–12, 180. *See also* membership

poverty. *See* income inadequacy; welfare

power relations: about, 27–28; institutional ethnography, 27–28

power relations in enforcement: about, 11, 135–38; direct federal enforcement, 135–38; disciplining power, 135, 138, 143–44, 148–49, 155; symbolic power of enforcement, 60, 137–38, 142–44; in workplaces, 148. *See also* deportations and removals; enforcement, federal (direct); multi-sited enforcement

power relations in workplaces: about, 63, 65–66; barriers to exerting rights, 65–66; closed work permits, 52–54, 69, 73–74; disclosure of status to authorities, 145–46, 148; employer-worker relations, 63–66; employment standards, 93; fear of reprisals, 65, 93; labour mobility, 72–73; passivity of workers, 94; in status spectrum, 65; workers' compensation, 93. *See also* closed work permits

PR status. *See* permanent residence (PR) status

Pratt, Geraldine, 142

precarious status: about, 9, 15–19, 37–40, 61, 136; as an analytical tool, 17, 61; Canada's illiberal tendencies, 15–17, 47–49; definitions of, 9, 15–19; detrimental long-term effects, 56; enforcement, 136; health care services, 105; hierarchy of membership, 4–5, 35, 46, 133, 136; lived experience, 19; "nothing to go back to," 56; permanent residence as goal, 19; recommendations for policy changes, 182–84; skill levels, 20; as spectrum, 16, 19, 37, 39–40, 52–55,

65; statistics, 18; uncertainty about status, 61; uneven effects, 16–18. *See also* status, migration
precarious status, types of. *See* refugees; temporary foreign workers; undocumented migrants
pre-departure programs, CIC, 48
privacy. *See* confidentiality
processing delays: about, 49–52; emotional responses to, 49–52; financial needs of migrants, 81; health care, 105–6, 108; health care for refugees (IFHP), 102; status uncertainty, 55–58; between work permits, 69. *See also* implied status (without physical documents)
protected persons, 113, 198n14, 210n11
provincial jurisdiction: about, 7–8, 40, 60, 167–68; concurrent jurisdiction, 40; *Constitution Act, 1867* (s 95), 197n2; education, 8, 109, 115; employment standards, 7–8, 63; vs federal jurisdiction, 7–8, 40; health care, 8, 126; human rights, 7, 167–78; selection of migrants, 40; social benefits, 7; welfare, 8, 126
public transit and enforcement, 144, 146–48

Quebec v A (2013), 164

race and ethnicity: historical background, 13; human rights codes, 168–72; uneven effects of precarious status, 17
refugees: about, 19, 21–22; barriers to social benefits, 102; claim process, 21–22; departure orders, 210n7; deportation orders with claims, 22; deservingness, 14; detrimental effects of uncertain status, 56; education of children, 113–14, 115, 116; failed claims, 129; health care (IFHP), 21, 101–2, 104, 106–7, 129, 203n4; historical background, 13–14; lived experience, 6; open work permits, 21; permanent residency eligibility, 21–22; precarious status, 16, 21–22; pre-removal risk assessment, 129; processing delays, 102; skill levels, 21–22; social benefits (health, education, welfare), 21–22; statistics, 21, 194n27; stereotypes, 14–15, 17, 18; uncertainty in status, 61; unenforceable removal orders, 129; welfare benefits, 128–31
regularization programs, 14–15, 156
regulations and laws. *See* laws, immigration (federal); multi-sited enforcement
removals. *See* deportations and removals; enforcement, federal (direct)
research study: about, 6–9; agency participants, 23, 27; author's position, 5, 25–26; feminist approach, 27, 64; holistic approach, 31; institutional ethnography, 23–24, 26–29; interviews, 7, 23–24, 39, 189–90; key questions, 7, 154; legal research, 26, 31–34, 196n55; limitations, 34, 60–61; lived experience, 8–9, 18, 28; location (Vancouver), 18; overview of chapters on, 9–12; power relations, 27–28; recommendations for policies, 182–84; status in multi-sited enforcement, 29
research study, migrant participants: about, 8–9, 23–26, 187(t)–88(t);

children of, 108; confidentiality, 34, 58, 195n34; deskilling, 66; gender, 23, 27, 66; lived experience, 8; nationality, 23, 187(t)–88(t); occupations, 63, 68, 187(t)–88(t); profiles of, 187(t)–188(t); recruitment for study, 23, 34, 58, 60–61; self-identification, 8, 23, 39; statuses, 8–9, 19, 23, 60–61
restaurant industry: class action lawsuits, 201n38; study participants, 66; wages and hours, 78
restricted work permits. *See* closed work permits
revocation of status. *See* deportations and removals; enforcement, federal (direct)
Reynolds, Vikki, 25–26
rights, human. *See* human rights
Rubin, Herbert J. and Irene S., 24

safety, workplace. *See* workplace health and safety
sanctuary cities, 181
sanctuary schools, proposal for, 117–18
School Act (1996, BC): about, 109–10; definition of residents, 110, 114–15, 117, 207n50; legal research on, 31–32. *See also* Education, Ministry of; education of children
school boards: about, 112–15; eligibility and status, 108–11; fees for non-residents, 6, 110, 113–14, 196n57; legal research on, 33–34, 113, 115–16; policy changes, proposal for, 178–79; sanctuary schools, proposal for, 117–18. *See also* Education, Ministry of; education of children

Seasonal Agricultural Worker Program: about, 68; barriers to asserting rights, 70; control of worker pools, 203n61; eligibility for future seasons, 97; employment standards complaints, 91–92; job insecurity, 70, 97; labour market needs, 43; study participants, 70; wages, 75, 91; workers' compensation claims, 97–98. *See also* temporary foreign workers
SELI Canada, CSWU Local 1611 v (2008, BC Human Rights Tribunal), 169–70, 173–74
sexual abuse: in the workplace, 86, 170
SIN. *See* social insurance number
Singh v Minister of Employment and Immigration (1985), 14–15, 213n9
skills: about, 43, 66–67; barriers to return to country of origin, 56–57; high-skilled workers, 42–43, 46, 56–57, 66–68; live-in caregivers, 46, 66–67; low-skilled workers, 20, 21, 43, 67–69; permanent residence, 43; precarious status, 20; refugees, 21–22; study participants, 66; trends in, 20, 68; uneven effects of precarious status, 17. *See also* deskilling
skills, programs for specific. *See* Live-in Caregiver Program; Seasonal Agricultural Worker Program
Smith, Dorothy, 26–29
social assistance. *See* welfare
social benefits (health, education, welfare): about, 10, 100–1, 132–34; administrative bureaucracies, 29–31, 132–34; barriers to asserting rights, 10, 100–1, 126, 132–34, 148–49; deservingness and moral scrutiny,

10, 132–34, 136; disclosure of status to authorities, 108, 181; eligibility and status, 10, 15–19, 131–34; enforcement sites, 136, 148–52; ethical issues, 133; fragmented system, 126, 132–34; hierarchy of membership, 133–34, 136; international rights, 166; power relations, 149; provincial jurisdiction, 8, 126, 134; recommendations for policy changes, 182–84; stereotypes, 10, 100, 133; visitors, exclusion, 102. *See also* education of children; health care; welfare
social class and precarious status, 17
social determinants of health, 89, 181
Social Development, Ministry of: legal research on, 33–34, 127; welfare policies, 129. *See also* welfare
social insurance number: barriers to EI benefits, 120; bias in hiring, 71–72; numbers with "9" (temporary workers), 22, 68, 71–72; statistics on, 22
socio-economic status: long-term effects of uncertainty, 56. *See also* deskilling
South Coast British Columbia Transportation Authority Police Service, 146–47
spouses: health services, 204*n*11; open work permits, 20, 42; permanent residence, 193*n*16; and precarious status, 15–16, 20; sponsorship of, 41, 197*n*11
status, migration: about, 3–8, 11, 29, 37–39, 60–62, 176–84; access to state benefits, 8, 11, 132–34, 153–54; barriers to asserting rights, 54–55, 144–45, 176; Canada's illiberal tendencies, 15–17, 47–49; definitions and descriptions, 38–40; as dynamic force, 29, 52; effects of, 16–18, 136; fear of asserting rights, 54–55, 93; hierarchy of status, 4–5, 15, 35, 46, 133; historical background, 13–15, 42; human rights codes, omission in, 168; institutional ethnography on, 23–24, 26–29; language of illegality, 58–60; lived experience vs legal constructs, 8, 38, 62; in a multi-sited regime, 11, 29, 135–38; "neither here nor there," 55–58, 60–61; as outsider, 175; as personal identity, 38–39; recommendations for policy changes, 182–84; rights to states to determine, 167; and social exclusion, 11, 136–37; spectrum of, 16, 19, 37, 39–40, 52–55, 65; of study participants, 187(t)–88(t); as a text, 28–29; visibility in society, 46; and workplaces, 98–99; written documents as, 44–46. *See also* implied status (without physical documents); membership; precarious status
status, types of. *See* permanent residence (PR) status; precarious status; study permits; undocumented migrants
status, types of work permits. *See* closed work permits; open work permits; unauthorized work (outside of work permit); work permits
stereotypes: historical background, 14–15; justification for exclusion, 10, 100, 133–34; *Law* test for analogous

grounds, 160–61; of motivations of migrants, 18, 47; of refugees as "bogus," 14, 18, 100. *See also* deservingness

Still v M.N.R., 124–25

study on exclusion and status. *See* research study

study permits: about, 41; education of children of holders, 112, 113–16; exclusion from social benefits, 41, 127; financial needs of students, 80–81; as foreign nationals, 41; health care, 41, 102, 103, 105, 106, 107; study participants, 66; Temporary Resident Permit, 113, 204*n*16, 206*n*34, 206*n*36; unauthorized work, 81; work permits, 41

subnational rights, 167–75. *See also* provincial jurisdiction

Supreme Court of Canada (SCC): *Andrews* (equality rights), 161, 162–63, 164–65, 172; *Charter* protection for non-citizens, 157; comparator groups, 162, 172, 214*n*21; *Corbiere* (analogous grounds), 162–63; *Law* test (analogous grounds), 160–61; *Singh* (non-citizens' rights), 14–15, 213*n*9. *See also Charter of Rights and Freedoms*

Surrey School District, 113–14, 116. *See also* school boards

Temporary Foreign Worker Program, 13, 193*n*24, 199*n*4

temporary foreign workers: about, 19–20; class action lawsuits, 201*n*38; closed work permits, 20; countries of origin, 20; EI benefits, 119; employment standards, 20; historical background, 13, 42; international agreements (NAFTA), 42; labour market needs, 13, 42, 50, 65; permanent residence, 43; precarious status, 20; skill levels, 43; social benefits (health, education, welfare), 20; social insurance numbers with marker, 22, 68, 71–72; statistics, 19–20, 22, 193*n*24; study participants, 8, 23; welfare benefits, not entitled, 20. *See also* precarious status; work permits

Tim Hortons and others, Chein and others v (BC Human Rights Tribunal), 170

Toronto, City of, 181

Toronto District School Board, 108, 182

tourists. *See* visitors

Toussaint v The Attorney General of Canada (2010), 159–65, 172, 174, 214*n*21

transit systems and enforcement, 144, 146–48

transnational membership, 175–76, 180. *See also* membership

tribunals: about, 32; human rights tribunals, 30, 168, 173; judicial review, 30–31; legal research on, 31–32. *See also* Employment and Assistance Appeal Tribunal; Employment Standards Tribunal; *Human Rights Code* (BC); Workers' Compensation Appeal Tribunal

Trudeau, Justin, 185

UN. *See* United Nations

unauthorized migrants. *See* undocumented migrants

unauthorized work (outside of work permit): barriers to EI benefits, 57, 120–21, 124–26; barriers to workers' compensation, 95–96; construction work, 68–69; deskilling, 67, 68–69; employer offence of hiring, 44, 140; employment standards claims, 95–96; financial needs of migrants, 59, 74–75, 80–81; good behaviour, 125–26; *IRPA* offences and penalties, 44, 59, 93, 140; labour rights, 95–96; language of illegality, 58; lived experience, 57; live-in caregivers, 82, 141–42; precarious migrants, 68–69; processing delays between permits, 69; reports to CBSA, 143; status differences, 78–79; wages and hours, 78–79, 95; workers' compensation claims, 93, 95–96. *See also* informal economy

undocumented migrants: about, 19–20, 22, 43–44, 140; access to services, proposal for, 181; amnesty programs, 14–15; barriers to EI benefits, 120, 124–26; Canada's illiberal tendencies, 15; CBSA policy manual on, 109*n*2; confidentiality of study participants, 195*n*34; deservingness, 14; education of children, exclusion, 113, 115; fear as enforcement, 149–50; historical background, 14–15; informal economy, 68–69; *IRPA* residual category, 41, 43–44; labour rights, 92; language of illegality, 58, 60; minimal enforcement, 22, 44, 59, 137, 140; overstays, 22, 44, 115; overtime, 79; precarious status, 16; statistics, 14, 22; stereotypes, 14–15; study participants, 8; symbolic power of deportability, 60, 137, 142–44; *Toussaint* (*Charter* rights for non-citizens), 159–65, 172, 174, 214*n*21; transit police enforcement, 146–48; wages and hours, 78–79; welfare benefits, exclusion, 127, 130. *See also* deportations and removals; enforcement, federal (direct)

unenforceable removal orders, 127, 129

unions, labour, 74, 166

United Nations: Migrant Worker Convention, 165–67, 174–75; Refugee Convention, 13

Vancouver, City of: access to services by undocumented migrants, 181
Vancouver Coastal Health, 33–34, 106–7, 150, 205*n*20. *See also* health care
Vancouver School Board, 114–18. *See also* school boards
Varsanyi, Monica, 180
Vega Jiménez, Lucía, 147–48
Villegas, Paloma, 145
visitors: exclusion from social benefits, 41, 102, 105, 107, 109, 113, 127; as foreign nationals, 41; study participants, 8, 23

wages: about, 75–82; agreements, 91; employer power relations, 78–79; employment standards, 75, 79, 82, 90, 95; fear of reporting illegal acts, 65; frequency of payment, 76; human rights, 168–70; LMO and wage rates, 91; minimum wage, 75, 78–79; overtime, 75–79; *SELI* (differential wages), 169–70; UN Migrant Worker Convention on, 166; unauthorized work, 78–79; written contracts, 95. *See also* employment standards; hours of work; income inadequacy wages paid "under the table." *See* informal economy

WCAT. *See* Workers' Compensation Appeal Tribunal

welfare: about, 100–1, 126–34; barriers to asserting rights, 129–31, 152; Canada's illiberal tendencies, 15; case law, 128–32; citizen children, 128, 131; disability benefits, 128–29, 130–31; eligibility and status, 20, 74, 131–34; as enforcement site, 137–38, 152; fear of risking permanent status applications, 130, 131; implied status, 128–29; international rights, 166; for mothers without status, 208*n*79; policies, 127–28, 131–32; proof of status, 127; provincial jurisdiction, 8, 126; refugees, 21, 128–31; residency requirements, 127, 132; stigma and moral scrutiny, 100, 127; study participants, 129–30; tribunal appeals, 128–32. *See also* disabilities and social benefits; social benefits (health, education, welfare)

Wexler, Steve, 31

Withler v Canada (2011), 160, 162, 164

women: feminist approach in research, 27; pregnancy and health care, 5–6, 104–5, 151; sexual abuse in the workplace, 70, 86; study participants, 23, 27, 187(t)–88(t)

work and workplaces: about, 9–10, 64–65, 148; barriers to asserting rights, 65–66, 144–45; as direct enforcement site, 144–48; employment standards, 98–99; feminist critiques of, 64; legal assumption of permanent status, 65; power relations between worker and employer, 65–66; provincial jurisdiction, 8; public transit as enforcement site, 146–48; study participants, 9–10, 187(t)–88(t); working conditions, 98–99. *See also* employers; employment standards; hours of work; power relations in workplaces; wages; workplace health and safety

work permits: about, 68; barriers to EI benefits, 120–24; change from closed to open, 50; education of children, 112, 113, 116; emotional responses to, 51–52; health care, 104, 105, 106, 107, 150; and identity, 45–46; lived experience, 45–46; not to confer status, 129; and precarious status, 15–19; processing delays, 51–52, 104; statistics, 20; on status spectrum, 16, 52–53, 61; study permits, 41; Temporary Resident Permit, 113, 204*n*16, 206*n*34, 206*n*36; uncertainty about status, 61; welfare, exclusion, 131. *See also* closed work permits; open work permits; temporary foreign workers; unauthorized work (outside of work permit)

Workers Compensation Act (1996, BC): about, 83; application of law to workers, 63–64, 83, 89, 93, 95–98; legal research on, 31–32; offences and penalties, 83; reports by employers and workers, 83–84. *See also* workplace health and safety

Workers' Compensation Appeal Tribunal, 32, 92–93

Workers' Compensation Board: about, 92–99; appeal processes, 92–93; claims by precarious migrants, 64,

95–97; employee-employer power relations, 93–99; injuries at work, 83–84; legal research on, 32–34, 64, 92; newcomer programs, 83; provincial jurisdiction, 63; remedies, 92; reports by employers and workers to, 83–84, 95–98. *See also* workplace health and safety

working holiday visas, 20, 106. *See also* temporary foreign workers

workplace health and safety: about, 83–89; abuse of workers, 84–89; barriers to asserting rights, 16; caregivers, 84–88; health problems, 84, 88–89; injuries at work, 83–84, 88–89; and precarious status, 16, 83; provincial jurisdiction, 8. See also *Workers Compensation Act* (1996, BC); Workers' Compensation Board

written contracts. *See* contracts